Houdini in a confidential mood. One of his favorite publicity
photographs.

THE SECRETS OF HOUDINI

BY

J. C. CANNELL
VICE-PRESIDENT OF THE MAGICIANS' CLUB

DOVER PUBLICATIONS, INC.
NEW YORK

This Dover edition, first published in 1973, is an unabridged republication of the work originally published in London by Hutchinson & Co. Ltd. in 1931. Twenty-four new illustrations have been added in the present edition.

International Standard Book Number: 0-486-22913-0
Library of Congress Catalog Card Number: 72-93609

Manufactured in the United States of America
Dover Publications, Inc.
180 Varick Street
New York, N. Y. 10014

CONTENTS

CHAPTER I

CHAPTER II

HOUDINI'S SPECTACULAR ESCAPES—HIS REMARKABLE
FAILURE AT THE MAGICIANS' CLUB—ESCAPE FROM
BANK-SAFE—IRON BOILER—PAPER BAG—MAIL-BAG—
WALKING THROUGH A BRICK WALL—BURIED ALIVE—
ESCAPE FROM IRON BOX—PACKING-CASE UNDER
WATER—THE VANISHING HORSEMAN—BOX AND SACK—
THE NEEDLES AND THREAD—THE VANISHING ELEPHANT
—THE MYSTERY OF THE MILK-CAN . . . 25

CHAPTER III

HOUDINI'S SPIRITUALIST ACTIVITIES—" GHOSTS " FROM
THE VASTY DEEP—SECRETS OF THE LOCKED BOX—
MENTAL EVIDENCE—MYSTIFYING PASSENGERS IN A
LINER—" SPIRIT " WRITING ON SEALED SLATES—
MEDIUMS " CONTROLLED "—THE SUN WORSHIPPERS—
TABLE LIFTING—" SPIRITS " DEFY BONDS—MESSAGES IN
BLOOD—PERSONAL SÉANCE-EXPERIENCES . . 63

CHAPTER IV

CONTENTS

CHAPTER IX

LIST OF ILLUSTRATIONS

THE SECRETS OF HOUDINI

CHAPTER I

HARRY HOUDINI, HIS LIFE-STORY—FAMOUS SPIRITUALIST
LEADER WHO BECAME HIS FRIEND—ACCIDENT WHICH
BROUGHT HIM A LIFE-PARTNER—EARLY STRUGGLES—
ULTIMATE TRIUMPH AND PREMATURE DEATH

THIS is the story of one of the world's most remarkable men, Harry Houdini, genius, prince among professional deceivers, a wizard of our times.

Though of slight education, Houdini was richly gifted with personality and natural resourcefulness.

Beginning his professional career as a circus boy, he became a famous figure in a class of entertainment which he himself created.

From early youth he understood the lure of magic for the crowd and set out to establish himself as a maker of mysteries. In this he succeeded eminently. He was obsessed by magic, escapes and illusions. When a dying man he staggered through his last stage performance in defiance of his doctors and friends who watched anxiously from behind the scenes. He collapsed at the end of the performance and was carried to hospital never to return to that stage which had been the centre of his life.

It may be said, above all things of Houdini, that he cast out fear. Possessed of wonderful physique and an extraordinarily quick mind, he defied the efforts of experts in

11

almost every part of the world to devise a restraint from which he could not free himself. He escaped from iron boxes, paper bags, bank safes and from packing-cases in which, handcuffed, he was thrown into the sea. Buried in a coffin six feet below the surface of the earth, he emerged smiling an hour later from his living grave.

" My chief task," he once said, " has been to conquer fear. When I am stripped and manacled, nailed securely within a weighted packing-case, and thrown into the sea, or when I am buried alive under six feet of earth, it is necessary to preserve absolute serenity of spirit. I have to work with great delicacy and lightning speed. If I grow panicky I am lost. And if something goes wrong ; if there is some slight accident or mishap, some slight miscalculation, I am lost unless all my faculties are free from mental tension or strain. The public see only the accomplished trick ; they have no conception of the tortuous preliminary self-training that was necessary to conquer fear. Another secret of mine is that by equally vigorous self-training I have been enabled to do remarkable things with my body. I make not one muscle or a group of muscles but every muscle a respective worker, quick and sure for its part, to make my fingers super-fingers, in dexterity, and to train my toes to do the work of fingers."

A remarkable fact about Houdini's career as a magician was that his secrets were preserved with such completeness. Although his performances were seen by many hundreds of thousands of people in different continents, few among all the public could tell how he performed even one of his wonders. The only explanation that the average man can offer is that Houdini was able to contract his wrists.

I am afraid that the ability to contract his wrists does not go far to explain his escape from a steel safe, an iron boiler, a sealed sack or from that type of handcuffs fitted with ratchets so that they can be fastened to the wrists with the tightness of a vice.

Houdini's physical strength and dexterity formed only one part of his methods of escape. Added to that was his extensive knowledge of locks and other forms of restraints. But, above all, he owed his distinctive success to his natural capacity for deception. He had the mental agility of ten men and his mind never slept.

His achievements caused such wonderment among mankind that many attributed to him super-normal power.

Among these was the late Sir Arthur Conan Doyle, who once wrote to Houdini, "My dear chap, why go round the world seeking a demonstration of the occult when you are giving one all the time? Mrs. Guppy could dematerialise, and so could many folk in Holy Writ, and I do honestly believe that you can also. My reason tells me that you have this wonderful power though I have no doubt that, up to a point, your strength and skill avail you."

In spite of their acute differences of opinion concerning spiritualism, Houdini and Sir Arthur Conan Doyle remained good friends until the end, although the creator of Sherlock Holmes held firmly to his belief that Houdini was a medium who was using his psychic powers to make a fortune.

Shortly before his death Sir Arthur Conan Doyle wrote an article for a magazine in which he set out to explain the mystery of Houdini by asserting that he was in reality a great medium. This article was shown by Sir Arthur to my friend Will Goldston, founder of the Magicians' Club, and one of the few people who have known the secrets of Houdini, for he was in the confidence of the magician. Mr. Goldston is a spiritualist, but after reading the article he advised Sir Arthur not to publish it in that form because the conception of Houdini which it contained was entirely erroneous. I believe that Sir Arthur was ultimately prevailed upon to modify the article.

Another prominent spiritualist who held similar views concerning the work of Houdini is Mr. J. H. McKenzie, President of the British College of Psychical Science. He wrote: "Houdini . . . is enabled by psychic power (though this he does not advertise) to open any lock, handcuff or bolt that is submitted to him. He has been imprisoned within heavily barred cells, double and treble locked, and from them all he escaped with ease. This ability to unbolt locked doors is undoubtedly due to his mediumistic powers and not to any normal mechanical operation on the lock. The effort necessary to shoot a bolt within a lock is drawn from Houdini the medium, but it must not be thought that this is the only means by which he can escape from his prison, for at times his body can be . . . dematerialised and withdrawn."

Houdini was usually annoyed by such assertions, which placed him in a slightly embarrassing position, for he could not dispute the words of the spiritualist without revealing exactly how he made his escapes, and that, of course, was impossible. He once wrote : " I do claim to free myself from the restraint of fetters and confinement, but positively state that I accomplish my performance purely by physical means. My methods are perfectly natural. I do not dematerialise or materialise anything. I simply control and manipulate material things in a manner perfectly well understood by myself and thoroughly accountable for by any person to whom I may elect to divulge my secrets."

During one of his visits to England the magician made a particularly smart escape from a packing-case and after this feat had been reported in the Press, Sir Arthur Conan Doyle sent a long telegram to Houdini declaring that, for his own good, he should acknowledge his wonderful occult power. " You should get your proofs soon," telegraphed Sir Arthur, " unless all proofs and all higher personal development are cut off from you, because you are not playing the game with that which has been given to you already. This is a point of view to consider. Such a gift is not given to one man in 100 million that he should amuse the multitude or amass a fortune. Excuse my frank talking, but you know this is all very vital to me."

I have much respect for Sir Arthur Conan Doyle. He was in every way a fine man, utterly sincere in his work as a crusader for spiritualism. As a journalist I had the opportunity of talking with him on several occasions, but

I am afraid I must say quite frankly that this telegram which he sent to Houdini shows that his enthusiasm for a cause got the better of his judgment. Had he been faced with the mystery of the escape from a packing-case, Sherlock Holmes, keen and cautious, would not have jumped impulsively to such a theory.

He would have said to himself, " Is it possible for a man to escape by trickery from a packing-case in which he has been secured ? " Moreover, Sherlock Holmes would have demanded, first of all, to know everything about the packing-case ; the manner in which Houdini was secured in it ; the length of time required for the escape and other vital details. Sir Arthur often talked about the necessity for procuring the correct " conditions " in which a medium can work. Like every spiritualist he declared that even the attitude of the sitters was important, so delicate a thing was communication between the living and the dead. He defended the darkness of the séance room, pointing out that it was a necessary condition, a kind of law over which neither the spirits nor the mediums had any more control than has a photographer who must develop his plates in the dark.

Yet Sir Arthur was eager to believe that Houdini could, in the full glare of footlights, and in the presence of two or three thousand people, reproduce twice nightly, to order, manifestations which would have been astonishing even under the best séance conditions. Apparently, Sir Arthur had little or no knowledge of the principles of magic nor of the possibilities of organised illusion.

In all his life's work he did not, I think, go more sadly astray than in forming this conception of Houdini.

There is no doubt that Houdini, particularly after he lost his mother, to whom he was passionately devoted, was eager to discover if there was any truth in spiritualism. He tried hard to obtain some communication from her and after each series of failures he used to stand at his mother's grave, and say aloud : " I have heard nothing yet." Lady Doyle, an admirable and charming woman, possessed, it is claimed, some powers as a medium and during one of her visits to

America, Houdini sat at a private séance over which she presided.

This is how Houdini describes the experience : " I walked with Sir Arthur to the Doyles' suite. He drew down the shades so as to exclude the bright light. We three, Lady Doyle, Sir Arthur and I, sat around the table, on which were a number of pencils and a writing pad, placing our hands on the surface of the table. Sir Arthur started the séance with a devout prayer. I had made up my mind that I would be as religious as was in my power to be and not at any time did I scoff at the ceremony. I excluded all earthly thoughts and gave my whole soul to the séance. I was *willing* to believe, even *wanted* to believe and with a beating heart I waited, hoping that I might feel once more the presence of my beloved mother.

"Presently Lady Doyle was 'seized by a spirit' . . . her hands beat on the table, her whole body shook and at last, making a cross at the head of the page, she started writing. As she finished each page, Sir Arthur tore a sheet off and handed it to me."

The message purporting to come from his mother which Houdini read, was : " O my darling, thank God, thank God, at last I am through. I have tried, oh ! so often, now I am happy. Why, of course, I want to talk to my boy—my own beloved boy. Friends, I thank you with all my heart for this, you have answered the cry of my heart and of his—God bless him a thousand-fold for all his life for me—never had a mother such a son—tell him not to grieve—soon he will get all the evidence he is so anxious for. Happiness awaits him that he has never dreamed of—tell him I am with him—and just tell him that I will soon make him know how close I am all the while—his eyes will soon be opened. Good-bye again— God's blessing on you all."

At the end of the séance, Houdini, who knew of Lady Doyle's great sincerity, appeared so sympathetic, that the Doyles were almost convinced that they had set him on the road towards belief, but in his heart he was thoroughly disappointed at what he regarded as a vague and meaningless message, just a collection of pious platitudes. Houdini, the magician, the man with an ultra-shrewd mind, could not accept such a message as evidential or important. In life Houdini's mother spoke only a few words of English; her native tongue being Yiddish, she always spoke to him in this dialect.

He could not accept the belief that in death she would speak to him in English, nor did Sir Arthur's assertion that the spirits could use any language they chose reconcile him.

Houdini was unbelieving, too, because, although the date of the séance happened to be his mother's birthday, she made no reference to this fact. Not one of the intimate phrases with which she was used to address him, it was later pointed out by Houdini, was used by the spirit of his mother. I think that this failure to get into communication with her embittered him against spiritualism. Towards the end of his life, he waged a relentless crusade against the mediums at séances which he knew to be bogus, dragging the medium before the police courts. He lectured against them and on the stage produced mock séances in which he showed the public the possibilities of trickery on the part of mediums.

I describe in detail in another chapter the methods of psychic frauds as revealed by Houdini. The effects produced at some of Houdini's " séances " were brilliant, and had he claimed the possession of genuine psychic powers he would have made a fortune.

I agree most earnestly with Mr. Harold Kellock, friend of the magician, when he said : " Had Houdini put his abilities to evil uses he would undoubtedly have been the greatest individual menace ever known.

" He could enter or leave any building or chamber at will, leaving no trace of breakage behind him, and he could open the strongest steel vault. He could solve any lock system in a few minutes and pass through the most elaborate door. Had he chosen the crooked path, society would have been compelled to put him to death for its own protection, for nothing short of the capital penalty would have served.

"Doubtless Houdini would have wrought even greater havoc in human society had he perfected his genius for illusion to make himself the central figure of a new religious cult. He could have done this without difficulty. Moreover, he was aware of what he could accomplish in setting himself up as the inspired prophet of a new mystical religion."

When Houdini was a baby his mother's chief anxiety was that he slept so little. A keen-eyed child, he was always staring at the walls and ceiling.

His first exploit as a lock-picker was directed on a cupboard where his mother kept her jam tarts. A number of these disappeared mysteriously, although the cupboard was always kept locked. The boy Houdini had discovered means of opening the cupboard, stealing two or three jam tarts, afterwards leaving the cupboard exactly as he had found it. He continued this for some time, then his mother, much puzzled, added a padlock to the cupboard. This made no difference and the pastry continued to disappear until the boy was once caught in the act.

He never lost his fondness for pastry and in later years delighted to extract cakes from his wife's cupboard by the same method he had employed as a boy to help himself to his mother's pastry. More than once his wife found the cupboard empty although locked, with Houdini's visiting card on one of the plates.

The son of Dr. Mayer Samuel Weiss, a Jewish Rabbi, Houdini was born in Appleton, Wisconsin, U.S.A., on April 6, 1874. He died in Detroit on October 31, 1926, at the age of fifty-two, when he had been a performer for forty-three years. His real name was Ehrich Weiss. Houdini's family came from Hungary.

As a boy he was restless and eager, showing distinct signs of those tendencies, the development of which was to make him famous.

At the age of six, Houdini's hobby was conjuring. The first trick he learned was making a dried pea appear in

any one of three cups. Possessed of a fine body he practised
acrobatics and at the age of seven was astonishingly agile,
outdoing most of the boys with whom he played. His
family were not well-to-do, and the boy did odd jobs as a
newspaper seller and boot-black.

The arrival of a circus in his native town when he was
nine was an important turning-point in Houdini's life.
He persuaded the manager of the circus to let him show his
repertoire of tricks. The man was astonished at the boy's
cleverness in releasing himself from rope ties and picking
up pins with his eyelids when suspended head downwards
from a rope ; the result was that the lad was given an
engagement which lasted during the stay of the circus in
the town, but in spite of his pleas Ehrich's father refused
to allow him to go off with the circus.

When eleven years old, the boy Weiss obtained a job
at the local locksmith's and was soon able to pick any lock
submitted to him. As the locksmith gave up his business
shortly afterwards, Houdini returned to blacking boots
and selling newspapers, and later obtained work as a
necktie cutter, at which he was employed two years,
distinguishing himself in his spare time as an athlete.

His mind was set on being a magician for he had
already achieved considerable fame locally by his performances at concerts. It was a book, a memoir of Robert
Houdin, which finally decided Ehrich Weiss to become a
professional entertainer. In the book the famous French
magician described conjuring and some secret codes
for tricks with a few coins. When he had finished
reading it, young Weiss was in a state of excitement,
and made up his mind at once. With a friend named
Hayman he started as a professional entertainer and the
pair were known as the Houdini Brothers. The name was
an adaptation, by the addition of " i " to the name of the
French magician.

Before his death in 1892, Houdini's father made him
promise solemnly that he would always help his mother.
This promise was kept most faithfully by Houdini.

In his struggling days he never forgot to send some money

to her, and when, in later years, he was handed what was really his first cheque as a star performer he requested that he should be paid the money in gold. A bag of gold was brought and Houdini hurried off to pour it into the lap of his mother.

Houdini separated from Hayman following a disagreement and his real brother Theodore became his partner.

The Houdini Brothers could not, however, obtain enough professional work to maintain themselves, and in the intervals between engagements found casual jobs of various kinds.

They went to Chicago and performed at a side-show, and later in the same city Houdini appeared alone in a " dime museum," earning twelve dollars a week for giving twenty performances a day. An escape from a specially prepared packing-case and a handcuff release were the chief items in his programme.

His colleagues at the " dime museum " were sword swallowers, jugglers, fire-eaters and fat ladies.

At the age of nineteen, while he was carrying out an engagement at a beach resort in New York, Houdini met and married Miss Beatrice Rahner. It was through spilling some acid on her dress during a conjuring performance at a girls' school that Houdini came to know Miss Rahner. Houdini's mother made a new dress for the young woman, who agreed, when he called at her house with the garment, to go for a walk with him. Shortly afterwards they became man and wife. His married life was always most happy, and he remained deeply in love with his wife until the end. Houdini could not have made a better choice than Miss Rahner, as she was precisely the right type of young woman to make a perfect partner for such an extraordinary man.

Coming from a family of strict ideas, Miss Rahner at first believed that she had married the devil disguised as a handsome young man. She believed in witches and hobgoblins, and some of her husband's mysterious tricks seriously frightened her.

A hitherto unpublished picture of Houdini and his wife.

Photographs showing Houdini's excellent physique.

One such trick was that in which he made the Christian name of her dead father appear, as though by magic, on his arm. She was so frightened that she ran from the house, but Houdini followed and brought his scared bride back to show her that it was but a simple trick.

Houdini taught his wife the principles of conjuring and " mind-reading," so that soon she was qualified to act as his assistant in stage performances, and thus to begin a long professional partnership.

The play-bill which advertised the first appearance of " The Great Houdinis " was specially drawn up by the magician, who described imaginary successes of the pair in the English music-halls.

The engagements obtained by the partners were mostly in beer halls and their combined salary amounted to twenty dollars a week, that is four English pounds. For this sum they gave about ten performances each day, working from ten o'clock in the morning until ten at night. Card tricks were made up and sold by Mrs. Houdini between the performances. Her husband bought up playing-cards at cheap rates from the gambling-houses which he visited specially for this purpose at night when he had finished his work at the beer hall. The re-sale of the cards added to the slender Houdini income.

Houdini was proud and hopeful when, at the age of twenty, he and his wife were engaged to appear at Tony Pastor's famous hall in New York, but they were given only a minor place in the programme and were not mentioned in the newspapers.

Not without a feeling of disappointment, the Houdinis obtained work at a circus, where he had to operate the Punch and Judy show, perform his tricks, and strangest of all, play the part of a wild man caught in the depths of the jungle. He was shown to the crowds in a cage, growling and eating raw meat.

Mrs. Houdini says that, as they were both quick tempered, they arranged in these circus days various means of avoiding domestic quarrels. When Houdini, in company, raised his right eyebrow three times it was a signal to his wife to stop talking. If she became angry, he would leave the house, walk around for a while, and then, returning, throw his hat into the room. If it were thrown out, he would take another short walk and repeat the operation until his hat was allowed to remain in the room.

The cleverest part of Houdini's performance in the circus, his work with handcuffs, was the least successful, because the audiences believed that he was using faked 'cuffs, but that was not the case. It was not until later years that he learned the importance of being spectacular as well as expert.

Houdini was not a good business man, and a venture in which he had an interest failed. It was a burlesque show, and the magician invested his savings from the circus engagement. The Houdinis knew what it was to be hungry at that time.

One day, Houdini, in New York, went to the offices of several newspapers and offered to sell for twenty dollars the secrets of his handcuff releases and other escapes, but he could not find a buyer. Not many years later, his secrets could not have been bought for ten thousand times that amount.

Tiring of circus work Houdini turned his attention with his wife to " psychic " demonstrations. Playing the part of medium, Houdini's wife acquired the trick of falling into a " trance," and, following the lines laid down by her clever husband, achieved interesting results in halls specially hired for the purpose. As the " Professor," Houdini compiled a book containing lists of people who attended séances in various towns. To add to his stock of information, the magician visited graveyards to make careful notes from tombstones and attended places where local gossip was to be heard. In the guise of a canvasser he would call at houses and obtain opportunities to inspect family Bibles which often contained much useful information.

The Houdinis employed a local tipster to give signals as to the identity of those who had come to the hall to receive messages. The result was that some remarkably impressive

" messages " came through, for Houdini, with his quick mind and retentive memory, could outdo the most seasoned " medium." A clever woman, Mrs. Houdini soon gained a considerable reputation as a medium.

The pair undertook this type of work to avoid the atmosphere of the circus, and to show the possibilities of fraudulent mediumship, but the truth is they were too successful and became almost frightened at the effect of their successes upon the minds of those who were seeking " messages."

Neither of them liked the situation in which they were accepted as genuine mediums. Both clever performers, they could hoodwink all those who came with critical minds to see their demonstrations. When a prophecy which was no more than a vague guess made by Houdini came true, he decided that he must leave the medium business. In later years, he realised the advantage of having played at being a medium, because it had taught him how easy it is to deceive people who are pathetically eager to believe.

In his general travels as a performer in the days which followed these experiences, Houdini never missed an opportunity to study phases of magic and mystery unfamiliar to him. Although he did not know it, he was treading the way to fame.

His escape from handcuffs in a Chicago prison was one of the turning-points in his career because it brought him much publicity, and his decision to spend his savings on a visit to London in 1900 was another such point. He was received quite coldly in England, but when he proved that handcuffs at Scotland Yard could not hold him he attracted attention.

Engagements in London and Berlin came his way and Houdini then began to realise what it all meant.

" Not bad for dime museum Harry," he wrote in his diary when he found himself the star feature at the Alhambra, London. The circus performer had become a star.

Quick to follow up opportunities, Houdini looked only

a head, and nothing could stop him. He accepted challenges to free himself from fetters and to escape from prisons in various parts of Europe, gaining great publicity from these feats. His progress was rapid, and he was as happy as a boy to find that " the great Houdini " was being appreciated at last. He bought for his mother a gown once worn by an English queen and spent a large sum of money so that his wife could drive up to Drury Lane Theatre in a luxurious car to occupy a box at a Royal command performance.

There were set-backs in Houdini's career after this, but none of them serious and he leaped from triumph to triumph.

In his best years in Europe and America he never spared himself. Handcuffed, he dived into icy-cold waters; confident he defied the locksmiths of two continents; buried alive and trussed in iron boxes, he escaped to smile and prepare himself for his next " miracle."

At fifty, he was incredulous that he was so old, but not long afterwards he met his death when at the height of his fame. In the magician's dressing-room, at Montreal, a student who had heard that Houdini could receive hard blows on the stomach without feeling discomfort, struck two or three experimental blows. Houdini was not prepared for them, and the blows caused his death some days later. His body was taken to New York in a stage coffin in which he had been making experiments under water.

So a swift end came to Harry Houdini.

We shall not look upon his like again.

CHAPTER II

HOUDINI'S SPECTACULAR ESCAPES—HIS REMARKABLE
FAILURE AT THE MAGICIANS' CLUB—ESCAPE FROM BANK-
SAFE—IRON BOILER—PAPER BAG—MAIL-BAG—WALK-
ING THROUGH A BRICK WALL—BURIED ALIVE—ESCAPE
FROM IRON BOX—SACK—PACKING-CASE UNDER WATER
—THE VANISHING HORSEMAN—BOX AND SACK ILLU-
SION—THE NEEDLES AND THREAD—THE VANISHING
ELEPHANT—THE MYSTERY OF THE MILK-CAN

THERE were minor failures in Houdini's career,
some of them caused through temporary defects
in apparatus, others through the stupidity or
obstructiveness of a committee man. Yet, with his quick
resourcefulness, Houdini was often able to evade the
embarrassing consequences of the mishap. He had, too, a
great knack of winning the sympathy of the audience if
something went wrong.

Two of the failures in Houdini's life, I think, are of outstanding interest. One of them occurred when he was a
young performer, but the second happened when he was
at the height of his fame.

His first failure, caused by lack of experience, happened
when he was giving a demonstration of an escape from
handcuffs at a side-show. The challenge he made was that
he would escape in a few seconds from any pair of regulation
handcuffs.

Accepting the challenge, a detective smiled as he fastened
the handcuffs on the magician. Houdini noticed the smile
but did not then understand the reason for it. When he
turned aside in order secretly to release himself, he found
that he could not do so. The lock of the handcuffs did not
move because it was jammed, and Houdini was a prisoner.

He suffered the humiliation of having to be cut out of the handcuffs. The reason he could not open the 'cuffs was that the detective had forced a tiny steel pellet into the lock, which made it impossible for anyone to undo them. It was a low trick, but it taught Houdini a sharp lesson. From that time onward, when about to be handcuffed by a challenger, he always insisted that the handcuffs should be locked and unlocked in his view before he permitted them to be placed on his wrists. Thus he obtained proof that the 'cuffs were in normal working condition.

In his later years when he visited the Birmingham area, where most British handcuffs are made, he sometimes had to deal with challengers who presented rusty handcuffs to him. They had been deliberately soaked in water for a week or more with the result that the mechanism worked only with the greatest difficulty. In such cases, Houdini would either denounce the man at once, or say nothing before he went to his cabinet to release himself, waiting to expose his challenger later.

In the hollow poles of his cabinet there were secret hiding-places for a number of useful accessories for the escaper, and among these was a length of fishing-line. Houdini would insert the end of the line into the lock, in which it became entangled. Standing on the part of the line trailing on the floor, he would tug hard so that the lock was pulled back by the fishing-line. Emerging from his cabinet Houdini would then denounce the man, telling the audience of the trick played upon him.

The other failure was more remarkable. As Houdini did not like to have it mentioned in his lifetime, the story is now being told in print for the first time. The peculiar incident occurred when Houdini, visiting England to perform at the climax of his fame, was chairman at a social gathering of the Magicians' Club, London, of which he was then President.

The entertainment was being given at the headquarters of the Club, but before the programme was half over, all the lights went out. There was some commotion, and

Houdini asked to be shown the meter connected with the electric light system. He was taken by Will Goldston, the founder of the Club, to the lower part of the premises occupied by a tradesman, who at that time had gone home. The door of the cellar which contained the meters was locked and no one in the building had the key. Remarking that no key was needed, Houdini produced from his pockets three or four fake-keys which he always carried. Holding a lighted candle, Goldston looked on.

Houdini started confidently, using a suitable pick. It had no effect on the lock, however. He used a second and a third, but the door still remained fastened. Then Houdini got down to the task with a sort of grim impatience, but although he applied every trick he knew from the repertoire which had made him famous and earned him a fortune, he did not succeed in opening the lock. At last he became disgusted and turning to Goldston said : " Fetch some candles and get on with the show."

Prince of handcuff performers and lock-picking experts, Houdini had failed to open this lock, though it belonged to a well-known patent type, hundreds of which he had conquered at various times.

The entertainment at the Magicians' Club continued by candle-light, and the chairman, Mr. Harry Houdini, was not in a good temper. He was hurt by the incident and never referred to it later. Yet it was really no reflection upon him, because locks are uncertain things. Much depends upon their condition.

Houdini was sensitive about this particular failure because so many professional magicians were present and knew of the incident.

The prominent members of the Magicians' Club were careful never to mention it in his presence, but one tactless person who had heard of it did so, and the result was that Houdini stormed for ten minutes, leaving the offender frightened and apologetic.

In one of Houdini's greatest successes, he took a great chance of disastrous failure. For cool daring I cannot imagine anything to surpass it.

BANK-SAFE ESCAPE.—It is the story of an escape from a huge bank-safe on a music-hall stage in London, and is a most remarkable narrative, showing Houdini's great resource and ingenuity. So far as I know he never repeated the performance in England.

He was at that time performing at the old Euston Palace of Varieties, King's Cross, and as a change from his usual programme, announced that he would undertake to escape publicly from any bank-safe in London. Rather to the surprise of some of Houdini's friends, the challenge was accepted by a well-known firm of safe-makers who happened to have in their showrooms an enormous new safe of which they were proud. They were certain that no one could escape from their safe, and they communicated with Houdini.

Only one condition was made by the magician, and it was that the safe should be delivered at the theatre twenty-four hours before the challenge was to be put to the test. The firm readily agreed to this condition. Houdini, they said, could have the safe for a week if he wished, as they were sure that it would stand his closest scrutiny. The huge safe was taken to the Euston Palace, a considerable number of men having to be employed in its removal. So heavy was it, that special supports had to be built under the stage to prevent a possible collapse.

On the night of the challenge, the theatre was crowded and a large number of people could not gain admittance. Always an expert at publicity, Houdini had taken care that all London knew of his new and daring undertaking.

When the curtain went up for Houdini's performance, the audience saw the formidable-looking safe, large enough to hold a man, standing on the stage. Wearing only a dressing-gown and a bathing costume Houdini came forward before the footlights and addressed the audience.

He explained that he was undertaking something of a dangerous character and he might fail. A man could not breathe for long inside the safe, he said.

After some further talk, Houdini invited on to the stage a committee from the audience, which included a well-

known local doctor and a representative of the safe firm
who held the only key to the safe.

The safe was examined inside and outside by the committee, who were satisfied that it was really a stronghold
of steel from which no man could possibly escape.

Discarding his dressing-gown, Houdini expressed to the
audience a wish to be searched and examined medically
before attempting to escape from the safe. The doctor on
the committee agreed to do this, and when the magician
suggested that the medical examination should take place
inside the safe with the door half open, the committee and
the audience approved. A further suggestion by Houdini
that a member of the committee should enter the safe and
act as umpire during the examination was also regarded as
fair and proper.

When the examination was concluded, the three men
emerged from the safe, and the doctor announced to the
audience that he, as a medical man, would testify that it
was impossible for Houdini to have anything concealed
about him and that he had also made a close search of the
safe. The umpire concurred in this opinion, and stated
that the examination had been most thorough.

Turning to the doctor and the umpire, Houdini shook
each of them by the hand, thanked them for their services,
and walked into the huge safe. The door was closed and
carefully locked by the committee. A large screen was
placed round the safe in such a way that no one could
approach it without the knowledge of the audience.

The committee and the audience watched eagerly for
fifteen minutes but nothing happened. When nearly half
an hour had gone by the audience became restless and
excited, and some shouted that the safe should be opened.
Houdini, however, had given his attendants instructions not
to request the man who held the key to open the safe unles
they heard knocking. A series of knocks, he had sai
should be regarded by them as a distress signal. Outsi
the screen the attendants were alert, listening for
knocks, but none came.

After forty minutes, one or two frightened wo

appealed to the management to stop the whole thing. When three-quarters of an hour had passed, the audience saw the screen pushed aside, and Houdini, still in his bathing costume, emerge. There was a great deal of applause, for Houdini had conquered the safe, the door of which remained securely locked. The safe and the lock were re-examined by the committee, but they could find no clue to the mystery of how Houdini had made his escape. To many it was a sort of miracle, and the public have never known the explanation, which I now give.

In the first place, Houdini's request to have the safe in his possession for a few hours before the test was not so innocent as it looked. He really wished to have a chance to tamper with, or temporarily to alter, the mechanism of the safe, and that is what he, in fact, did. With his mechanics, he removed the stiffly working new springs and replaced them with springs of his own. In other words, he so altered the effectiveness of the mechanism that, by the time he had finished, the safe was not the honest and formidable piece of work which the firm had turned out. Yet to the eye, nothing was wrong, as the alterations were interior. Houdini had his own fake-key made to open, from the inside, the altered locking-arrangement. Obtaining possession of the fake-key, after having been searched by the doctor, was one of the chief difficulties, as there was no possibility of hiding it inside the safe, but when I inform you that the man who stepped forward from the committee to volunteer as umpire was Mr. Will Goldston, Houdini's closest friend, and that he shook hands with the umpire as well as with the doctor when thanking them, you will see the possibilities.

The fact is, that attached to an ordinary ring on Mr. Goldston's finger was the special fake-key made so that it could be drawn from the ring by Houdini as he shook hands with Goldston. Had Houdini failed to draw the key from the ring, or, once inside the safe, had the key failed to operate, the situation would have been difficult and unpleasant for the magician.

He did not remain, as it appeared to the audience, forty-

five minutes in the safe. After a few minutes he opened
the door, locked it quietly and carefully again, and sat
behind the screen reading a novel until he thought the
right time had come for him to reveal himself.

The fake-key which enabled Houdini to escape from the
safe was made of steel and had two prongs at the end.
It was cut by him after some experiments with the safe
when the special soft springs had been inserted.

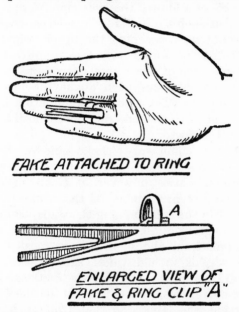

FAKE ATTACHED TO RING

ENLARGED VIEW OF
FAKE & RING CLIP "A"

THE FAKE-KEY WHICH ENABLED HOUDINI TO ESCAPE FROM
THE BANK-SAFE. THE TOP DRAWING SHOWS HOW IT WAS
ATTACHED TO HIS CONFEDERATE'S HAND

No one but a man with an expert knowledge of locks
and of the art of escaping, as well as great self-assurance,
would have attempted such a feat as this escape. It had
distinct risks.

The safe was returned to the makers on the day following
the performance, but, by that time, the real springs had
been replaced and no examination of the mechanism could
show how the trick had been done, for Houdini and his
assistants had left no trace.

I think that the episode of the safe stands out as a remarkable example of the daring deceptions which made Houdini a great performer.

It is impossible to conceive of greater trust than that placed in Goldston by Houdini on the night of the escape. A mishap or a false move on the part of Goldston would have wrecked Houdini's career.

Had some other member of the committee also volunteered to act as umpire, the magician would not have refused him, as such a refusal might have caused suspicion. Houdini would have accepted the other volunteer, with the remark that he would have two umpires to see fair play. No member of the committee or of the audience would have felt any suspicion about the fact of there being two umpires. The medical examination completed, Houdini would have shaken hands with both umpires as well as with the doctor.

The important thing was to shake hands with Goldston, and it did not matter how many were thus treated. The situation did not arise, however, as Goldston looked the part of the innocent member of the committee, taking great interest in the safe, tapping the walls, and appearing to be much engrossed in the whole affair.

This escape from the bank-safe is most interesting, because it reveals with distinct clearness the mind and methods of Houdini. He misled the bank-safe firm, the doctor, the committee, the audience in the theatre and the public outside who later read that Houdini had escaped from a locked safe. He smiled as he left the theatre that night. He had no conscience about his trickery—was, in fact, proud of it, as he had a right to be. His business was to deceive, and the more daring and spectacular the deception, the richer and more popular would he become. The public like to be deceived in the way in which Houdini tricked them.

While the newspapers were full of stories and pictures of Houdini's escape from the safe, and the whole of London was wondering how it had been done, Houdini continued his usual performances with handcuffs, ropes, chains and

Top: Houdini with Will Goldston in London.
Bottom: Houdini in film work.

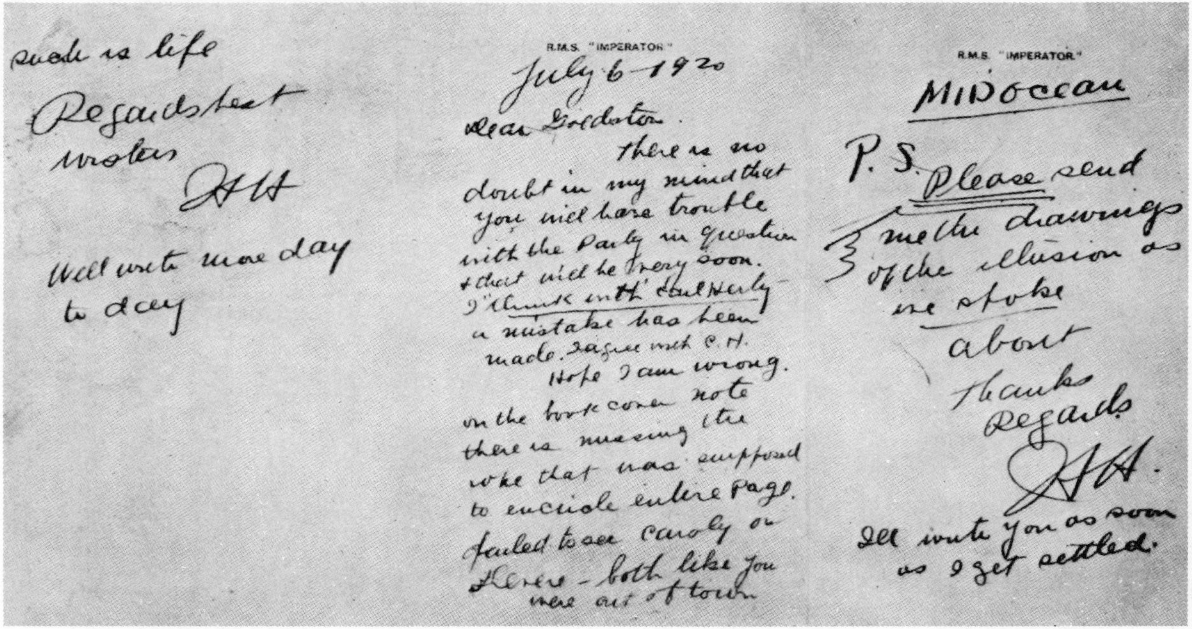

R.M.S. "IMPERATOR"

July 6 1920

Dear Goldston.

There is no doubt in my mind that you will have trouble with the Party in Question and that will be very soon. I think with Carl Hertz a mistake has been made. I agree with C.H. Hope I am wrong.

On the book cover note there is missing the … that was supposed to encircle entire page. … failed to see … Both like you were out of town.

R.M.S. "IMPERATOR"

MIDOCEAN

P.S. Please send me the drawings of the illusion as we spoke about. Thanks Regards HH.

Ill write you as soon as I get settled.

Such is life

Regards best wishes HH

Will write more day to day

Facsimile of a letter written by Houdini to Will Goldston.

iron boxes, filling theatres wherever he went. He had obtained an enormous advertisement.

The public were not aware that Houdini had the safe in his possession for some hours before the performance. Even had they known, I am not at all sure that the significance of it would have been realised. I assume that when the firm delivered the safe beforehand, they were confident that the mechanism was so effective and complicated that it would be impossible for anyone to make a duplicate key, at any rate, in the time available. I do not think it occurred to them that Houdini would, or could, alter the mechanism of their safe.

BOILER-ESCAPE.—Although this escape did not figure in Houdini's usual repertoire, it had a definite relationship to other feats which he constantly performed with excellent results to his pocket and fame.

In the escape from an iron boiler into which he was actually rivetted on the stage, the deception was so clever that the boiler-makers themselves, constantly at close quarters during the performance, did not detect it.

Houdini's magic was divided into several classes, but in most of the different tricks and escapes there was a similarity of principle, although the method varied according to the requirements of the particular illusion.

In the case of the boiler-escape, there was practically no risk, and that is why Houdini was able to repeat it almost everywhere he performed without ever being found out. It was, in fact, the perfect trick, performed at close quarters without a confederate.

Some time before Houdini was due to arrive in a particular town, large posters appeared on the hoardings announcing his arrival and the fact that he would escape in the presence of the audience from a boiler made by any local firm and actually finished on the stage.

The firms who made boilers in the town were usually eager to accept a challenge which meant free advertisement, and Houdini had sometimes to choose between the firms so willing to compete with him.

The firm accepting Houdini's challenge to make the

boiler, did so according to his specifications, but there was really no trick in this. It was a boiler so constructed that escape from it appeared to be impossible.

Made of iron, it was large enough to hold a man and its plates were secured with rivets. The lid of the boiler was so constructed that its edges fitted over the top of the body of the boiler, and there were holes both in the lid and in the boiler at the top, enabling two bars of hard steel to be pushed through crosswise, keeping the lid firmly in position.

It was certainly an inspiration on Houdini's part to arrange for the completion of the boiler on the stage in full public view, as it gave a stamp of honesty to the boiler and provided something of a spectacle.

Following an inspection of the partially completed boiler by representatives of the audience Houdini would be placed inside it while the local workmen came forward to make him a prisoner by driving the final rivets. The boiler completed, the steel bars would be pushed into position so that they held the lid firmly.

To provide secrecy, the boiler, containing Houdini, was always placed in his cabinet, his assistants standing on guard outside it.

The orchestra had its part—the playing of lively music.

At a signal from one of the men the music would stop and Houdini appear from inside the cabinet, a free man. When the boiler, on each occasion, was again shown to the audience, it was found to be intact and as secure as when the workmen had left it. The closest examination by the committee and the workmen revealed not the slightest clue as to how Houdini had escaped from his prison, and the boiler-makers were usually invited to take the boiler back to their works for further inspection.

This trick never failed to baffle the town in which it was performed.

Once again the wizard of escape had worked his old trick by having the boiler delivered to him at the theatre some time before the performance. In this case, hours of preparation or of tampering with the boiler were not

necessary. Houdini's purpose would have been fulfilled
had the boiler been delivered to him only a short time
before the curtain went up. There was no actual tampering with any part of the boiler. The secret was one of
exchange. Houdini knew that if he were imprisoned in the
boiler with the lid kept in position by the *hard* steel bars he
could not escape from it, as hard steel bars cannot be bent

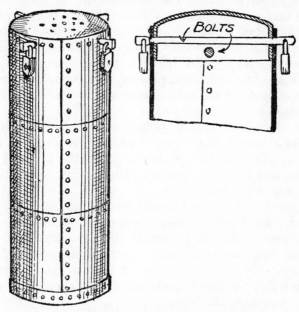

IRON BOILER INTO WHICH HOUDINI WAS RIVETTED AND
YET ESCAPED

or "worked" in such circumstances. What Houdini did
know was that *soft* steel bars can be cut or bent with the
proper implements. He knew, further, that in appearance
soft steel bars are the same as those made of hard steel, and
that, normally, it requires some kind of test with a saw or
other implement to discriminate between them. He
therefore exchanged the bars, hiding the genuine ones in
the hollow poles of his cabinet, innocent looking and
specially made for such a use. This was done before the
performance began.

Neither the committee nor the workmen noticed the change, as the bars inserted appeared to be the original ones. At that early stage of the trick, everyone was, as usual, off their guard, and no one thought of putting the bars to a workshop-test. Those who watched imagined that the trick, if any, was to come later, but the real part of it had already been done. All that remained for Houdini, when imprisoned in the boiler, was to cut with his special tiny saw through the soft steel bars. This involved some effort, but Houdini was strong and unafraid of work. The committee and the workmen were off the stage, during the actual escape, and between the audience and the cabinet was the orchestra, playing loud enough to drown any noise made by the cutting process, though this was not great, as it was inside the boiler.

When Houdini had freed himself by cutting through the bars he removed them, and replaced the original bars securely. The cut bars were hidden in the poles of the cabinet, and the saw concealed there or in his clothing which was not searched.

Houdini deserves much credit for this escape. A boiler made in a local foundry would be accepted by most people as fool-proof. Houdini specialised in employing in his illusions materials ordinarily regarded as being above suspicion. His whole life appeared to be directed towards finding a flaw in honest craftmanship, or, even if no such defect existed, to create one.

PAPER-BAG RELEASE.—Houdini's escape from a paper bag was another interesting example of trickery.

For this deception he used a bag shaped like a foolscap envelope and large enough to contain him. The bag had at the top a gummed flap, which, when sealed down, made it apparently impossible for anyone to escape without tearing or destroying the paper.

When Houdini had placed himself in the bag and the flap was carefully gummed down by the committee, they invariably inscribed their names or initials to make an exchange impossible. When this had been done, the cabinet was placed round the bag which held the magician prisoner.

It will be readily understood that the use of a covering was necessary in escapes of this kind, so that the public would not know how Houdini made his escape. The trick would have been spoiled for ever had he performed it openly. There is no trick when you know how a thing is done. Without mystery there is no interest, although certain smaller tricks which depend for their effectiveness upon diverting the attention, misdirection, or swiftness of

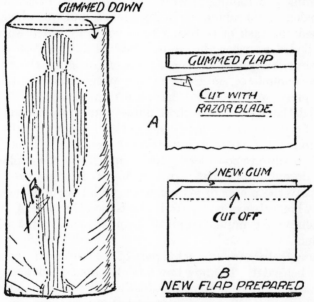

THE PAPER-BAG ESCAPE

manipulation, can be done successfully without resort to concealment of any kind. Houdini was a master of both types of trickery, but in his escapes secrecy in execution was unavoidable.

So, in the paper-bag escape, he always remained in his cabinet for a short time, and then walked out carrying the bag in his hand. The names and initials of the members of the committee were still there and the bag had certainly not been changed, though it was undamaged. This trick provided a nice problem, and no scrutiny of the bag gave the committee the slightest hint as to the solution.

The paper-bag escape is, I think, delightful, because it is so utterly simple. The first thing which Houdini, imprisoned in the bag, did when his screen or cabinet was placed around him, was to produce from his pocket a safety-razor blade and cut the bag carefully in a straight line exactly along the top. Then he drew himself out and commenced to remove all trace of his means of exit. This involved nothing more than making a new flap by a simple gumming and folding process. The gum and brush were concealed in his cabinet or in his pocket, and when he had finished the task of restoring the bag, it looked precisely as it had done when the committee had finished the work of sealing, *except that the bag was about two inches shorter.*

The committee, in their examination after the trick, paid great attention to the condition of the bag and assured themselves that their names and initials had not been forged or reproduced, but none of them thought at any phase of the test of measuring the length of the bag.

When you are considering the simplicity of the explanation, do not forget that in presenting it, Houdini brought into play the power of his personality and the influence of *talk*, which always tends to distract the attention of even the shrewdest minds from the fundamental point of a problem.

These factors are as much a part of the trick as the actual secret behind it. To know how a trick is done is not enough. The vital thing is to have the dazzling or soothing personality to present it in such a way that the audience cannot think, but yet the secret of an illusion must be sufficiently ingenious to bear the closer examination of retrospective thinking.

The materials used by Houdini to achieve spectacular and interesting effects in his escapes were widely different in character. Wood, iron, glass and paper were all employed by him. When he turned his attention to canvas and mail-bags he accomplished what he regarded as the neatest trick of escaping in the whole of his repertoire. Houdini made a close study of standard mail-bags, and after some experiments presented a trick the solution of which would never occur to the average mind. He selected the American mail-bag for the trick because it was a well-made, formidable article. The British mail-bag would have been useless to Houdini as it is little more than an ordinary sack.

MAIL-BAG TOO.—The American mail-bags are made of sail-canvas, part of the bag being sewn and rivetted to the canvas. They are tightly fastened by passing a strong leather strap through a number of eyelets, and a padlock of a modern type keeps the mouth of the bag firmly closed.

Houdini gave himself a hard problem when he set out to discover a means of escape from such a bag, but he did succeed, and the fact that in his performance he used only the regulation pattern of mail-bag added to the mystery. Houdini liked to encourage people to inspect the bag before and after the escape, because he knew there was nothing for them to find out.

At his own request an inquisitive man was once placed in a mail-bag of this type by Houdini. By being so imprisoned, the man hoped to find the secret. Locked in the bag, he soon realised his helplessness and had to shout for help. There was, he said, no air in the bag and no room in which to move.

The value of this trick was greatly increased by the fact that it involved no tampering with the bag. Nothing was altered or removed, and therefore, in that sense, it was an example of perfect trickery.

When performing in American towns, Houdini would often invite those who could do so to bring mail-bags to the theatre, and when they accepted this invitation their astonishment at Houdini's escape was all the greater because they knew the genuineness of the bag provided.

It was sometimes suggested that Houdini actually cut himself out of the mail-bag provided and replaced it with another bag into which he fastened himself. This theory did not, however, explain how he could have locked himself into the second bag. Another theory was that he never got into the bag.

Houdini's escape from the mail-bag caused more speculation among those who were intrigued by magical problems than his greater and more ambitious illusions.

I know of a university professor who was so much attracted by Houdini's escape from the mail-bag that he obtained a similar bag himself in order to make experiments at home. He was placed and locked in the bag by his friends, who soon had to rescue him, however. The bag was subjected to the most intensive scrutiny by the professor, who not only examined all the materials used in it, but measured the bag so carefully that he accounted for every inch. He made efforts to find a way of tampering with the bag in order to make escape possible and yet to defy the notice of those who had examined it beforehand. He did a lot of hard work in this direction with knife and needle. The result of it was that he damaged the canvas irretrievably.

The persistent professor bought another bag and continued his experiments, and this time he drew up a series of diagrams, approaching the escape as a mathematical problem. In this he was as unsuccessful as he had been in the practical experiments.

He placed the problem before his fellow-professors, and they spent many nights trying to find the answer.

Some of the professors submitted the problem to their students, and for a while little else was talked of in that particular university, but neither the professors nor the students could think of a practical way of escape from the mail-bag.

The execution of the escape involved a good deal of determined effort on the part of Houdini. In the first place, he had concealed about him a duplicate key to the bag. It was easy for him to make or obtain such a key, and this was fastened to his belt by a length of string concealed in his clothing. Once inside the mail-bag and concealed in his cabinet, Houdini would commence to make use of the only possible avenue of escape from the bag. This was the tiny space where the flap came over the top of the bag and in contact with it. You can imagine how small that space would be in a well-made Government mail-bag. It was, in fact, just big enough to enable Houdini to force the key and the string through it. By such means, he was able to get the key, attached to the string tied to his belt, outside the bag, and thus make important progress.

His next move was to grope along the canvas until he got hold of the key *through* the material. When this was done he would manœuvre his hand, forcing the flexibility of the canvas to its utmost, until he got the key into the lock from

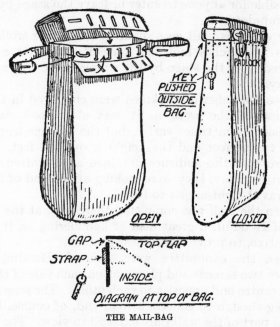

THE MAIL-BAG

the outside. To do this and to turn the key in the lock was not an easy business, but Houdini was well practised in it, and could do it with remarkable speed. Although the canvas was stout, Houdini had trained himself to grasp and operate things through canvas. The opening of the lock had to be done quickly, as there was little air in the bag.

THROUGH A BRICK WALL.—The illusion of walking through a brick wall in front of an audience was another of the picturesque possibilities which attracted the attention of this remarkable man, whose mind and body were never at rest.

As in the escape from the iron boiler, the illusion made a strong appeal to the audience because the wall was actually built on the stage in their view by local workmen.

Before the bricklayers began their work, Houdini always pointed out to the audience the fact that the entire stage was covered by one large carpet which made it impossible for anyone to enter or leave the stage by means of a trap-door.

The wall was built on a small steel frame or trolley with wheels two inches high, so that afterwards it could be removed from the stage by the simple process of wheeling it away.

Quite a number of workmen were employed in the construction of the wall, as it was of a good size. The dimensions sometimes varied, but the average length was about twelve feet and the height about ten feet. It was built so that the audience obtained an elevation view of it, that is to say, they were looking at the end of it. The wall was at right angles to them.

When the wall was completed there was, at the suggestion of Houdini, a great deal of hammering on it by the committee, to prove that it was genuine.

When the committee were satisfied, Houdini would produce two screens and place one on each side of the wall, in the centre and opposite to each other. The screens were just big enough to conceal a man and, of course, left the greater part of the wall fully exposed to view. The screens did not reach to the top of the wall, so that climbing it was obviously impossible. When all was ready Houdini would walk behind one of the screens, shouting, " I am going," and, after a pause, " Here I am now." At that moment, he would appear on the other side of the wall, emerging from behind the screen there. It is important to emphasise that the screen did not in any way cover the wall but was used simply to conceal the actual movements of the performer.

Few tricks could be more bewildering in their effect than

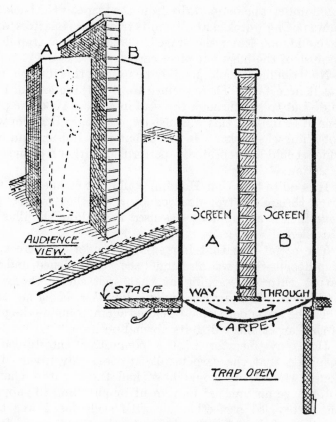

WALKING THROUGH A BRICK WALL

this. There seemed no solution to it, and most people soon gave up their attempts to find out how it was done.

It was, as I have said, impossible for Houdini to have climbed the wall in view of the audience ; he certainly could not escape temporarily from the stage at the back, as he was being watched at all points from close quarters, and he could not leave the stage by means of a trap-door because of the huge one-piece carpet.

No " double " could possibly be used in this illusion, nor was it necessary. There seemed to be nothing left for him to do but to get through the wall in some way, as he pretended to do, but this was also impossible, as Houdini was not a miracle-worker. It was a first-class illusion and one which could be repeatedly performed without chance of detection.

It is quite true that Houdini could not escape from the stage through a trap-door or by any other means, yet nevertheless a trap-door was used in making the illusion possible.

The secret was that immediately under the screen, a trap-door—which was also under the wall—opened, and the carpet naturally sagging at that spot under the wall, enabled Houdini *to crawl under to the other side of the wall.* Then the trap-door would be closed again, bringing the part of the carpet affected to its normal position.

Had any member of the committee entertained a suspicion that the carpet was in some way involved, I doubt whether he would have had the slightest chance to observe an unusual movement or anything to support his theory, so perfectly and with such speed was this function of deception carried out. As a matter of fact, however, no one ever stumbled upon the secret.

Concerning this illusion of walking through a wall, Houdini had a difference of opinion with at least one other magician. I believe the dispute referred either to the invention of the illusion or to the right to perform it. It is, however, not part of my purpose to discuss such a matter here.

Archiv für Kunst u. Wissenschaft, Charlottenburg.

Harry Houdini

One of Houdini's autographed pictures. He is holding a copy
of one of his early books.

Casket containing Houdini being submerged in the swimming pool of the Hotel Shelton, in New York, on August 5, 1926. Houdini stayed under for an hour and a half by using intensive breath-control to conserve oxygen, thus disproving claims of Egyptian fakirs who supposedly lived that long without air.

BURIED ALIVE.—When *Houdini was buried alive*, it meant hazard and much careful concentration for him.

The appropriate announcements never failed to attract a large crowd to the plot of ground, usually just outside a big town, where the demonstration was to take place. A good deal of excitement attended these demonstrations and the presence of the police was a necessity. Houdini, as a good showman, made the most of the moments before he began the work of being buried alive for an hour. Sometimes he made a speech, and he was listened to with curious feelings by those who thought that perhaps, too daring, he was about to make his last spectacular experiment.

After a hole six feet deep had been dug, Houdini would be placed inside an ordinary coffin. The rest of the procedure followed the lines of real burial, the coffin being lowered into the grave, which was completely filled in again.

As the minutes went by, at each of these tests, the crowd became uneasy, and Houdini's managers, watches in hand, showed a measure of concern which was by no means unreal.

At the end of about fifty minutes the work of digging the grave open would begin, and was quickly completed. Raised out of the grave with ropes, the coffin would be unscrewed and Houdini released. Often he showed signs of the strain of being buried alive for such a length of time.

I have discussed this trick with many people who have been mystified by it. Some of them assert that Houdini never went into the coffin and that by some smart ruse he was able to make people think he had done so. Others have expressed the view that he had concealed about him apparatus to provide him with oxygen, but neither of these theories is correct. Houdini was genuinely buried alive with no artificial aid of any kind.

The secret was simply one of intensive breathing-control, of which Houdini was a master. The method of breathing employed by him was that while in the coffin he took breaths of extreme shortness, thus conserving the supply of oxygen in the coffin.

It will be readily understood that deep breathing uses up, or I might say burns up, the vital constituents of the air around. Had Houdini breathed in the normal way in the coffin he would not have lived long. No doubt it was a dangerous business, but Houdini never hesitated to take risks to maintain his reputation as a " great magician." He never rested on his laurels and had to live dangerously to keep his place at the top of the theatre bills.

To a man not possessing abnormal physical powers and the ability to concentrate for a long period, this experiment of being buried alive would certainly be fatal. Houdini used to train himself for it by holding his breath under water. He acquired the ability to stay in the coffin for a long period by a series of experiments in which he would gradually increase the duration of his voluntary burial until he became became sure of himself.

I have seen a number of letters written by him in which he referred proudly to these experiments and to the length of time he was able to stay in the coffin. This and other evidence makes me believe that Houdini was proud of his ability to be buried alive. He had good reason to be proud of it. Sometimes his friends attempted to dissuade him from making these dangerous experiments because they feared that some unforeseen mishap might result in his death, a fear that was not without foundation.

He did not, however, listen to advice or reason in such matters and regarded the performance of being buried alive as a hobby to which he could turn when he wanted to give the public " an extra thrill."

Houdini's interest in the possibilities of being buried alive for a considerable time was first aroused through a performance of the same kind by a fakir. Houdini asserted that nothing supernormal was involved and set about to train himself to repeat the performance of the fakir. He succeeded admirably and then turned his achievement to purposes of publicity for himself. One other thing he learned in developing the trick was that the coffin should be slightly larger than usual. As the size of coffins vary, the little extra space gained by Houdini in this way passed unnoticed, and even if it had been observed, there could have been no reasonable objection to it because, fundamentally, the trick was one of extreme difficulty and considerable peril.

One of Houdini's obsessions was to reproduce by normal means the wonders of fakirs and fraudulent mediums. He was always annoyed if anyone suggested that an achievement in this category must be supernatural. Had his great strength temporarily failed him during one of these demonstrations of being buried alive, as it might have done, Houdini would have met his death in a way that he would have liked—being picturesque to the last.

Another coffin trick which Houdini often performed was of a different character. It was designed for stage performance.

Members of the committee from the audience were invited to inspect the coffin most closely, and often they spent considerable time in doing so. It was stoutly made and screws were used to fix on the lid. The screws, as well as the coffin itself, were invariably examined with much care. Houdini did not mind how cautiously the coffin was inspected for he was sure no one would discover the secret of his escape.

Although he performed this trick hundreds of times no ordinary member of the public ever did find out how it was done.

After the preliminary business of inspection had been gone through, Houdini would be placed inside the coffin, the lid of which was securely screwed down, seals, usually wax, being pressed over the screws.

This escape belonged to the class which had to be performed in the privacy of Houdini's cabinet, and here it was carried out. The length of time which elapsed before the magician appeared again varied according to his mood and to the effect he desired to create among the spectators. It was always of sufficient duration, however, to make the audience believe that a most difficult escape had been accomplished.

For them, it was certainly a mysterious achievement, because, when the committee re-examined the coffin, they found it intact and the seals on the screws unbroken. It was the intact condition of the seals which chiefly puzzled the audience, and some believed that after forcing the lid of the coffin in some way he imitated and remade the seals. This supposed solution was, however, wide of the mark.

The seals and screws did not trouble Houdini because, in order to escape from the coffin, he had no occasion to lift off the lid. Houdini escaped by removing *the bottom of the coffin*, pushing upwards against the inside with his shoulders.

The coffin was so constructed, in a secret way, that the upper part of it was lifted from the bottom. The screws in the bottom of the coffin did not, as they appeared to do, hold the bottom securely against the sides, because these screws fitted into dowels, or wooden slots shaped like a screw, attached to the bottom edge of the sides of the coffin. The screws which appeared to keep the bottom of the coffin securely against the sides merely fitted into these dowels, thus keeping the bottom of the coffin only temporarily in position, and yet so ingeniously that anyone would think the screws had been driven into the bottom and into the sides in the ordinary way. Considerable force had to be employed by Houdini to escape in this way, because the bottom of the coffin had to be fixed to the rest of it with sufficient security to defy such an examination as the committee would make. The trick in the coffin really made the screws ineffective in the bottom because they were driven into the dowels or wooden encasements instead of into the wood of the sides of the coffin.

The replacement of the bottom of the coffin by Houdini was quite a straightforward task, and so long as it was carefully done there was no chance of the committee suspecting during their re-examination that the bottom was detachable.

As a trick, this was by no means among Houdini's best performances. It involved the use of faked apparatus, the secret of which the public never had any real chance to detect. Yet it was puzzling in its execution and much ingenuity was shown in the structure. It was just a neat little example of misdirection, but it did not demand from Houdini the resourcefulness and coolness he was compelled to exercise in his bigger achievements.

There is no end to the possibilities of tricks with specially faked magical apparatus.

FROM AN IRON BOX.—In a much better class as a trick was Houdini's escape from an iron box. There was nothing false in the box which Houdini produced. An examination of it under a powerful glass would have revealed nothing wrong or suspicious. Made of iron, one-eighth of an inch in thickness, the box was heavy and solid. It was rivetted strongly at each corner and angle, and the lid which fitted over it was similarly treated. There were four holes in the sides of the lid, and these corresponded to four holes in the top part of the iron box. The holes were used for bolts, which kept the lid in position. The box, the nuts and the cotter pins, were all subjected to the usual scrutiny by the committee. Engineers often figured in the committee which went on the stage for this trick, but none of them was able to find a defect in the iron box or in the accessories. The box and the rest of the things were all genuinely made and might have been produced in any workshop.

When Houdini had taken his position in the box the lid would be adjusted by the committee, to whom he would push through each of the holes the bolts so that the nuts could be fastened on from the outside, and the cotter pins placed.

Again, the escape was made while Houdini was screened by his cabinet, and there was the usual astonishment when he appeared on the stage with the box still fastened and all the bolts, nuts and pins in place.

It was really a clever trick, and Houdini repeated it many times without discovery.

The solution of this mystery is that, when he got inside the box, Houdini *did not push through the holes the bolts he had shown to the committee* but other bolts which were

cleverly faked and looked precisely the same as the original
bolts, which he had concealed after getting into the box.

The heads of the faked bolts which he pushed through
the holes *could be unscrewed by Houdini from the inside,* so
that he had merely to unscrew these bolt-heads with his
fingers and push the bolts through the holes until they fell
onto the floor of his cabinet. Of course, nothing remained
to hold the lid in position and he could lift it off and step

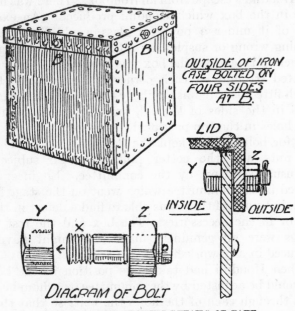

THE IRON BOX, SHOWING DETAILS OF FAKE

out. He would next replace in the holes the original bolts
which were shown, and the heads of which did not screw off.

This replacement of the original bolts was somewhat
complicated and involved the use of string. Houdini was
a master of the process, however, and it did not take long.
With the box restored to its original condition of security,
it was again ready for an examination that would reveal
nothing.

Houdini did not appear from the cabinet as soon as he
had completed the trick of escape and restoration, but

waited for awhile reading or amusing himself. He could have performed this trick with any iron box of this type provided he had a chance to make or obtain bolts with faked heads.

It is important to distinguish between the escapes in which Houdini was searched and those in which there was no such examination. In tricks of this type he was not searched because there was apparently no need for such a precaution.

The noise caused by the bolts as they fell to the floor when he pushed them through was not heard by the audience because of the orchestra. For some of his escapes, Houdini required loud music during the critical moments, and the necessity for it will be realised easily when you think of the noise produced by Houdini's freeing himself, for example, from the iron boiler, where the work of sawing bars had to be carried out.

OUT OF A SACK.—One of the qualities which made Houdini a successful performer was his insistence upon using, wherever possible, the simplest materials. An admirable example of this was a sack escape. In this case, nothing was used in the trick except good canvas and stout thread, such as is used for sail-making. The great novelty and appeal of the trick consisted chiefly in the fact that Houdini was actually sewn into the bag on the stage.

Two or three members of the committee did not need much time to complete the bag, and the needlework was efficient, if not elegant.

They were greatly surprised when Houdini walked from his cabinet holding the sack, which they had marked for identification, in his hand. Naturally the committee made an immediate examination of the stitches to discover if they had been tampered with, but they found nothing.

There were many people who liked this trick of Houdini's better than anything else he did. It was certainly mystifying, but the explanation is absurdly simple. When Houdini, inside the bag, was placed in his cabinet, he merely cut the threads at one edge of the sack and then sewed up the bag once more. Although the bag had been marked for identification, to make an exchange impossible, it never occurred to the committee to *mark the thread* used by them. Stitches in such cases are so much alike that the average person would certainly not be able afterwards to say of a particular row of stitches that they were not his.

After releasing himself, Houdini would have a good look at what remained of the row of stitches he had cut, and should there be any outstanding characteristics in the way it had been sewn, he would carefully imitate it. Even in stitching, personality shows itself, and had Houdini not taken the precaution of imitating the type of stitching he had cut through, he might have been discovered when showing the bag for re-examination.

Asked to sew one end of the bag, a member of the committee would do so with remarkable care and deliberation, making a neat row of small stitches. Another man, while doing his part of the work quite effectively, would make his stitches large and irregular.

Some of the stitching was done out of the range of Houdini's vision, as his position when the bag was being sewn round him would not permit him to see all of the work. This examination of the type of stitching employed was really the only precaution Houdini had to take in performing a trick of delightful simplicity.

Houdini provided his own materials, but there was no reason why he could not have performed the escape with canvas and thread brought to him by a member of the audience, provided that he could obtain a piece of the thread of the same type as that being used. As a matter of fact, on at least one occasion, Houdini did this for the fun of the thing. When a sail-maker challenged him there was a little addition to the trick which was distinctly clever and daring. During the preliminaries, when the man who had brought his canvas, needles and thread, was producing them to the committee and to Houdini, the magician saw the chance for which he was watching—to steal a length of the challenger's thread. Seeing that he had to cut it from a length of thread, it must have been a nimble movement, because there were six or eight people immediately around him. Houdini was particularly proficient at deception at close quarters.

The man who challenged the wizard on this occasion was most astonished when the escape had been performed, for his professional experience enabled him to sew the sack expertly. He was assisted by another committee man, and Houdini took care in escaping from the bag *not to cut the edge of the sack made by the sail-maker*. He suspected a trick in the sail-maker's stitches, or that, in any case, the stitches would be so distinctive that he might have difficulty in reproducing them.

The sail-maker who challenged Houdini thought himself clever and believed that the magician would not be able to escape from a sack of his making. Yet he was not so clever as he thought or, rather, Houdini was much cleverer than he had imagined. Not only was the poor sail-maker's thread cut and stolen under his eyes, but he was hood-winked into making *only a part* of the bag himself.

The incident is typical of Houdini's audacity and remarkable quickness.

UNDER WATER.—No feat of Houdini's attracted the public more than his spectacular escape from a packing-case under water. The fascination of it lay, among other things, in the fact that it was not a stage performance but took place on a river or canal. Houdini presented this escape with a great display of showmanship, in which he was so accomplished.

Such a sensational phrase as " My challenge to death " was freely used in the advertisement-matter, for Houdini exercised no restraint in the language he applied to his own performances.

When a sufficiently large crowd had gathered, two or three local carpenters would begin the work of assembling a large packing-case, the parts of which they had made. When the case was ready, Houdini, handcuffed, would be placed inside.

Ordinary wire nails of the type generally found in packing-cases were used on these occasions. The carpenters took great care over their work. A small hole was bored in the lower side or bottom of the box so as to make it sink, thus, apparently, depriving Houdini of any chance of escape.

The final stage in the imprisonment of the magician was the tying round the packing-case of a rope in the same way as ribbon is tied round a chocolate-box, excepting, of course, that the rope was tightly tied and well knotted.

By the time all this had been done a tug hired by Houdini would come alongside the pier, or jetty, where the demonstration was being given. The packing-case would be hoisted over the water by means of a crane swung out from the tug and then slowly lowered into the water until it was submerged. This caused among the crowd the excitement which Houdini had calculated upon. In a minute or two the crowd would see the packing-case being hoisted up again and the magician sitting on the top.

When the tug drew alongside the quay once more an inspection of the packing-case by the Press and public would show nothing, for the case looked exactly as when Houdini had been put into it, the lid still being securely nailed down. This feat required dexterity, some daring and a little deception.

The packing-case was certainly genuine, but what the public did not know was that Houdini had concealed about him a pair of small nail-cutters. The handcuffs he used on these occasions were faked and could be opened instantly by touching a secret spring. *As soon as Houdini had been fastened into the packing-case he would release himself from the handcuffs and, with his nail-cutters in hand, prepare himself for rapid work as soon as the case was lowered into the water.* It needed only a few seconds to cut a sufficient number of the nails to enable Houdini to push open one or more planks, forming the lid, to squeeze himself out, and his next step was to sit on the case so as to force the planks temporarily into position.

It was certainly remarkable as a quick under-water feat, but Houdini was an expert swimmer and accustomed to stay under water for several minutes.

Top: Houdini manacled and about to dive into the Mersey.
Bottom: Houdini being picked up.

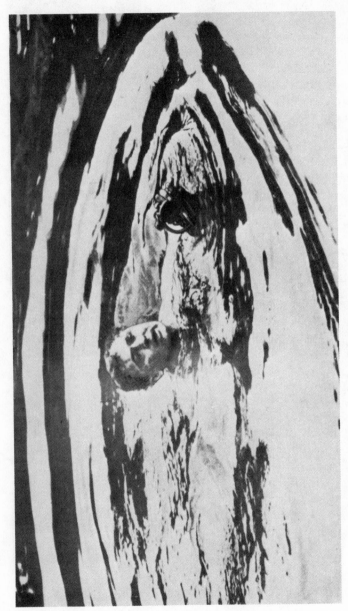

Houdini in the water after releasing himself from the handcuffs.

The deception in the demonstration concerned the restoring of the packing-case, with its cut nails.

As soon as the packing-case was hauled on board it was seized by two of Houdini's men who, in a cabin on the tug, which was not yet alongside the jetty, quickly removed the pieces of broken nails and substituted new nails of the same kind as those used by the carpenters. *The inspection*

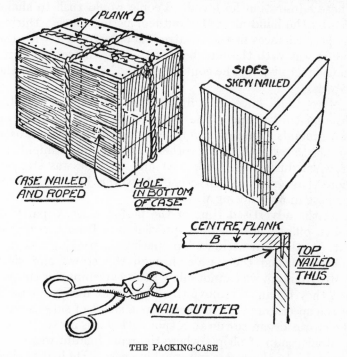

THE PACKING-CASE

of the packing-case by the Press and members of the public did not take place until the tug drew alongside the jetty again, when it was bundled out for further examination.

Everyone seemed to forget, as the public always forgot on such occasions, those moments when the packing-case was *out of their sight.* They were vital moments in the task of making the case look what it had been when the performance began.

This escape has been regarded by the public as one of

Houdini's most mysterious accomplishments. There was not, as I have said, much mystery about it, but as an example of physical courage and coolness it was a distinctive achievement. It is also interesting because it is so characteristic of Houdini's methods. He liked to perform it, as it brought him a great deal of publicity and also drew him into closer personal contact with the public whose admiration he loved. People would rush to shake him by the hand after this outdoor performance. During his performances in the theatre, his only contact with the public was with the members of the committee, but here, on the pier or jetty, he could enjoy the hero-worship of the crowds.

More than once, Houdini found himself in trouble through this escape. The police took objection to it on two grounds : one of them, that obstruction was caused by the crowds and the other that Houdini might be drowned during the trick. At any rate, he was stopped more than once. At Liverpool, however, he achieved his purpose in an amusing way.

At the advertised time of the performance, a party of police officers was sent to prevent him from carrying it out. As the carpenters were preparing the packing-case, the officers pushed their way through the crowd and said, " Mr. Houdini, we cannot allow you to attempt this thing," and they began to remove the box, to the disappointment of the spectators. Then there was a shout of surprise and the crowd began to run to a spot fifty yards away, joining another group of people where the real Houdini was being lowered into the water in a packing-case. He had tricked the police by using a " double " at the advertised place and by himself performing a short distance away. The constables ran, but they were then too late, for the demonstration was being completed. Houdini laughed at the success of his ruse, and it brought him much publicity.

THE VANISHING HORSEMAN.—A smart deception which formed part of Houdini's stage programme was one in which a white horse was used. The illusionist, dressed in a blue uniform, would ride on the stage on a fine animal with his retinue of attendants, dressed in white, around him. Two of the attendants would produce a huge fan which they held up so that, for a moment, the magician was hidden from the view of the audience. When the fan was lowered, Houdini had vanished.

No trap-door was used in this illusion. How, then, did Houdini succeed in vanishing from the stage ? The answer is that he did not leave the stage, though he was unobserved by the audience, because in the moment during which he was concealed by the fan, he tore off the blue uniform, specially made of paper for the purpose, and pushed it under the white uniform he was wearing under the blue uniform. To jump off the horse required only a second or two and then he could mingle with the attendants on the stage without being recognised, *as no one had troubled to count the attendants.*

One of the smartest rapid-escape illusions ever performed by Houdini was presented by him when he first visited England.

BOX AND SACK.—In this illusion, Houdini showed on the stage a strong wooden box and a sack. While the audience watched carefully, his woman partner was placed in the sack which, tied tightly at the neck, was lifted into the box. When the lid had been fastened, a piece of thick rope was tied around the box.

The next move was to lift the box, containing the sack in which the woman was imprisoned, into Houdini's cabinet on the stage, and then to draw the curtain, the illusionist standing on the stage some distance away. Houdini always made a spectacular dash into the cabinet, and when the curtain was pulled aside by one of the attendants a second or two later, he had vanished and his woman partner walked from the cabinet in which the box, still screwed and tied, was to be seen. The woman walked to the footlights while the attendants dragged the box from the cabinet to the front of the stage. Then, when the box was opened, and the mouth of the sack untied, Houdini was discovered in the sack. The box, screwed and roped, had certainly not been changed and there was no doubt as to the identity of the man found in the sack inside the box which, but a few seconds earlier, had contained the woman.

Skilfully concealed, a secret panel in the box made this illusion possible. By means of a simple movement, the

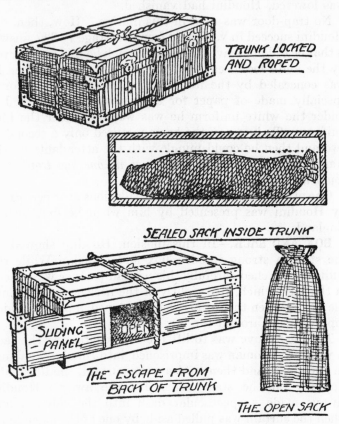

TRUNK LOCKED AND ROPED

SEALED SACK INSIDE TRUNK

SLIDING PANEL

OPEN

THE ESCAPE FROM BACK OF TRUNK

THE OPEN SACK

THE BOX AND SACK ESCAPE

panel could be pushed back from inside the box, thus enabling anyone to escape from or to enter it quickly.

The actual procedure in performing the illusion was this: as soon as the woman partner, tied up in the sack, had been lifted into the box, she opened the bottom of the sack by cutting the seam, and then crawled out of the sack, ready to emerge from the box at the right moment. When

Houdini, concealed by the cabinet, entered the box through the sliding panel, he pushed himself up into the sack. He was found in a *sitting position* when the lid of the box was opened by the attendants and the neck of the sack untied. *He did not move from that position,* so no one suspected that the bottom of the sack, which, of course, they could not see, had been cut. The chief merit of this illusion was the great speed with which it was carried out.

NEEDLES AND THREAD.—For many years Houdini regularly performed the trick with the needles and thread. He would produce a number of needles and a piece of thread and then invite the committee to examine his mouth. They would find nothing in his mouth. Then Houdini would slowly place in his mouth the needles as well as the piece of thread, which was not in any way attached to the needles. There was no doubt whatever that the needles and the cotton did go into Houdini's mouth.

He would close his mouth and perform a swallowing motion and, immediately after, pulled from his mouth the cotton with the needles all threaded on it in a row. Sometimes the thread with the needles would extend right across the stage.

Houdini liked this trick and practised it hundreds of times before he performed it in public, for it was a piece of conjuring not without its dangers.

Houdini was able to baffle the committee because, in spite of their examination of his mouth, there *was* something hidden there. It was a bundle of needles all ready threaded on a piece of cotton, and the real part of the trick was *in concealing the needles from those who inspected his mouth.*

When Houdini placed in his mouth the needles and cotton he had produced in the first place, he at once, by the swallowing movement, caused them to move into another part of the mouth. These needles, by the way, had blunt ends, a fact which would not be noticeable to the committee as they were not given the chance to examine them. The needles they were allowed to examine were quite genuine, because as Houdini pulled them from his mouth in a certain way there was little danger of his being pricked by them. He used to have a knot between each needle on the cotton which he pulled from his mouth to prevent the needles slipping, and thus jamming against each other.

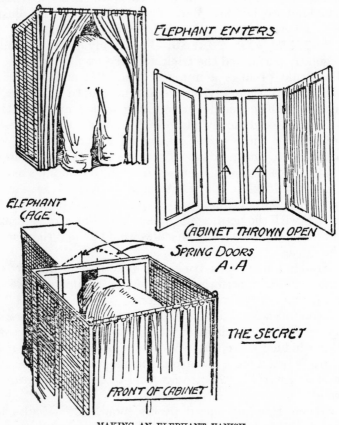

MAKING AN ELEPHANT VANISH

VANISHING ELEPHANT.—In contrast to this example of intimate conjuring, Houdini performed many times a spectacular illusion in which an elephant was made to vanish. I have been told that Houdini experimented with this illusion because someone had told him that even he could not cause an elephant to disappear. The problem

Theo Hardeen, brother and successor of Houdini, laced in a strait-jacket ready to escape.

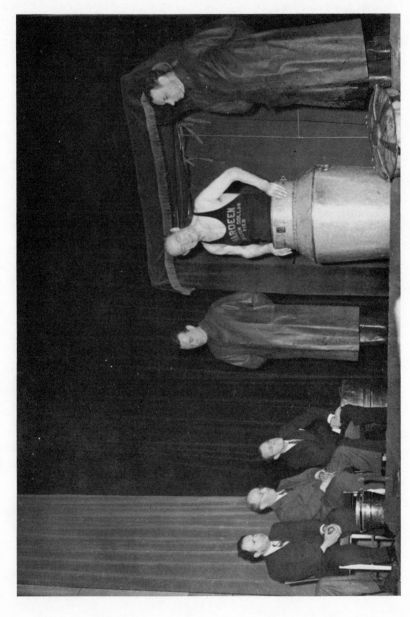

Hardeen, as Houdini's successor, entering a water-filled milk can after its examination by a committee from the audience. (Photo taken nearly twenty years

certainly presented some difficulties, in the face of which both the conjurer's sleeve and the trap-door would be useless.

The effect of the illusion as presented by Houdini was this : on the stage the audience would see a large and yet collapsible cabinet. Lumbering on to the stage, the elephant would walk straight into the cabinet. Almost simultaneous with the animal's entry into the cabinet, its flimsy walls would be pulled back and the elephant had vanished. A trap-door could not be used and it was impossible for the elephant to go behind the back curtain without his being seen. " Even the elephant does not know how it is done," Houdini once said.

The strange thing about the illusion was that the elephant never left the stage, and yet the audience could not see him after he had walked into the collapsible cabinet. No mirrors were used, but the secret was that *the elephant walked into another cabinet situated immediately behind the one which the audience saw.* The second cabinet into which the elephant walked was so constructed that it was hidden by the huge folding parts of the front cabinet when they were made to collapse. The elephant was trained to walk into the second cabinet because he knew that some dainty tit-bits were awaiting him there. The vanishing of the elephant was always highly effective as an illusion. It was done quickly so that the audience could have little time in which to think.

Houdini's escape from a milk-can filled with water was a favourite item in his programme. The can could be submitted to the keenest scrutiny, for its secret was ingenious.

The lid of the can was kept in position by several pad-locks, and as these could be provided by members of the public, the secret of his escape was really most mysterious. It was not possible for Houdini, standing in the water-filled can, to reach the locks on the outside.

The secret was that the can had a double lining—there were really two cans, one fitting tightly into the other. As the inner lining was locked on the bayonet principle, the fact of its existence could not be discovered by an ordinary examination of the can.

When imprisoned in the can, Houdini was certainly immersed in water, some of which, through displacement, flowed over. It required only a few seconds, however, for him to release himself, the procedure being to twist the lining around until the catch was released and then to push

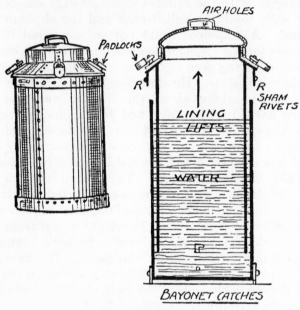

THE MILK-CAN

this interior frame away from the solid outer structure of the can.

The locks, in fact, merely fastened the lid to the top part or shoulder of the can, which appeared to be fastened on securely with rivets. These were really only half-rivets. Therefore, when Houdini, having twisted round the interior lining of the can, pushed up against the lid, the shoulder could be removed. The lid itself was not pushed away, nor could it be. It was fastened to the shoulder of the can and the point of separation was lower down where what appeared to be genuine rivets were placed.

CHAPTER III

HOUDINI had brilliant qualifications for the
task of exposing bogus spiritualistic mediums.
His comprehensive knowledge of trickery of all
kinds made him a formidable enemy to the fraudulent
" psychics," who feared and hated him.

Whatever may be the truth about spiritualism, certainly
some fraud creeps into it. Spiritualist leaders of the calibre
of the late Sir Arthur Conan Doyle are themselves stern
in denouncing and exposing the tricksters in their ranks.
Houdini, however, was much more sweeping in his
denunciations, and phenomena claimed as genuine by
believers were often declared by him to be fraudulent.

He attended hundreds of séances to obtain his evidence,
and observed what he believed to be the conjuring methods
of certain mediums. He claimed to have discovered a
large number of trick methods used at séances, and devised
what he called improvements upon them. Both on the
stage, and in private, he gave many mock séances at which
remarkable results were obtained. It is fair to say that if
some of these results had been observed at serious séances,
they would have been regarded as " manifestations." He
could produce by trickery a great deal of " psychic phenomena " and found ways of providing " mental evidence "
by means of thought-reading tricks.

It is an interesting fact that most magicians of distinction have the same attitude as that of Houdini towards spiritualism, though one of the exceptions to this is Mr. Will Goldston, the founder of the Magicians' Club and lifelong friend of Houdini. Formerly an illusionist, and now builder of magical apparatus, whose intimate knowledge of tricks is undeniable, Mr. Goldston is a convinced spiritualist.

My concern here is not with the merits of spiritualism, but with the methods of fraudulent mediums as revealed and practised by Houdini at his mock séances.

There are many ways of producing bogus manifestations in séance rooms.

In a few cases, the medium insists on being completely isolated by being covered with a large gauze net, the edges of which are fastened to the floor. This is done to convince the sceptical that the manifestations produced must be genuine as the medium is unable to move or operate because of the security of the net.

In such cases, however, manifestations can be produced by a confederate, although I do not think this method is much favoured by " mediums." It is a fact that most of the people who sit at séances have little or no knowledge of conjuring, or of securing a medium so that he is really incapable of movement. Many fake mediums prefer to perform the trickery themselves and they do not, as a rule, permit themselves to be imprisoned in a net. Mediums have so many excuses or reasons to offer as to why such drastic restraints should not be applied to them. Chief among these is the statement that a wrong atmosphere, disliked by the spirits, is created. A number of mediums do submit to some sort of control by the sitters, in order that the effects they produce may appear more impressive. This control is often of the simplest character, such as the linking of arms of the whole of the circle, a precaution which can be evaded in several ways. Frequently, however, there is no control by the sitters, who have implicit faith in the medium. This leaves him free to do anything he wishes, and as most séances are held in the dark the possibilities of cheating are great. The way of the fraudulent medium is made easier by the fact that sitters usually give a solemn undertaking not to touch anything during the proceedings. Impressive reasons are always forthcoming for exacting this condition. A remarkable state of mind is expected of the sitter by many mediums.

A SULKY SPIRIT.—When I attended a séance, at which the medium was a woman, on one occasion, she told me that a spirit whose name was Charlie was standing beside me. I asked her how she knew his name was Charlie and she said he had told her and had actually spelt out the name.

"Charlie says you know him well," said the medium. I replied, "I have known, and still know, lots of men named Charlie. Which one is this?" The medium continued, "Charlie says you must remember him. He is dressed in khaki, is five feet ten inches in height, and has a smiling face." I suggested to the medium that as Charlie could communicate to her his Christian name perhaps he would also be good enough to tell me his surname, as that would be much more helpful. The medium's next comment was, "Charlie has gone. He does not like your attitude. It makes it difficult for him."

I smiled and was sorry that the mysterious Charlie had vanished again into his psychic fastnesses without being kind enough to let me know that part of his name which I might have recognised. I was sorry to have met a sulky spirit and a peevish medium.

The woman on my left at the séance was much more fortunate because when the medium announced that a spirit named Mary was near her, she at once recognised the name and plunged into a series of questions about her welfare and surroundings on "the other plane," all of which were fully and vividly answered by the medium.

I cannot say whether or not there are such things as ghosts, but I do know, and Houdini knew, that realistic "ghosts" can be produced by trickery. Houdini often told of séances he had attended where trick ghosts produced by bogus mediums were addressed by the sitters in an attitude of great affection and reverence. It appears, however, to be the custom of these ghosts not to answer questions, although it is claimed that some of them have occasionally broken this rule.

The trick-ghost is most emphatically a material affair.

One of the most important pieces of apparatus in the tool-bag of a fraudulent medium is a pair of lazy-tongs. When closed they take up little space in the pocket, but they can easily be extended to reach across a room. The ends of the tongs are fitted with a simple spring-grip, which can hold any light article used in the séance, including a trumpet or even a " ghost." Tongs of this type have figured in police court cases in which bogus mediums have been sent to prison because of some exposure at a séance.

Houdini demonstrated, on a number of occasions, the many uses to which these tongs could be put. He once showed at a private mock séance how all the " properties " necessary for the production of trick spirits could be stowed away in the seat of a chair. The " head and shoulders " of the spirit in this case were composed of a light wire frame, with a small air balloon for the " head," the " body " being merely light gauze. A " form " of this description can easily be made to float about in a darkened room by means of the lazy-tongs, and when the sitters have been deeply impressed by its appearance, the figure melts away—in other words, the medium or his confederate folds it up, releases the air from the balloon and puts away all the compact apparatus in its original place in the seat of the chair.

There is no darkness like that of a séance-room and no atmosphere which can compare with it. After an hour in dark silence, even a highly sceptical person often becomes susceptible and finds himself thinking that, after all, there may be something in it. The creation of such an atmosphere is part of the bogus medium's business ; indeed the chief part, for the least unusual movement or sound of a voice after a long period of waiting in darkness will startle or interest the sitters. Those taking part in the séance are, when the manifestations begin, generally at the lowest ebb of their powers of scrutiny and critical observation.

Another use for the lazy-tongs is to operate, at some distance from the medium, a tiny bellows, which creates draughts, attributed to the movements of the spirits. They can be used, too, as a means of conveying an impression of seeing " astral lights " in the séance-room. The use of sulphur paint can aid in this deception.

Flowers and other articles are sometimes projected mysteriously into séances. To the sitters, these have come from another plane, transported by some spirit miracle, but when the bogus medium is at work, his useful implement, the lazy-tongs, which are not so lazy as their name would suggest, have been used again.

In such cases, the flowers are kept in the medium's rubber-lined pocket, where there is a little block of ice, until the right moment. The ice produces the correct touch of coldness compatible with the mystery of the séance-room. The usual explanation of this chilly condition of the flowers is that they have travelled many miles to the circle.

Houdini once attended a séance at which the medium was able to describe, in the dark, articles handed to him by the magician and other sitters.

Accurate descriptions of the various articles, some of which were of a complicated nature, came through a trumpet in a husky " astral " voice. The effect was so uncanny that most of those taking part believed that only psychic power could account for what had happened.

SECRETS OF LOCKED BOX.—The first step in the procedure at this particular séance was the production by the medium, before the lights went out, of a strong wooden box. At his suggestion, each of the sitters placed in it some personal article in such a way as to make it impossible for him to see what was being put in. One of the articles was a carefully folded piece of paper upon which had been written two words of the sitter's own invention—they were half French and half German. A French fifty-franc note was the contribution of another to the collection of articles, and a woman deposited an old ring, the inscription inside being so faded that it was difficult to read, even by daylight. A fountain pen without a nib, a fragment of an American newspaper, a crumpled visiting-card, and a small pocket diary containing many entries, were also included.

The box was locked and sealed by one of the sitters who retained the key and handed the box to the medium. The lights were immediately switched off and the medium went into what was said to be a trance. Meanwhile, soft music came from a gramophone in the room, operated in the dark by one of the medium's friends.

Ten minutes elapsed, then a voice came from the trumpet, which was part of the apparatus used for the séance, and the sitters heard the various articles described with accuracy.

The owner of the diary placed in the box was astonished when he heard five or six entries from it being recited by the trumpet-voice. Nearly half an hour was occupied by intimate descriptions of the articles and not one mistake was made. When this process had been completed, a gurgling noise was heard from the direction of the medium and one of the sitters remarked that he was coming out of the trance. Five minutes later the lights were restored, and the box was seen upon the floor in the centre of the room alongside the trumpet. Some of the sitters pounced upon the box and searched for signs of tampering. There were none—the seals over the lock were untouched.

A pretty mystery this, but Houdini recognised the trick by means of which articles locked in a box can be described in the dark. Some of the sitters were established believers and loudly praised the mediumship which had made such " manifestations " possible. Houdini said nothing, but the next day each of those attending, as well as the medium, received an invitation from him to a séance at which he would preside. All of them were surprised to learn that Mr. Smith, who had been one of the circle, was Houdini, the magician. The invitations were accepted by the sitters, but the medium did not respond.

At the mock séance conducted that night by Houdini, the

same procedure as that of the " real " séance was followed in every detail. The magician even went farther than the medium, for he suggested that envelopes, gummed down and containing messages, should be placed in the box. This suggestion was accepted by two or three of the sitters, and afterwards the envelopes were found intact in the locked box, the messages having been read out through the trumpet during the séance.

The general character of the test to which Houdini, acting the part of medium, submitted himself, was, on the whole, more difficult than that of the first séance. A friend of the medium, who had accepted Houdini's invitation to the mock séance, gave some trouble by insisting that the box at this séance should be fastened by him with a length of window cord which he produced.

Houdini's answer to this was, " I have undertaken to reproduce in exact detail the procedure and the effect of the séance last night. I am in the hands of the sitters on the question of following the exact procedure."

The majority of the sitters agreed that as no cord was tied round the medium's box, it should not be tied round the one produced by Houdini. Most of them declared that if Houdini could reproduce results obtained at the first séance, they would be satisfied, and the séance proceeded without the box being tied with the cord. Houdini, did not, as you have seen, fail in his promise to do at least as well as the medium.

The suggestion made by the medium's friend revealed to Houdini that he, also, was a rogue, and shared the secret of the medium's fraud.

The box used by Houdini was similar in structure to that of the medium. It contained no sliding panels, and yet it could be opened without touching the locks. The secret lay in the fact that the thin wire rod which ran through the two hinges of the box could be pulled out by a certain movement. This enabled the box to be opened from the wrong side, thus giving access to the articles inside it. The real use of the trumpet was to conceal the lighting apparatus used to allow the medium to inspect the articles. The medium carried in his pocket additional adjustable apparatus which was fitted to the trumpet by him after the lights had been turned out. This apparatus contained a tiny electric bulb and battery, giving sufficient light for an inspection of the articles. The attachment was fitted into the bottom or broad end of the trumpet in such a way that the light was thrown *downwards only*. It would not, therefore, shine on to the medium's face as he peeped through the top of the trumpet into the box to examine the articles.

The process of opening the box and fitting the metal attachment inside the trumpet involved a little noise which would have been heard by the sitters but for the sound of the gramophone playing soft music. The medium had said that the music was necessary to create the " vibrations " which would help the spirits to do their work. This was a picturesque excuse to avoid any suspicious noise being heard. Had those at the mock séance agreed to the suggestion that the box should be tied with cord, Houdini would, I do not doubt, have found a way of removing and afterwards restoring the cord, although this would have involved more time and trouble.

There were several methods which Houdini could have employed to open the gummed envelopes, or temporarily to remove their contents. In this case, a piece of special apparatus was used. It was made of wire and so constructed that it could be pushed under the flap of the envelope in the tiny space at the top where there is no gum.

In this position, the wire was twirled round, causing the paper containing the message to roll up. Attached to the wire, it was withdrawn at the top for inspection. The note was replaced in the envelope in a similar way, the apparatus causing it to unroll and resume its original position.

Many people have been deceived by such boxes used by bogus mediums. Houdini always had one of them in his magical equipment.

Variations of this trick are practised. In one of them neither trumpet nor box is produced by the medium, who simply asks for articles to be handed to him after the lights have been turned out. He holds the articles in his lap, goes into a trance and while " under the influence of his spirit guide," describes them.

Although this is different from the box method, the principle is the same, for the medium has in his pocket what is called a " reading bell " which is really a folding trumpet. In this case, also, a tiny electric light is attached. Sometimes a blue light is used to minimise the risk of discovery when the concealment afforded by the box is not employed.

The importance of a trick in which it is possible, after all, to see in the dark, is great and opens up wide possibilities of deception in the séance-room.

MENTAL EVIDENCE.—Some mediums insist that " mental evidence " is of greater value than " physical manifestations " and, accordingly, concentrate upon them. There are many ways in which people can be made to believe that a page selected by them in a book, or a written message, has been read by the spirits. One of these methods is much favoured by the type of medium who works in the daylight, red light, or subdued light. Houdini, too, liked the trick, and performed it during his mock séances.

I saw it used by a bogus medium a few years ago at a séance in half-light. A book, which happened to be a copy of one of Thackeray's works, was produced, and a sitter was requested to push a plain card given to him by the medium into some part of the book, leaving half of the card projecting. The man did so, and it was certain that his choice was not in any way forced by the medium, who immediately took the book and handed it to another sitter, he himself returning to his chair in the circle. The medium then requested that the man holding the book should open it at the place where the card had been thrust between the pages. As he did so, the medium went into a trance and began to describe the contents of the two pages laid bare. At first incoherent, the description given by the medium of the letterpress on the two pages became remarkably accurate in detail. Once or twice he quoted whole paragraphs verbatim from the pages, and when he had completed his descriptions, nothing of importance remained unmentioned. The medium claimed that it was the spirits who had made it possible for him to perform this wonder, but the truth is that it was a neat conjuring trick.

Beforehand, the medium had memorised the contents of the two pages. It was not necessary for him to memorise both pages verbatim, but merely to get into his mind a good detailed description of the contents, in addition to learning two or three paragraphs word for word.

When the medium produced the book in front of the sitter, requesting him to push the plain card between the leaves, he himself had already inserted a similar card between two pages, the contents of which he had memorised. While handing the book to the other sitter, he turned it round in quite a natural manner so that the end of the book from which *his* card was protruding was seen by the second sitter, who, of course, assumed that it was the card inserted a moment before. This was not so, as the original card had been pushed into the book out of sight.

In some cases, the bogus medium invites the sitter to insert his visiting-card in the book, and this increases the mystery. The only circumstances in which the medium can do this, however, are those in which he has had a previous opportunity to obtain a visiting-card of his " client " to use as a duplicate. Such circumstances are not rare, because when a visitor arrives at a house where a séance is to be held, he will often send in his card, unless he is attending the séance under a disguised name. Sometimes, a bogus medium will retain a visiting-card belonging to someone he meets socially—for future use.

I know of cases in which much cruder methods have been used by fraudulent mediums for discovering the contents of an envelope. This trick consists of handing to the " victim " another bundle of envelopes or a tablet of writing-paper as " something to write upon." He does not realise that as he is writing his " secret " message, an impression is being made through a sheet of carbon paper inside the envelope on top of the bundle, or between the leaves of the writing-tablet.

It may be surprising that people can be deceived in this way but the trick has often been successful.

A similar effect can be obtained without introducing carbon paper. If a specially hard pencil and soft paper are used, a distinct impression will be left on one or more of the immediately underlying sheets of the writing-tablet. Sometimes charcoal powder is spread over the writing-sheet thus impressed, as the use of the powder brings out with distinctness the words written.

Alcohol has many uses, but it is not generally known that it can be a valuable aid to those who wish to read a message written on a strip of paper in a sealed envelope. It has certainly been used by bogus mediums and will, I have no doubt, often be used again. By smearing an envelope with a sponge soaked in alcohol, it is possible to read the contents of the message written on the slip of paper. The moisture produced in this way dries with reasonable quickness and leaves no trace.

The precise manner of its use is this : the bogus medium asks the person who has come to consult the spirits through him, to write on the back of a visiting-card any question he wishes to be answered by some dead relative. The question is usually so vague that an impressive answer can easily be given by the medium. I have heard and seen many such questions, which, I think, reflect most unfavourably on the intelligence of the questioner. Here is an example, " Is Uncle Jim here, and, if so, is he happy ? "

For the medium, the rest is easy. Taking the envelope from his client, he quickly and secretly smears it with the alcohol-soaked sponge, and then goes into a " trance."

The duration of the trance is, roughly, the time it takes him to read the card through the envelope, and to let both dry. If he is working in the light, the problem is easy, but, if in the dark, his trumpet with its secret light is brought into service.

How can his client avoid being impressed when he is told by the medium, still in a trance, that " Uncle Jim is happy." Of course, Uncle Jim is always happy. The medium frequently adds to the answer a number of vague statements.

The medium will sometimes allow more questions, but should they be of a definitely evidential nature, he can always resort to the excuse provided by the " difficulties in maintaining communication with the spirits."

To those who expressed doubts as to the power of mediums so to impose on their sitters, Houdini's answer was to show them on the spot a number of tricks and to watch their bewilderment, pointing the moral, which was, that the average person is no match for the trained trickster. Without the aid of darkness or of the medium's cabinet, Houdini would produce deep mystification in the minds of those who were watching the intimate tricks, although they knew—and this is highly important—that they were about to see a trick. The average sitter at a séance, sceptical though he may be, finds it a little difficult to resist the idea in his mind that, perhaps, he is about to come into contact with the unknown. It is that feeling which makes the tricks of the medium much more easy to perform. The fact that a man or woman is at a séance means that they are wondering if there is something in spiritualism.

Personally, I have found myself in some embarrassing positions after performing tricks which are particularly mysterious in their effect, so willing are people to believe in the occult.

Let me give concrete cases, which are parallel with the experiences of Houdini in presenting illusions of this kind.

A LINER MYSTERY.—Not long ago I went on a trip to New York. I made the outward journey in the Cunard liner *Aquitania,* and the return trip in the *Berengaria.* In each of the ships it became known that I was a prominent member of the Magicians' Club and something of an amateur illusionist.

" Show us some tricks " was the request or command I constantly heard, and, though I wished to read in a quiet corner of the ship, finally I had to yield. There was a general clamour in the smoking-room that I should

" show them something." I performed a number of small tricks with cards, matches and handkerchiefs, but these were not enough—they wanted to see more. So denying myself of the leisure to which I had looked forward, I set out thoroughly to deceive those who wished to be deceived.

On board the *Berengaria* during my return journey to England I held a " magic session " each night in the large smoking-room. At first I performed only for an intimate circle of friends, but news of the " magic " spread, particularly among the several hundreds of American girl students on board.

One night when nearly a hundred and fifty people were present, I announced that I was about to demonstrate my powers as a thought-reader. *The truth was that I intended to demonstrate a thought-reading trick, the principle of which is extremely old, and to discover how many of them would realise how it was done.*

Fearing that they might afterwards think it too simple, I began with an apology, which, strange to say, was received by everyone as a sure sign that a most baffling mystery was about to be seen by them. They thought it merely a conjurer's apology, designed to throw them off their guard, so they watched intently.

I handed out forty slips of paper, borrowed from the ship's supply of stationery, and said I wished each of the forty people to write on the slip of paper some brief message. When this was done I gave instructions that the slips of paper were to be folded carefully in a certain way which I indicated and placed by the members of the audience in a large salad bowl which I handed round.

I brought the salad bowl containing the forty slips of paper to my table in front of the audience, and then explained that I should need an assistant to sit beside me in order to keep observation at close quarters.

A young American woman offered her services, and took up a position at the table.

Then I began my performance. With my eyes tightly closed, I placed one of the folded papers, picked at random, on my forehead, and, after some hesitation, read out the

contents, much to the surprise of the writer. Unfolding
the paper I handed it to the young woman to check the
accuracy of my thought-reading. She signified to the
audience that it was correct. I repeated the process until
all of the forty slips had been read in the same way.

An unexpected incident occurred during my demonstration. I had just read out the contents of one of the slips of
paper and was unfolding it to show to my woman assistant,
when the man who was the author of the message, inter-
rupted and shouted, " That paper you have in your hand
is not mine, although you have just read out what I
wrote ! "

I showed surprise and appealing to the audience, said,
" Here is an interesting challenge. This gentleman does
not believe that this slip contains his message. If he will
kindly come forward he may satisfy himself by examining
the paper."

The man did come forward and I handed him the slip he
wished to examine.

He was embarrassed when he found that it actually
contained his message exactly as he had written it. He
apologised and returned to his place, while I continued
my demonstration.

When I had finished I was surrounded by a group of
people with puzzled faces. Some of them were trying to
think it out, but others were awed, as they believed that,
by some mysterious means, I had been able to read their
thoughts. One woman told me that I *must* have psychic
powers because the message she had written was in code—
a code she had previously arranged with her friends to use
in a cablegram.

Several women came to me the next day to ask if I
would tell them their fortunes, and they were disappointed
when I said that I could not do so. I tried to assure them
that what they had seen on the previous night was merely
a trick, and, in theory, a simple trick at that, but the more
I attempted to do this, the stronger became their belief that
I possessed super-normal powers. I found to my amusement that the thought-reading demonstration was the talk

of the ship, and I caught people casting curious glances in my direction. I thought to myself that if it were possible for me so easily to convey the impression that I was " psychic," how much easier it must be for a medium with his dark room, trumpet, mysterious phrases and the rest of it, to succeed.

The manner in which I worked was this : before starting, I had arranged with a man in the audience that he should write a certain message on his slip of paper. I asked him to write " Home rule for Ireland," and he did so. While I was collecting the papers, I gave my friend's paper a little twist so that I would recognise it among the others. The young woman who volunteered to act as my assistant was also a confederate, and she played her part well in pretending that everything was " all right."

Leaving the slip of paper with the twist to the last, I picked up one of the other slips, closed my eyes and placed it on my forehead. With appropriate hesitation and pretence of difficulty, I then read out " Home rule for Ireland," at the same time looking around the audience innocently and asking if anyone had written that. Of course my secret confederate in the audience acknowledged that he had done so. Then came what was the most difficult part of the trick, the principle of which is simple enough—reading at a single glance the contents of each slip of paper I had held to my forehead. After opening it I handed it to my woman assistant with an audience watching keenly. Even the slightest pause at this moment would have been dangerous. Not only had I at one glance to read the real contents of this slip, but also to maintain a flow of talk about the mystery and difficulties of mental telepathy. It was, I suppose, the fact that there was no perceptible pause, which made the audience believe it impossible for me to have, at any phase of the trick, a chance to read the contents of the slips without their knowledge. My woman assistant was the only person, apparently, who was reading the slips, and, of course, the audience imagined that she was merely checking what I had read out. As a matter of fact, the message on the first slip I read was, " Who will win the deck tennis tournament ? " By taking up another slip and placing it against my forehead I had to continue the talk, keeping that sentence at the back of my mind. This process was repeated until the whole of the forty slips had been read. I had to take care that my friend's slip was left until the last. I tricked the interrupter by getting hold of his real paper as he came forward to the table to see it.

Although the theory of the trick is elementary, a certain amount of mental agility and concentration is necessary for its performance. My explanation of it in these pages is the result of my surprise at finding, (1) that not a member of a mixed audience on board an Atlantic liner knew the trick, and (2) that so many people among the audience should attribute to psychic influence something they could not understand or would not take the trouble to think out.

The first time I performed this trick was at a children's party when I was a boy, twenty years ago, and yet here it was still possible not only to deceive a grown-up audience, but to make some of them humbug themselves in the way I have indicated.

On the night following this performance on the *Berengaria*, I showed them another trick which produced even greater wonderment, and converted more people to the belief that I possessed some mysterious powers.

"SPIRIT" WRITING.—I showed two ordinary school slates, fastened together by a length of blue hair-ribbon in the same way in which a chocolate box is tied. Several members of the audience acceded to my request that they should place their initials, first of all, on the two outer sides of the slates then exposed. When this was done, I untied the ribbon and turned the slates so that these initials were then inside. I fastened the slates in the same way once more, and invited other members of the audience to write their initials on the sides of the slates then exposed. Thus the initials of members of the audience had been placed *on all four sides of the two slates*.

I handed the slates, still securely tied, to a member of the audience, who held them up in full view. At no time,

Houdini visiting Ann Eva Fay, the famous vaudeville "mind reader," following her retirement.

Houdini and a former spirit medium, Anna Clark Benninghofen, about to demonstrate how a trumpet can speak with "ghostly" voices while "floating" in mid-air.

during any phase of the trick, were the slates out of sight of the audience. No exchange of the slates took place.

While the slates were being held by the audience, I announced that I wished to obtain the assistance of some-one and, in order to avoid suspicion on the part of the audience that I was employing a confederate, I suggested that the assistant should be selected by means of a pack of cards. My suggestion was that the first person, man or woman, to draw an ace from the shuffled pack, should be the selected assistant. This was agreed to by the audience, several members of which gave the cards a thorough shuffling. Placing the cards on a tray so that I could not force a choice, I moved among the audience, starting with those nearest to me and working my way along the rows of chairs. Each person drew a top card from the pack and at last a man indicated that he had drawn the first ace. Returning to my place at the table, I announced that I wished my assistant to write on a sheet of ship's note-paper any message he wished and to place it in an envelope, which he would retain in his possession. I handed the man the note-paper and envelope as well as a pencil, and warned him to be sure when writing that no one could possibly see, or discover by any means, what the message was. To write his message, the man went into a corner of the large smoking-room away from the rest of the audience and myself. When he had finished writing, he placed the sheet of note-paper in the envelope, which he gummed down and put in his pocket.

At a signal from me, soft music was played for a minute or two, the slates still being held by the audience. Then I shouted, " Stop ! " and the music ceased.

Stating that I wished to discover if the " spirits " had helped us, I requested that the slates should be untied, and this was quickly done by a member of the audience.

A remarkable impression was made when it was found that inside the slates was a message. The man who had acted as my assistant read it out, and declared that it was the same as the one he had written on the note-paper. He produced the note-paper with his message to show to an astonished audience. Examining the message written on the slate the audience found that it was in slate pencil on the insides of the slates securely tied and held by them, and that the writing was not that of the man who had been my assistant.

Remembering Houdini's policy in these matters, I made an emphatic declaration to the puzzled audience that they had seen nothing but a trick, and that my references to mysterious powers were made only as a joke to increase the effect of the trick.

The expressions on the faces of some of the spectators, however, showed me that they did not believe me and some of them said so quite definitely. One woman declared I was a medium without knowing it. What could I have done to convince them ? Only one thing—to have given away the secret of an excellent trick, and I was certainly not prepared to do that. I repeated my assurances, heard some denials, and shrugged my shoulders. The way of a mystery man is sometimes hard.

Although I did not reveal my secret to the audience on the *Berengaria*, I am going to tell now how I performed this " miracle."

In the first place, the innocent-looking hair-ribbon was not used, as I told the audience, for the purpose of securing the slates so that the inner sides of them could not be tampered with by me without their knowledge. It certainly did tie the slates together, but its real object was to hide the message written on the slates before the trick began. The message was written in small handwriting and was completely covered by the ribbon stretching lengthwise across the slate.

I took care when handling the slates to have the outer sides initialled, to approach only women and elderly men, because they would be more unlikely to attempt to interfere with the ribbon, either carelessly or through curiosity.

When the outer sides of the slates had been initialled, I returned to my table and untied the ribbon, taking the necessary precaution of having the side of the slate on which the message was written towards my body, and the

clean, uninitialled side towards the audience. I placed
the slates together again, the initials and the precious
message then being inside. When I had tied the ribbon
again, I handed out the slates to have the clean sides
initialled, but this time there was no danger of discovery.
The message was safely tucked away inside, and I actually
held the slates by the ribbon boldly inviting spectators to
write their initials on any part of the slates they liked,
under or outside the ribbon. I did not mention the ribbon
the first time or suggest that initials should be written *on
any part of the slates*. No one seemed to have noticed that
I did not give such a wide choice when I first handed out
the slates.

The most difficult moment of the trick was certainly that
when I handed to members of the audience the side of the
slates on which the message was concealed under the
ribbon. I held the slates in quite a normal manner, my
hands on the wooden edges, but I kept my hold on the
slates. A precaution was to have only two initials on the
dangerous side, as I wished to get that part of the business
over as quickly as possible. The time taken to put
initials on the other side of the slates did not matter as the
really critical moments of the trick had passed.

When the side of the slate with the message written on
it was being initialled, I had my mind screwed up to a high
pitch of alertness, and had anyone attempted to interfere
with the ribbon over the message, I would immediately
have created a diversion—part of the magician's art—
moving, quite unconsciously as it were, to some other
member of the audience.

How did I know what the man, who was selected as my
assistant, would write ? The answer is that, when he
retired into a corner of the lounge, he wrote on the note-
paper exactly what I had told him to write, because he was
my secret confederate. I had tricked the audience by means
of the cards. It was true that the pack I handed out was
genuinely shuffled, but when the cards were again handed
to me, I made a rapid exchange as I turned to lift from the
table the tray on which I placed the pack. There were

several other articles on the table, and it was the work of a swift moment to make the exchange while still talking. The pack which I handed round on the tray was a prepared one and I knew the exact position of the ace. It was the fourteenth card down, as my confederate was occupying a chair which would be the fourteenth to be visited by me.

When he drew this card I moved rapidly to the next person so as to show no sign by even the slightest pause that I was expecting the ace at that moment.

My confederate was well selected for his part. He was a cool, reliable man, who could feign innocence without difficulty.

Nevertheless, I had an emergency measure prepared. Suppose, for example, my faked pack of cards had been accidentally knocked over while I was handling them round to the audience, the trick would have been ruined, had I not taken some precaution. I had, in fact, two emergency measures : the first was to have a second faked pack similarly arranged on the table, and, had the occasion arisen, I could have returned t , the table and repeated the card shuffling with the trick of exchange. There would, however, have been definite danger of discovery in doing this a second time.

The more important of the two emergency measures consisted of a note hidden between the leaves of the note-paper. Assuming that, through some unfortunate accident, I had been compelled to accept someone else as my assistant, I would myself have conducted him towards the corner of the room, apparently to place him in a position where it was quite impossible for anyone to see what he was writing, but really, when handing him the note-paper, to point to a note concealed between the leaves. The note, which was a kind of "S O S " read, " To avoid spoiling this trick, please write——," and then followed the message I had written on the slates. Anyone would respond to such an appeal, and although my secret would have been in a stranger's hands, the audience would have been none the wiser.

My own confederate knew that the " S O S " note lay

between the leaves of the note-paper, and he removed it before he began to write, so that the note-paper and envelope could afterwards be examined by the audience.

Like the thought-reading with the slips of paper, this method of deception shows the possibilities of imposing on a crowd of people by means of nicely organised conjuring.

Houdini was an expert in this type of trickery and could produce a large number of mystifying effects. I remember a clever method employed by him to deceive some of his friends during a visit to England. He was being entertained at a party, and the inevitable request came that he should show some of his magic.

" Very well," said Houdini, " I will show you something new."

From his bag he brought five London newspapers of the same date, and they were scrutinised by his friends who were convinced that they were in every way genuine.

Houdini said he would retire from the room and he requested that someone should, in his absence, select a paragraph or news item from one of the newspapers.

THE MYSTERY OF THE NEWSPAPERS.—" To avoid the possibility of a choice being forced upon you by a confederate of mine," he said, " I suggest that one person selects a newspaper, another person a page, a third a certain column, and a fourth an item in the newspaper. As four people will thus be involved, any possibility of a forced choice is removed. The nature of the item selected does not matter. It can be a leading article, an advertisement, a wedding anouncement, or anything else you like. It is important that everyone should know what has been selected so that all the people in the room can concentrate upon it. When I return, I shall try, by means of thought-reading, to discover the item chosen. I shall be waiting in a room at the end of the corridor and I suggest that when you are ready for my return, you open the door of the room and strike loudly on this gong, which belongs to our host. If someone came to summon me, you might suspect him to be my confederate communicating your choice to me.

One further point. Let there be no talk or even whispering while the choice is being made, so that it will not be possible for me to overhear anything. You will find it quite easy to make your selection without talking."

Houdini retired from the room, and within a minute or two the guests had decided upon a news item in one of the newspapers. It happened to be an account of a boy's fall from a barge into the river, and his rescue by the crew of a passing barge.

The door was opened and the arranged signal given on the gong. Houdini at once answered the summons and, entering the room, closed his eyes. After some hesitation he began to describe the news item selected. He told not only how the boy had fallen from the barge and was rescued, but gave also the boy's name and his address, the name of the barge and of the man who had actually pulled the lad from the river, all of which details were given in the news item.

Houdini repeated the performance several times, and in turn described a chosen advertisement, a shipwreck and a new invention. He made no mistakes and did not open his eyes until he had completed his descriptions. When he returned to the room in each case to perform the thought-reading, he did not move about nor did anyone else. No one spoke or approached him.

There were several magicians in the party and each of them was deceived. Houdini had no means of knowing which item would be selected. He was entirely at the mercy of the people who selected the item, but one of them, the host, was his confederate.

The first part of Houdini's secret was that in the room to which he retired, five similar newspapers had been secreted by him. They were duplicates of those held by the guests, and were also genuine newspapers of the same date. The second part of the secret was, that running from the room where the guests were to the other room, was an ordinary electric wire laid under the carpets of the rooms and down the corridor. At Houdini's end was a simple electric lamp, and in the room where the selection was made a tiny switch under the carpet was operated by the foot of the host, a close friend of the magician. The papers were secretly numbered, and when Houdini, in his room, saw two flashes, he knew that they meant paper No. 2, *The Daily Telegraph*, for example, had been chosen. Houdini would then pick up his copy of that paper and watch the lamp.

If seven flashes were made he turned to page seven. The number of the column and of the news item from the top of the column were communicated in a similar way. All that remained for Houdini to do was quickly to read the news item and, roughly, to memorise it, particularly outstanding names and facts. This was not difficult for a man with a mind so quick and retentive as that of Houdini. If page 22 of a particular newspaper were chosen, the lamp would not flash twenty-two times, as that would have been clumsy ; it would flash twice, with another two flashes immediately following.

The chief quality of the trick was that the apparatus required was not elaborate. Special signals were arranged between Houdini and his confederate to deal with a situation in which something unusual in a newspaper was selected. The choosing of the date on the front page of one of the newspapers was an example of this. As a rule, the date on the front page of a London journal is not in a column, and occupies more space than the width of one column.

" GHOSTS " AND HOW TO MAKE THEM.—Houdini knew several ways of producing ghosts by trickery, in addition to that I have already described.

Ghosts of the séance-room vary drastically in type. Some are fully-fledged ghosts, with faces and hair and even clothes. Others, however, are not so complete, and the sitters may not see more than a " materialised hand." Sometimes an article or an answer to a message is dropped into the lap of the sitter by the materialised hand, which can be seen in the darkness of the séance-room. Houdini knew this trick well, and often used it at his mock séances. To many, a materialised hand can be explained in only one way—that it is a genuine ghost-hand, for it moves, or rather floats, in the darkness.

Acting the part of medium on one occasion, Houdini produced a ghost hand perfectly. Secreted about him, before the séance began, was a black silk robe which covered his head and hands. The other part of his apparatus was a false hand dusted with sulphurous paint. When the lights were turned out, Houdini moved from his chair, as the ghost, and carefully produced the sulphurous hand. Thanks to the black silk robe, nothing else could be seen. It was easy to make the hand appear to float and to deposit articles in the laps of the sitters. To avoid creaking noises, he removed his shoes and moved cautiously in the circle stocking-footed.

There were other variations of the pranks which this black-robed ghost could play. A sulphur-painted tambourine could be made to appear above the heads of the circle and then to drop on the floor. As Houdini wore black gloves also, the sitters could see nothing but the tambourine, and they were suitably impressed.

Sometimes, masquerading as a ghost, Houdini would not use articles smeared with sulphurous paint, but confine himself to touching, with a finger cold from contact with ice secreted in his pocket, the faces of sitters.

As he stood on a chair and spoke in a husky voice, it would appear that " spirit guides " were talking.

There are mediums who claim to be " controlled " on occasions by the ancient sun worshippers, and they say that, while so controlled, they are immune from the effects of fire or burns. As a rule, the mediums who make these claims are women. While under the " control " of a sun worshipper, such a woman can hold her fingers in the flame of an oil lamp or candle without burning it. She can even pass her hair through the blaze, and it will not catch fire.

A recipe for this wonder given by a bogus medium to Houdini is as follows : dissolve half an ounce of camphor in two ounces of aqua vitae ; add one ounce of quicksilver and one ounce of liquid styrax, which is the product of myrrh and prevents the camphor igniting. Shake and mix them well. Paint the inside of the hand and fingers with this preparation, and allow to dry.

To make possible the contact of the hair with a flame without burning, the formula, as given by the bogus medium, is as follows : dissolve all the salt a tea-cup of water will contain, and, in another cup, place a tea-spoonful of soda in warm water. Pour the two together, and, after they are well mixed, wash the hair, or that part of it to be employed in the experiment. Then comb until dry.

To walk on a bar of red-hot iron, the medium informed Houdini that it was necessary only to add to the first preparation for passing the hands through flame pulverised red stones, which should be stirred with the rest of the ingredients, and afterwards rubbed on the bottom of the feet.

A method of making a spirit hand with fingers was given to Houdini by another fraudulent medium whom he had exposed. Here it is : " Paint on a piece of card-board an open hand with the fingers spread out. Do not cut out the outline of the hand, but fill in between the fingers with black. Just trim off the parts of the card in excess of the width or length of the hand. Now turn the card over and proceed to paint the same-sized hand with the difference that the fingers are not spread out. Paint all the rest of the card black.

" During the séance put the painted hand into your lazy-tongs or lifting-rod, and by quickly turning it, first on one side and then the other, to your audience in the dim light, it will present the appearance of an open hand with the fingers spreading and closing."

TABLE LIFTING.—Table lifting is easily possible by trickery, although most of the methods require the use of small tables.

The table used by Houdini to demonstrate possibilities in this direction, contained a trick which would defy detection by the average person. Houdini would place his open hand upon the table which was ornamented with a floral design let into the wood. At the word of command the table, which he tilted, would rise. The fingers of his hand were wide apart and the sitters had a clear view of the top of the table and of the hand. In some mysterious way the table seemed to cling to the tops of Houdini's fingers. It could be swung round and lifted into any position.

Examination of the table and of Houdini's fingers would not disclose the secret, which was that two of the conventional berries in the design on the top of the table were really the tops of *two small metal pegs* fitted into the wood. When the table was in its normal position, there was nothing to show that these berries were not part of the design, but, as soon as the table was turned over, the metal pegs fell to their full extent, though, being fastened, they would not fall away from the table.

Houdini had merely to open his right hand, place the tips of his fingers on the top of the table and press against the pegs with his thumb and little finger. The pressure was sufficient to enable him to raise the table, swing it about, and hold it in any position. Finally, he took the table with his left hand, while it was still above the eyes of the audience, and returned it to the floor, causing the pegs to sink back to their original position.

A simple wrist-lever strapped to Houdini's arm and hidden by his sleeve enabled him to make a table tilt from the floor as though it were pushed upwards by some unseen force. The services of a confederate, equipped with a similar wrist-lever, were necessary when the table was to be lifted completely from the floor.

Whether there are such things as genuine spirit raps, I do not know, but there are certainly more methods than one of producing them by trickery.

Mediums have been discovered using what is known as a hammer-belt. It is a useful piece of apparatus, by means of which many people have been deceived.

Attached to the belt worn by the demonstrator, is a movable hammer, usually made of lead, the head being covered with felt. The hammer is operated by the medium's foot placed in a sort of stirrup connected with it. This leaves the demonstrator's hands free, and, like the rest of the sitters, he places them on the table when the séance, in darkness, begins.

Using his apparatus, he can produce raps at will and, employing the code agreed upon by the sitters, and the "spirits," many questions can be answered.

It is easy for the medium to place the detachable stirrup in his pocket and readjust the belt so that there is no projection, before the lights are switched on again.

The tables used by some bogus mediums are specially constructed and contain a trick of one kind or another, making possible the production of raps by mechanical means. Such tables look innocent, and it would require a person of large experience and much alertness to detect the trick.

Some time ago, I saw such a table. It was small and round with a single leg-support on a base of four short legs. Hidden at the top of the single leg was a loose wooden-block with a rubber bulb under it. This bulb was connected with a rubber tube which passed down the main leg to one of the short legs. At the end of the tube was another rubber bulb. By sitting at the table and pressing one foot on the unseen rubber bulb at the bottom of one of the short legs, it was possible to cause the small wooden block at the top of the main leg to knock against the under part of the table.

A small hook protruding from the bottom of the medium's waistcoat has accounted for much table-tilting and also table-lifting. To *lift* the table the assistance of a confederate is again required. It is not easy to discover if such a hook is causing the " phenomena " because, while using the hook with his body, the medium can have his hands placed on the table like everyone else.

" Raps " can be produced satisfactorily by the use of the hands only as they are spread on the table. When the hands are outstretched, the thumb-nails should be brought into contact and pressed together tightly. If you allow your thumb-nail to slip against the other, a rap will be the result. Practice has made many " mediums " expert at this method of producing so famous a manifestation. It is important to remember that in the stillness of the dark séance-room, the tiniest sound can be heard, not only because it is quiet but also for the reason that the sitters are tense and waiting for the least noise.

A still better method is to place your shoe against the leg of the table, slipping it up and down.

By way of diversion, it is possible to cause occasional tapping on the wall or ceiling by throwing tiny lead pellets skilfully from the table out of the circle against the wall or ceiling. Should the pellet come into contact with a sitter, the " medium " could say that he had been touched by a spirit. If a pellet were afterwards found in the room, the medium might claim it as "apport," one of those mysterious articles which are said to travel from another plane into a séance.

The Fox sisters of spiritualistic fame were accused of throwing small shot about the room, but whether they did so I cannot say.

Raps on a slate or book have been produced by holding the article in a certain way, so that the nails of the forefingers were in contact and slipped against each other as in the trick with the thumb-nails on the table.

The way of the bogus medium is not always smooth. He occasionally meets troublesome people who try to catch him out and he has to show resource and skill. In no branch of " mediumship " are these qualities so necessary as in the opening of sealed letters.

Some " mediums " specialise in this work, and receive a steady income from it. Sealed letters containing questions or statements are sent to the medium encased in an outer envelope with the request that the spirits should read the contents of the sealed letter.

Of course, the sender expects to have the letter returned to him intact with a message from the spirits through the medium.

In some cases the sealing of the letter is carried out so crudely that the medium has no difficulty in tampering with it, but another seeker after truth will be more painstaking, testing the ingenuity of the medium to the utmost.

SEALED LETTERS.—A certain " medium " known to Houdini, received such a sealed letter, which was enclosed in three opaque envelopes. The letter was folded to fit the smaller of the three envelopes and the edges were glued together. It was machine-stitched with red and blue silk thread.

Several spots of glue had been smeared on the sealed letter so that it stuck to the sides of the first envelope in which it was placed. Stitches had been passed through both envelopes as well as through the sheet on which the message had been written. The second envelope was also gummed on the outside, causing it to stick to the sides of the third envelope in which it was placed. The third envelope was sealed with furniture glue, and also sealing wax which was stamped with some kind of expensive die.

It is a tribute to the skill and patience of this medium that he succeeded in opening this sealed letter and afterwards restoring it.

He began by breaking off the wax from the outside of the envelope with a thin knife-blade. It came off in pieces, some as small as a pea, others much larger. He took great care not to break that part of the sealing wax containing the impression of the die, although the remainder of the wax did not matter, as it could be melted again. He opened the outside envelope by applying steam to the seams and placing it on one side to dry. The second envelope was disposed of in the same manner.

After examining the third envelope he decided he could duplicate it. So he steamed and cut it away from the original letter to which it was adhering because of the glue.

Over an hour's hard, cautious work was required to pick the silk thread from the letter, but it was finally accomplished.

The medium read and copied the letter, and as the sitter had mentioned his name and address to the spirits, the medium wrote to one of his friends in the town referred to, and in the course of a day or so had some interesting information about the sitter.

In the meantime, he was applying himself to the task of restoring the sealed letter and its covering. First, he had to obtain a duplicate of the envelope he had destroyed, but this was not difficult.

After glueing, the sheet containing the message was replaced in the envelope. It was necessary to put the thread back through this envelope by hand and it had to be held up to a powerful light, so that the holes caused by the thread in the original letter could be seen. Had the envelope been put on a sewing machine they could not have been seen. The patience and skill of the medium enabled him to imitate by hand the machine-work.

The last envelope was given a coat of glue on the inside even more liberal than that given by the sender. The object of this was that the second envelope would stick firmly to it and make it impossible to do much investigating *without destroying evidence, if any were left, of the medium's tampering with the letter*.

The most delicate part of the work of restoring was that concerning the sealing wax on the large envelope. The wax had left a stain on the envelope which guided the medium in putting back the pieces on which was the impression of the die or seal.

He gave these pieces a good coat of glue and stuck them in their place, being careful not to allow the glue to show beyond the edges of the wax. He let the pieces dry before replacing the remainder of the wax. When they were firm, he melted the rest of the sealing wax in a vessel and poured it where it had been before, taking care to make it cover all the stains and marks caused by it in the first place.

The medium had to exercise care to ensure that the wax which he melted did not *show a joint* where it met the pieces that he had glued on. He did this by heating a knife-blade and holding it close to the wax until the two edges, affected by the heat so close to them, melted together.

The sealed letter, with its formidable covering, was returned to its sender by the medium, who also forwarded a long message from the " spirits " in which the names of the sitter's relatives and family history were described. The sender was deeply impressed and wrote a grateful letter in reply.

Sometimes, it is impossible for the medium to reply to the contents of a sealed letter opened by him, because the writer, without giving any information about himself, asks questions like, " How old am I ? " Such letters try the patience even of bogus mediums !

Houdini once lectured on the methods of the medium who was responsible for this excellent deception of the sealed letters. With nearly twenty years' experience of spoof séances at which he produced various " manifestations," this medium was a remarkably able man. On one occasion, a séance which this clever fraud conducted was attended by a police officer who said he would like to apply a new test to the medium. The officer, who was in plain clothes, proposed that the medium should drink " a mouthful of port wine from my flask " before beginning the séance. " If you keep the wine in your mouth," he said, " it will prevent you from speaking, and, should we hear voices, we can be certain they are not yours."

Rather to the surprise of the police officer, the medium agreed, and to his greater surprise his mouth was still filled with the wine at the end of the séance in which many voices had been heard in addition to other manifestations beginning with the loud ringing of a bell, which would certainly have involved a great deal of movement on the part of the medium had he been responsible.

The believers in the circle received the demonstration as sound proof of the genuineness of the medium, and the officer himself went away puzzled.

The medium had cleverly tricked the police officer by emitting the wine from his mouth into the bell after he had rung it. The " voices " followed, as the medium was then free to speak. Before the lights were restored, he refilled his mouth with the wine from the bell.

Although Houdini knew scores of tricks with " spirit " slates he never lost an opportunity of visiting a medium who was reputed to have discovered a new one. He considered one of the best of these to be that with the four slates. As a rule, this " manifestation " was produced for the benefit of one sitter who had come to interview the medium, though it was not necessary to confine the demonstration to one person.

The medium produced the four slates and, wetting a sponge, requested that, first of all, the sitter should wash the slates clean.

The slates formed a little pile, one on top of the other. With the wet sponge the sitter gave the slates a thorough washing, and they were then placed on the table in front of him while the medium went into a " trance."

Later, the sitter would see that one of the four slates contained a message written in coloured crayon or chalk. As it was impossible in this case for the medium to use acids to produce the effect of delayed secret writing, the sitter would naturally be much mystified, especially as the message was personal and intimate.

The method by which the medium tricked his victim was as follows : standing on the left side and slightly behind the sitter the medium showed him the four slates, and requested him to remove the top one, to wash both sides and place it at the bottom of the pile. The same thing happened with slates 2 and 3, but, while the sitter was engaged in washing slate 3, the medium deftly placed slate 4 at the bottom, with the result that the fourth slate washed by the sitter was really slate 2, which was thus washed twice.

The message was written on the bottom side of slate 4. It was there from the start but through the feat of conjuring on the part of the medium, slate 4 escaped washing.

There are methods of producing messages on slates by the use of invisible chemicals and there are also many kinds of trick-slates so constructed that they contain a secret flap or false side.

Many forms of fakes are made possible by slates of this type, for the false sides can be used to cover messages previously written on the slates.

"**POEM**" **MYSTERY.**—For some time, the use of such slates in what was known as the "poem mystery" was popular for "mediums."

When the slates had been examined and found "satisfactory," a book of poems would be produced and someone attending the séance—held in daylight—would be requested to open it at any page. The slate remained on the table in full view.

The top verse on each of the selected pages would be read out by the person who had chosen them, and re-examination of the slate would show that the "spirits" had written there the verses from the poems. The secret of the slates you know, and that of the selection of the poem concerns the book, which was not all it seemed.

Each page, or rather each two pages, were the same, so that, wherever the book was opened, the same lines of poetry would be found in their correct places at the top of the pages.

The book looked genuine enough, but the medium was careful to take it from the hands of the client immediately after the verses had been read.

As the medium possessed several books with pages printed alike in this way, he could change the book for any particular séance, to avoid the suspicion which repetition might arouse.

It is prudent always to distrust locked slates produced by any medium, because there are many methods of faking them which only an expert could discover.

The secret tampering beforehand with the staple which holds the slates together, when locked, is among the chief of these.

One of the best slate mysteries is that in which a number of faces are drawn instantaneously by the "spirits."

FACES ON SLATES.—Houdini once caught a medium playing this trick and exposed him. The procedure followed by the medium on this occasion was to hold underneath the table a slate previously examined and found to be clean. After making a number of strange grimaces attributed to the functioning of mysterious "spirit powers," the medium showed the slate in the

circle, and it was seen that nearly twenty " recognisable " drawings of faces were upon it. As the slate had been under the table only a few seconds, it was impossible for the medium to have drawn even one of the faces. The slate appeared to have been covered by the " spirits " with white powder and the faces were produced as black lines on the white surface. Looking at the drawings, several people said they recognised friends or relatives.

As Houdini told the circle, there had been, first of all, a simple exchange of the slates under the table. The slate upon which the spirit portraits were drawn had been previously prepared.

The formula is : rub a clean slate all over with slate pencil until it is white, and then, with the ends of the fingers, rub lightly until the powder is evenly spread. Cut from a magazine or newspaper the faces which are to appear on the slate. You must not cut round the lines of the faces. A margin of about an inch all round should be allowed. Wet evenly the side of the paper opposite to the pictures, then lay it on the slate, wet side downwards, and hold it firmly in place. With a blunt pencil, trace all round the lines of the faces, putting some pressure on the pencil. Take off the paper and when the slate dries you will find an excellent reproduction or copy of the face on the slate.

The recognition of such faces by those taking part in the séance is another proof of the faculty of self-deception possessed by a large number of people.

Houdini was once fiercely attacked when he asserted that some mediums had trap-doors in their houses, but this was true, and he was later able to prove it.

It is well worth while to dishonest mediums to have a secret trap-door cut in a suitable room, as it greatly extends the range of their " manifestations." Some such mediums prefer to make a secret opening in a wall leading to the next room. This opening, covered by a sliding panel, is usually placed behind an innocent-looking wardrobe or cabinet. The back of the wardrobe is also constructed so that the medium's confederate in the next

Photograph of Houdini and his chief assistant, James Collins, taken in May 1923 by Alexander Martin, a self-styled "spirit photographer." Martin claimed that the surrounding faces were "spirit extras," but Houdini classed them as simply "double exposures" of cut-out portraits of persons taken during their lifetime. (See next page for later details.)

Photograph of a living woman taken by Martin the "spirit photographer" some time after Houdini's death. Among the ghostly "extras" is one of Houdini himself, closely resembling the portrait that Martin took of Houdini while alive. (See previous page.) This stands as strong proof that Martin dubbed in pictures of dead people for his "extras."

room can gain secret access to the séance and leave at the proper time without discovery. Suspicions felt by anyone in the circle concerning the wardrobe would not be supported by examination of it.

In one case investigated by Houdini, seven assistants were used during a séance by a medium. In various ghostly disguises they entered the room, separately, carried out their manifestations, and departed. When every man had played his part, he went home to supper, using the back door of the medium's house, having finished his day's work for which he would be paid the next day.

It is only by means of a trap-door that a certain method of answering questions written on a slate by a client of the medium can be used.

Investigating a specific example of this, the famous magician discovered that a sealed slate, brought by the client, was held by him and the medium under the table, so that the " spirits " could read what he had written. The medium and his client sat opposite each other at the small table, and each of them held with one hand a corner of the slate. After a while, the medium's hand began to shake violently, and for a second or two, owing to this " psychic " trembling, the slate left the hand of the client, who, with a quick, groping movement, regained possession of his end.

Some time later, the trembling on the part of the medium was repeated, and again his client had the slate forced from his hand for a moment.

Later, in the darkness, the medium left the table, leaving the slate in possession of his client, who, soon afterwards, heard through the medium's trumpet, " spirit voices " answering his questions and giving him advice. He was impressed then, and even more so when the lights were turned up and a close examination of the slate failed to reveal any evidence of tampering.

As you will guess, the trembling on the part of the medium was not due to psychic influences, but had as its object the withdrawal for a moment or two of the slate from the grip of the client. During this moment, the trap-door under the table was opened and the medium's confederate below whisked away the real slate and placed a substitute in the medium's hand. The trap-door was closed, and the confederate in the room below opened the slates to read the question. He then imitated the seals, and made the slates secure once more. He wrote the question on a card which he handed to the medium when he again opened the trap-door, took away the substitute slate during the hand-trembling, and returned the real one. The confederate used a small step-ladder to lift the trap-door, and when the medium moved away from the table, he did so in order to read the card by means of the secret electric light attached to the bottom of his trumpet. Speaking through the trumpet, he then answered the question more or less satisfactorily. The medium knew that his client would be mystified if he discovered the spirits knew what the question was, even though the answer was not understood by him. If the question were a vague one, the medium would have no difficulty in being equally vague in his reply to it.

Houdini once caught and exposed a fraudulent medium in a distinctly smart manner. In the company of a police officer and a journalist, he attended a trumpet séance. All three men, of course, gave false names, and none of them was recognised by the medium, who, when the lights were switched off, produced a number of " manifestations." Several voices were heard from the trumpet, which seemed to float about the room. Flashing an electric torch, Houdini sprang up and denounced the medium, whose face and hands were smeared with lamp-black. The man was completely confused, and well he might be, for just as the lights had been turned out, at the beginning of the séance, Houdini had rubbed lamp-black on various parts of the trumpet before it began to " float " in the air. The medium claimed that the trumpet floated about the room by psychic power, but had that claim been true there would have been no stains of lamp-black on his face and hands. He had himself been holding the trumpet and speaking through it.

A great deal of emphasis has been laid by spiritualists

upon the " evidential value " of moulds of spirit faces made
during séances. It is claimed that the spirits " materialise "
themselves and in the presence of the sitters make paraffin
moulds of their faces and hands with materials provided for
them by the medium. I will make no comment upon these
claims, except to state that fraudulent mediums sometimes
include this form of " manifestation " in their repertoire.
With them, the routine is to place on the table in front of
the materialising cabinet, a basin of hot water containing a
large piece of paraffin wax, which melts and floats on the
surface of the water. Also on the table is placed a basin of
cold water. The " spirit " comes from the cabinet and,
bending over, apparently dips its face first in the paraffin
wax, and then in the cold water. It requires, they say, three
dips to make the mould of paraffin wax sufficiently thick
to retain its form. After dipping, the spirit stands erect,
pulls the mould from its face and hands it to one of the
circle, all this being performed in a dim light.

The fraud lies in the fact that the medium plays the part
of the ghost after preparing in advance a mask of paraffin
wax which is fitted over his face as he emerges from the
cabinet. Although he appears to do so, he does not dip
the prepared mould into the paraffin, but he does dip it
into the cold water, so that when it is handed to someone
in the circle, it is wet and dripping.

Sir Arthur Conan Doyle once showed me the paraffin
wax mould of what he claimed to be the hand of a spirit
which had materialised at a séance. He pointed out to me
that although the hand itself was that of a full-sized man,
the aperture, through which the hand had to be withdrawn
after making the mould, was so small that a human hand
could not have passed through it. This appeared to be so,
but, as I was not present at the séance during which the
hand was made, I reserved my judgment and comment.

Some experts say that there are trick methods of making
such moulds which would account for this little mystery.
Frankly I do not know, because I have never experimented
with the making of moulds.

Sir Arthur Conan Doyle attached much value to this

wax hand and regarded it as something with which to confound his critics.

During a séance mediums are sometimes secured by ropes or in other ways, but frequently the work of tying the medium is carried out by people who have no qualification for it.

"SPIRITS" DEFY BONDS.—Houdini often demonstrated how fraudulent mediums, although secured by ropes the ends of which were held by two people, could produce "spirit manifestations." For the purpose of demonstrating this, Houdini used a small cabinet, similar in type to those seen at séances. In the cabinet, which could be examined, were placed a small stool, a slate, a bell and a tambourine. A length of examined rope would be tied tightly round Houdini's wrists, the centre of the rope being used for this purpose, so that the two ends could be carried out through holes in the sides of the cabinet, to be held by sitters or members of the audience on each side of it.

The curtains of the cabinet would be drawn, and although the rope was being tightly held at each end, the tambourine would be thrown from the cabinet, and the slate with a message on it thrown out. Had Houdini really pulled his hand out of the loops in the rope, those holding it would have been aware instantly that such a release had been effected. When the curtains of the cabinet were drawn back again, the position of the magician was the same as when the demonstration started, his wrists still firmly held by the rope.

The explanation was that the centre of the rope was "tapped," that is to say, it had been divided in half. In the centre of one half a tiny screw was fitted, and in the centre of the other, a corresponding metal thread. This meant that the two pieces of rope could be screwed together, and, if the fake were properly done, the joint could not be seen. When Houdini was having his hands fastened in the loops of the rope, he arranged it in such a way that he got the secret joint just between his wrists, and on top of them. After the curtains of the cabinet were closed, he held the rope, at the point where the joint was,

with his mouth and used his teeth to unscrew the two
pieces. He was thus able to get his hands free, but while
they were engaged in producing the manifestations, he
took care to hold the two ends of the rope firmly between

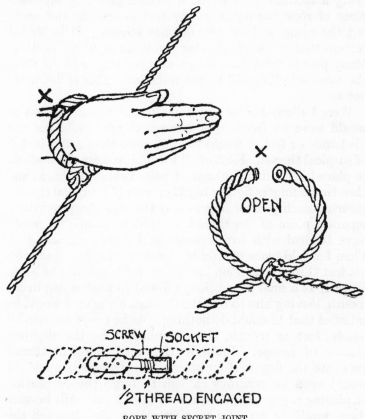

ROPE WITH SECRET JOINT

his strong teeth, so that no slackening of it would be
perceptible.

When the manifestations were finished, Houdini put his
hands back into the noose, and screwed up the rope again
with his teeth.

In his own work, Houdini proved hundreds of times that
he could release himself from the most drastic restraints

in which ropes were used. Fraudulent mediums have only a tiny part of his knowledge—but these men do study conjuring and can achieve a great deal.

If you were to give the average man the opportunity of tying a medium to a chair, he would probably choose a piece of rope twenty or thirty feet in length, and carry out the tying without any definite scheme. It is almost certain that the work of tying would be inefficiently done. Many people think that the greater the length of the rope, the more effective will be the restraint. This is definitely not so.

Were I allowed to tie a medium in such a position that he would have no freedom of movement and could not use his hands or feet, I would use not more than a few inches of surgical thread. First of all I would request the medium to place his hands palm against palm behind his back, and then tie his fingers tightly together with the surgical thread, securing each pair of fingers and the two thumbs with a separate piece of the thread, so that to escape he would have to deal with five separate and highly efficient ties. Then I would place him on his knees on the floor and push his feet through the loop formed by his hands at the back. Were I, as a final precaution, allowed to push a gag in his mouth, leaving him to breathe through his nose, I would be satisfied that he could do nothing. As he could not use his hands, feet or mouth, there would not be the slightest chance of escape. Properly tightened, surgical thread cuts into the fingers if an attempt to struggle is made. I would even be generous enough to forgo the precaution of placing a gag in the medium's mouth and still be sure there would be no false manifestations, for although the mouth can be used in a number of ways for holding and operating apparatus, it can be used efficiently only in conjunction with the hands. I would also take the precaution of examining the medium's mouth, whether I intended to use the gag or not.

I think it is correct to say that the method I have just described is the most effective of all means of restraint.

It will come as a surprise to most people to learn that

nothing but a few inches of strong thread are necessary to make a man utterly helpless.

Other contrivances figured in Houdini's repertoire of "spiritualistic tricks." He would sit on a stool and have his wrists tied tightly to rings firmly secured to a post on the stage. The post, rings and stool were all capable of close examination.

When Houdini had been bound to the post and the curtain drawn round him the "manifestations" would occur. Later, he would be found still bound to the post. Subsequent examination of the knots would show that they had not been tampered with.

The post was attached to a stout board, and Houdini's stool was placed on this board. One of the screws in the board was a dummy. When pressed down, it depressed a small lever attached to a wire running through the centre of the board and up to the top of the post. Near the place where the two rings were situated at the top of the post, this wire passed through a spring. The result of pressing down the dummy screw was that a latch or pin holding the two rings in place came out of the ring-fittings, and the rings could be drawn out of the post. They remained on Houdini's hands while he played the tambourine and played other tricks. The rings were replaced in position by depressing the dummy screw once more. This screw, which operated the whole mechanism, was depressed by means of a little pin fake attached to the centre of the rubber heel on Houdini's shoe.

One method of satirising the work of frauds among mediums is distinctly clever and interesting as a stage illusion, called by different names, although the principle is the same in each form of presentation. What is called a spirit cabinet is the chief piece of apparatus. The cabinet rests on a chair, and the performer draws back the curtain to show that it is empty. To prove this, he lifts the cabinet lightly from the chair and puts it on a sheet of glass placed between two other chairs.

Eventually, from behind the curtain, bells and musical instruments are thrown out.

The illusion is made possible in this way : when the performer draws back the curtain of the cabinet while it is resting on the first chair, the cabinet is really empty but an assistant, a boy, is behind waiting to enter it. The boy, hidden by the cabinet, is sitting on a ledge formed by the back of the chair which can be pressed down to the same level as the seat to which it is fastened, by a strong spring. When the performer closes the curtain of the cabinet, the boy pushes his way into it through a small trap-door, and the back of the chair automatically rises into position as the cabinet is being moved by the performer. As it would be impossible for the performer to carry the cabinet containing the boy without some suspicious movements of his body and arms due to the weight of the load, he has to be helped in a secret manner. This assistance is provided by wires, invisible to the audience, attached to the top of the cabinet. The wires run upwards to the flies and across to the wings. Heavy counter-balance weights are fixed at the end of the wires, so that the performer picking up the cabinet finds his burden light, due to the counter-weights on the wires.

A bogus medium once told me of a trick he had practised which I consider deserves high praise as a feat of conjuring.

This medium was in the habit of offering to have himself sealed in a muslin sack immediately after the lights were turned out and when the séance was about to begin. The offer was usually accepted by the sitters who were anxious to tell their friends afterwards that the manifestations they had seen were " genuine beyond all doubt."

The medium told the sitters that it was necessary for him to be placed and sealed in the muslin bag in darkness, so that the spirits who would help him to get free without breaking the seals could have the correct atmosphere in which to work.

The condition seemed reasonable, and, although it was dark, the sitters, by sense of touch, knew what they were doing, or thought they did.

The medium would step into the muslin sack, which was a large one, and take up a crouching position, holding up the neck of the bag to be tied and sealed.

Manifestations would take place in the dark, and, when they had ended, the medium would turn up the lights, showing that he was free and that the seals of the sack were unbroken, this being a final manifestation of spirit power.

The sitters, much impressed by this, did not know that another sack had been forced upon them. The second sack was concealed in the man's clothing, and, standing in the original sack, he would push up the mouth of the *duplicate sack* so that the sitters thought they were sealing the sack enclosing him. It was darkness that made this little example of clever conjuring possible.

The second muslin bag was hidden under the medium's waistcoat at the back when the séance began, and it was not difficult for him, crouching in the real sack, to pull up the mouth of the duplicate sack and push it into the hands of the sitters.

The result was that when the sitters returned to their places, the medium merely stepped out of the first muslin sack and hid it in his clothing, keeping the second one to show afterwards.

This fake medium told me that he had discovered a means of producing this effect in the light, or semi-light, but that it was more complicated and required the use of a large silk cloth, on some pretext or other, to hide the mouth of the original sack. Personally, I doubt whether it could be done in the light, unless the medium was a first-class conjurer or his sitters first-class fools. Even a performance in the dark requires a great deal of dexterity, although I have satisfied myself, by experiment, that it can be done.

An important precaution, which must be taken, concerns the original sack, which should not be allowed to flap down over the feet. The stooping position of the medium in the original sack means that he is able to prevent this happening by pulling the sack, which, as I have said, is large, well over the head, and by holding up the second sack in precisely the same manner as if he had offered the mouth of the real sack to be tied.

There are nearly a dozen ways of escaping from sacks,

and in one of them, also practised by psychic frauds, a piece of broomstick a few inches long is pushed by the medium near to the mouth of the sack as it is being tied over him. As the sack used in this case is of stiff canvas, the hardness of the small length of wood is not so noticeable to those tying the sack as might be imagined. The withdrawal later of the piece of broomstick, enables the medium to escape, because some of the cord or rope at the mouth of the sack has been wound round it.

Another system of escaping from a sack requires that the man inside must, with his fingers, pull down towards him a length of the cord in the mouth. A tiny space in the hem, at which the cord runs round the mouth of the sack, is sufficient to allow him to grip the cord with his fingers. Those tying the sack do not realise as they are fastening their knots tightly, that there is perhaps a foot unaccounted for, because it is held by the man inside. The principle of getting " slack " is highly important.

MESSAGES WRITTEN IN BLOOD.—I do not know whether the blood-writing test is still used at séances, but, years ago, it was a regular item. Here is the recipe for the mystery, given by a confessed fraudulent medium : at a convenient opportunity, wet the forearm with strong soda water and allow it to dry. Take a small sharpened stick from your pocket and write on the arm the name or answer to the question which you wish to appear, pressing hard on the skin. Wait until the red lines have disappeared and then announce to the sitter that your "control" will write the spirit's answer on your arm. Allow him to examine your arm, and when he is satisfied that it is normal, rub briskly a few times with the open hand, and the name or words will appear, in blood-red letters.

Another way of writing on your arm is to use varnish made thin with alcohol or turpentine. Request the sitter to burn his envelope containing the question, the nature of which you have already discovered by the old carbon trick. Take the charred paper and rub it over the writing. It will not stick to the skin except where you have written on your arm with the sharpened stick, thus giving a name or answer in black letters.

A few drops of alcohol on a sponge will remove the lettering.

Bogus women mediums are at least as full of tricks as the men, and they are often more difficult to deal with.

I remember such a medium who made considerable sums of money from what she claimed was the power given to her by the spirits to defy natural laws, and her best trick was that in which she showed how, with the aid of the spirits, it was impossible to lift her.

Not only could she defy attempts to lift her, but she could also control her weight, so that at one moment she was just a little heavier than her normal weight, and the next, twice as heavy, and so on, until the strongest man could not move her.

Moreover, the woman claimed to be able to transmit, by touch, her powers to someone else, and sometimes gave a display of her possession of " this faculty." In these cases, a boy would place his hands on hers, holding one end of a silk handkerchief while she held the other. Efforts to lift the boy were unsuccessful.

There was no real mystery in this ability to defy those who tried to lift her. The trick lies in the position of the body.

The elbows should be thrown slightly outward and back, the shoulder blades drawn together and the spine stretched to its full extent, with the body inclined slightly forward.

Those who tried to lift the medium had to hold her *by the elbows*, and this was the true secret of her weight-resisting powers. Anyone could lift her by placing their hands under her armpits, but no such opportunity was given to them. The forcing of the choice of the elbows on the would-be lifter was usually done in a neat way. It was not stated that the woman *must* be lifted by the elbows, but the suggestion was conveyed by one of her friends or assistants opening the display by attempting to lift her in that position. Everyone else appeared to accept this without question.

When the medium " imparted her power " to a boy near her, she did nothing but arrange the boy in the correct position, and if he were a stranger who lost the position and was actually lifted, the medium would explain that she could not operate on *all* subjects.

Much the same principle is involved when the medium falls to the ground in spite of all attempts to hold her, after the chair, upon which she has been standing, has been drawn away. Her elbows are thrown either forward or backward, and those attempting to hold her up are thrown off their balance and temporarily lose their power of lifting.

Some spiritualists who read this chapter will say that the days of physical phenomena, such as that exposed by Houdini, are over and that in modern spiritualism, mental phenomena are pre-eminent.

But this is definitely not the case as I know from experience. The manifestations may have altered somewhat in form, but fundamentally they are the same. There may not be so much of the ringing of bells and shaking of tambourines, but séance fashions have changed very little. Let me give you a recent experience which shows this.

I was invited to a séance in London at which the medium was a famous American. He has, in fact, been described as " the greatest direct voice medium in the world." Where other mediums are said to have only one " spirit guide," he claims to have ten.

I should explain that about a week before attending this interesting séance, I visited the house in the suburbs of London where the medium was staying as a guest of a well-known man. My visit on that occasion was for the purpose of getting an interview with the medium who had just arrived from America. I gave him my card and we had a chat. I found him a pleasant and well-dressed man of about forty-five, with apparently no conversation save that of his mediumship.

The invitation I received to attend one of his séances came suddenly. I was in Birmingham carrying out

journalistic duties when I received a telegram stating that
there was a vacancy in the circle for that night's sitting
and that I could fill it if I wished. I caught the next train
back to London and that evening, after dinner, presented
myself at the house.

The host was, in fact, Mr. Dennis Bradley, an able and
sincere man. Mr. Bradley gave his guests, including
myself, who were to sit at the séance, some light refresh-
ments. We smoked and talked for a while, and were then
led into the library where the séance was to be held.

I noticed as I entered the room that the windows were
heavily curtained and that chairs for the medium and
sitters were arranged in a circle in the centre of which two
trumpets rested on the floor. On each of the trumpets
there was a band of luminous paint so that they could be
seen in the dark.

Before the séance began, Mr. Bradley came to me and
asked for my promise *not to touch anything* during the
progress of the séance. I gave the promise and adhered
to it.

A SÉANCE REQUEST.—We sat down, but just before
the lights were turned out, the medium approached me
with a request. He asked me not to sit with my legs
crossed, a position which I had, out of habit, taken up as
soon as I occupied the chair. The medium said something
about the conditions being affected if people sat in such a
position. Without replying I uncrossed my legs and the
lights were turned out.

Those who have not experienced the darkness of a
séance-room can hardly realise how complete it is.

I could see nothing but the two trumpets, with their
luminous paint, in the centre of the circle.

A gramophone in the room was operated by someone
who, if I remember rightly, stood outside the circle during
the whole of the time.

We recited the Lord's Prayer more than once, and again
there was music. Over a half-hour went by, but no
manifestations occurred and I began to fear that the
séance would prove uneventful. It was, I think, about

twenty minutes later that we saw a movement of one of
the trumpets in the centre of the circle. It was slight but
definite. Another lapse of ten to fifteen moments occurred,
and during this time I moved my chair near to the
trumpets, away from the sitters, so that I might watch at
close quarters. In this I was not breaking the promise
given to Mr. Bradley who had not said that I must remain
in the place originally allocated to me, but had merely
stipulated that I must touch nothing, meaning, of course,
the trumpets or anything which might appear during the
séance.

While I was keeping as close a watch on the trumpets as
was possible in the dark, a loud voice suddenly roared above
our heads. "Good evening, souls," it shouted, in a peculiarly
strong and yet hoarse tone.   "Good evening," said the
medium, who said he recognised the voice as that of one of
his guides—an Indian who had died long ago.

Immediately after this, another voice was heard above
our heads, and this time it had a pronounced Irish brogue.
The medium recognised this "spirit," also. Two other
voices were heard and the medium addressed them with
the greeting : "Hallo, friends."

Then things began to happen. From under one of these
trumpets, the broad end of which was resting on the floor,
there came a deep voice which spoke two or three sentences,
and the trumpet began slowly to rise and float, in the
manner of an airship. I moved my chair cautiously back
to its original place in the circle as I wanted to avoid any
contact with the trumpet, for that would have been a breach
of my promise. The trumpet made a circuit of the room
at a height of about five feet from the ground, and then
headed straight for me. It came within less than a foot
of my face and hovered there. I felt a strong urge to grope
with my hands in the air near the trumpet to discover if
it were being supported by some artificial means, but I
overcame this desire, still remembering my promise, to
watch but not to touch.

A husky and quite inaudible voice addressed me through
the trumpet, but I could not understand a word of what

was being spoken, as this trumpet-voice was as indistinct as the voices previously heard above our heads had been clear.

I began to ask some questions rather in the manner of a Fleet Street journalist talking to someone on the telephone who has just come through claiming to have a remarkable piece of news. " Who are you ? " was my first question, but the answer was merely a husky spluttering.

" I am sorry, but I cannot hear you," I said.

The trumpet then fell to the floor and the medium said that this was due to loss of power. It did not remain there long, however, and again moved towards me. Once more I asked similar questions, but not one of the answers could be heard.

After further " loss of power," the trumpet made another ascent, but this time moved in the direction of one of the woman sitters, to whom a husky trumpet voice was addressed. The woman's first remark was : " Is that Auntie May ? " The answer to this question could be heard by the whole of the circle. It was " Yes," and I must confess I was not surprised that this establishment of identity was so obligingly assisted by the woman.

" Are you happy ? " was the question then put by the woman to the trumpet, and once more it answered : " Yes."

The woman seemed quite satisfied with this, and had apparently no more questions to ask. At any rate the trumpet moved away from her, and, rather to my surprise, again floated towards me. The same procedure was gone through, and at last I gave up my attempt to get an answer to my question, " Who are you ? " I was afterwards accused of being too sharp and direct in my questions to the spirits. I did not apologise for being so unhelpful.

I insist on being at least as exacting with voices claiming to be those of spirits as I would be with earthly telephone voices claiming to tell of some big item of news. I cannot imagine a bigger item of news than that which would convince me of spirit communication.

I was told that the spirits did not like my manner of addressing them. I am sorry, but a trained journalist naturally demands greater mental precision than that shown in the woman sitter's question : " Is that Auntie May ? "

Just after the trumpet had made its latest attempt to communicate with me it fell to the floor and I concluded that no further efforts would be directed towards me, but in this I was mistaken, for in a few minutes the deep voice of the medium's chief spirit-guide, by name Dr. Barnet, was heard inside the trumpet which was then resting, as before, with its broad end on the floor. The voice of " Dr. Barnet " said something about difficult conditions and I appealed to this voice to help, if possible, in the identity of what was claimed to be the spirit in the floating trumpet. After a brief pause Dr. Barnet's strong voice sounded from inside the trumpet, saying : " Sir, I will spell the name." What he spelt was " C-R-A-N-W-E-L-L."

Thus we had the name CRANWELL. You may say that this was quite a good shot at my own name, CANNELL. That is true, but I must make the following important observation on the matter. Although a simple one, my name is unusual, and most people who are not familiar with it address me as Cranwell or Crandon. It is remarkable that the spirits, being able to spell, should have made one of the mistakes frequently committed by people with whom I come into contact.

It is also remarkable, I think, that at the end of the séance, when we had returned to the drawing-room, the medium, to whom I made no comment whatever on the events of the evening, should have come to me and said : " You know, Mr.——"—even then he did not mention the name—" you gave me your card when you came to see me some days ago."

This was an extraordinary thing to say and conveyed to me the impression that the medium was anticipating the possible doubt in my mind as to the real identity of the voice which had spelt out my name. In other words, he was saying : " Had it been my voice in the séance, I would not have made that mistake, because I know your name," and yet he did not address me by name. I am not pointing here to any definite conclusion, nor am I asking you to believe that it was the medium who was speaking. I am simply describing the events of the séance with the utmost impartiality.

I want to emphasise the point that physical manifestations did play an important part in this séance. Floating trumpets are one of the best-known forms of physical manifestation and Houdini often produced this effect by trickery.

Moreover, during the séance a woman on my left said to me : " Did you see those astral lights ? " I peered into the darkness, but saw no astral lights. Ten minutes later, however, when I had forgotten the woman's question, I saw a number of tiny lights dancing before my eyes. Whatever caused them, I am certain that similar lights could be and have been produced by magicians.

Not long afterwards the same woman enquired if I had felt the " astral draught." I had often heard of astral draughts as being one of the commonplace things of the séance-room, but I had felt nothing and said so. It is also true that nearly half an hour later I did feel an icy draught sweep by me. Here again was one of the well-known " manifestations," so that our séance was not so up-to-date after all.

Summing up the occurrences of the séance I must say that there was nothing which could not have been achieved by trickery, although I do not say that the medium was faking. The voices above our heads could have been caused by the medium standing on a chair, and the methods of making trumpets float by means of the lazy-tongs have already been described by me. The " mental " side of the séance was a complete failure, and I think Mr. Bradley, who recorded the séance with the honesty and sincerity that characterise him, wrote it down as such.

There is one further observation that I must, in fairness, make. It is that I am unable to explain how a voice can be made to come, by trickery, from inside a trumpet resting on different parts of the floor less than a foot away from me. It is true that I suffered from the disability of not being allowed to make a search with my hands, and it may also be true that I have not yet learned all the tricks of producing voices from trumpets.

CHAPTER IV

FAKIR WONDERS—"MIRACLES" WHICH HOUDINI EXPOSED
—MY RESEARCHES—STOPPING THE PULSE AT WILL—
WALKING ON FIRE AND BROKEN GLASS—THOUGHT-
READING—HOUDINI AS CLAIRVOYANT—THE INDIAN
ROPE TRICK—THE BOY IN THE BASKET—THE MYSTERY
OF THE MANGO TREE—SAND AND WATER—NAILING A
FAKIR TO WOODEN BLOCKS

HOUDINI investigated with much energy the tricks of fakirs as well as those of bogus mediums. He reproduced their "super-natural wonders," and himself invented a number of deceptions of this type.

One of the best tricks of the fakirs is that of controlling the pulses by "highly developed will power." Houdini soon found out how it was done, and occasionally demonstrated the "miracle."

Not many people outside the circle of students of mystery and magic have the slightest idea of the secret of this remarkably clever deception.

In London, some time ago, I attended a "séance" or demonstration given by two fakirs. One of them specialised in pulse-control, and a group of people, including well-known authors and business men, were deeply puzzled by what this man did.

He was a tall, fine-looking young man with "mysterious" eyes, which I am sure he found a great asset in his work. He appeared before us dressed only in a flimsy cotton vest, with short sleeves, and shorts. After an explanation by his manager, who spoke of the "supernormal powers" possessed by fakirs, the demonstration of pulse-contro. began.

I was one of the two people asked to test the pulses of

the fakir, and I held his left wrist while a friend held the other one, and each of us held a watch.

The fakir appeared to go into what is called a trance and gave one or two low moans. During these moments his pulse was beating normally, but as I held his wrist, I realised that it was getting distinctly slower in speed. I checked this fact carefully with my watch and told my friend on the other side what was happening. The speed of the fakir's pulse on my side had gone down to less than half the normal, but my friend reported that, on his side, it was still beating at the usual rate.

The slowing down of the speed of the left pulse continued until I could feel no beat whatever, while my friend still noticed no change on his side.

We reported the mystery to the group of onlookers, who were much interested and, I think, astonished.

After a few seconds, the pulse on my side almost suddenly returned to normal, or rather to slightly lower than normal, and as I checked this with the watch, my friend stated that the pulse on his side appeared *to have stopped*. A moment later both pulses were at normal again, and about seven or eight seconds after that both pulses had stopped and the fakir was moaning once more. The duration of the stoppage was only a few seconds and then the alternating fluctuations in the speed of the respective pulses continued. The whole experiment lasted four or five minutes, and as I thought that the fakir had had enough I brought the demonstration temporarily to a close. It was repeated shortly afterwards to other members of the group.

Most of the twenty people present were convinced that they had seen a demonstration of super-normality. What they had really seen was an exceedingly smart trick, utterly simple in its explanation, but demanding concentration and some staying power.

It is quite impossible for a fakir or anyone else to make his pulse stop by means of mind control, although that is what he pretended to do.

When asked by those who had seen the display for my explanation I declined to give it to them, as I saw no reason why I should reveal the fakir's secret. I did, however, point out the interesting fact that the fakir had not given us a demonstration of *increasing the speed* of the pulse above the normal.

Pulse control, such as the fakir claimed to possess, would involve the power to make the pulse speed faster than the normal as well as slower. I do not doubt that the fakir could, if he tried, cause a *slight* increase of speed in the normal beating of the pulse, but he certainly could not bring about increased and regulated speed with the same surety as he could cause a slower beat. If anyone pauses to think what the genuine stopping of the pulse really means he will realise that it is an impossible feat.

The control of the pulse-beats by means of a trick which has nothing to do with the mind, is quite another matter.

The dress of the fakir was so flimsy and innocent looking that the idea of his having anything concealed about him did not occur to anyone. The apparatus he required was so simple that clothing was not necessary to hide it   Two small balls of solid rubber, one under each armpit, made the " miracle " possible.

The movement involved in pressing one of the balls into the armpit is so small as to be unnoticeable, and any tense attitude of the fakir would be accepted naturally as part of his " trance " state.

When the fakir wished to influence the left pulse, he merely applied pressure to the hard rubber ball under the left arm. The greater the pressure the slower would the pulse become. With the flow of blood to the wrist inter- rupted so drastically, the pulse is at once affected in strength and speed. To make both pulses slow down, or appear to stop, the fakir simply had to apply pressure on each ball at the same time.

I have met many shrewd people who have been deceived by this trick, and it is no reflection upon them that they were baffled. As a specimen of smart deception, it stands in the first class. Houdini found out the secret many years ago and rightly regarded it as one of the best of the fakir deceptions.

FIRE WALKING.—More than half the world has been mystified for many years by fakir demonstrations of walking bare-footed on fire or broken glass. Our fakir friend of the pulse-stopping trick did not perform this trick, but his colleague did.

Before the fakir walked on the burning cinders, he went through the usual preliminary process of going into a "trance," and thereby produced the right atmosphere for his performance. There was no doubt that he was bare-footed and that he did walk boldly on the fire, which was red-hot and smouldering, though there were no flames to burn the higher parts of his body. After a short interval, a large tray of broken glass was produced, and the fakir not only walked on it but stamped his feet among the fragments. He emerged from both the tests without any injury. After each performance, he came out of the "trance" most impressively. I was surprised that the audience were puzzled, because walking on fire or glass is a trick that has been performed in side-shows at fairs and even in street markets for the best part of half a century in many parts of the world.

The secret is that before the fakir or the performer walks on the fire and among the broken glass he must prepare his feet. There is more than one formula for this, but the following is a good one : dissolve as much alum as possible in a pint of water and add to it as much pink sulphate as will cover an English shilling. Soak the feet several times in this solution and allow them to dry. This toughens and prepares the skin for the demonstration.

Another exhibition of this type given by one of the fakirs was much cruder, and involved the piercing of his cheeks and arms with knives and needles. This was not so interesting because, with clean implements, a good deal of care and the proper use of loose skin, it can be done without much difficulty.

THOUGHT-READING.—Fakirs are fond of displaying their powers as thought-readers, but Houdini, good magician as he was, knew from his own experiments that the effects achieved were not so mysterious as they seemed.

I have seen a number of such demonstrations and, in order that you may understand what happens, I will describe some of the thought-reading activities of the young fakir of whom I have written in this chapter. More than fifteen of us were present in an hotel drawing-room. It was suggested that in the fakir's absence a personal article should be hidden efficiently in some part of the room.

We agreed, and selected a petite actress to take the leading part in the first test. Entirely without advice or suggestions from us, she hid a diamond ring in the soil of a flower-pot which stood on a small table. When she had done this, the fakir entered and was led towards her by his manager, who also had been out of the room during the hiding. The fakir placed his fingers lightly on the woman's wrists and began to move nervously in circles, the woman following him, or rather, as it sometimes seemed, being pushed by him. Together, actress and fakir moved around the room two or three times in this fashion. Several times the fakir stopped suddenly, and once picked up a book which lay on another table quite close to the flower-pot. He fingered the book nervously and then rejected it. Two or three moments later he was at the flower-pot, which he lifted, but, as he gathered from the attitude of the audience that he had not completely succeeded, he removed the earthenware pot from its outer case and suddenly groped in the soil, where he found the ring.

This was good, and the fakir got from the audience, including myself, the applause he deserved.

We sent him and his manager out of the room again, and this time a colonel over six feet in height was asked to carry out the hiding of an article. The colonel hid his fountain-pen behind a picture frame placed so high on the wall that, tall man as he was, he could barely reach it. When the fakir returned to the room, the procedure was the same as in the previous test. This time the fakir made two mistakes before he found the pen, but he did find it and in a reasonably short time.

Someone suggested that it would be interesting if a test were made in darkness, and, as the fakir and his manager agreed, the blinds were drawn and the lights switched off. During this test, an article was hidden by another woman of small stature. She hid her handkerchief in a vase on the mantelpiece, and the fakir went round the room three times with the woman before he stopped at the mantelpiece. He felt with one hand on the mantelpiece, and suddenly picked up one of three vases—the wrong one. He soon corrected his mistake, however, and, picking up the vase in which the handkerchief had been hidden, placed his hand inside and produced it.

All this was distinctly clever, and I gave the fakir the fullest credit for it. It was, however, no miracle, nor can it properly be described as thought-transference.

A friend of mine, a magician, can and does repeat this trick with distinct success, although not everyone could do so.

He, and others who perform it, assure me that in practically every case a tall man will hide the article in some high place, usually just within his reach, whereas a small person never strains or stands on tip-toe to conceal the article, but rather places it in some spot easily within his reach.

This tendency of people of different heights is the first piece of useful knowledge which the fakir uses to guide him. It is of much value, because it eliminates a great deal of the room.

The second part of the fakir's secret in finding the article is even more important, because it involves the skilful use of sensitive fingers and sharp eyes. It has been demonstrated many times that everybody " re-acts " when brought near the spot where the article is hidden. The re-action is usually expressed in *a slight increase in the speed of the pulse*. In the case of women, this increase is usually much more definite, because in such matters they are more responsive.

The fakir goes round the room several times so that he has three or four chances of testing the victim's re-actions. His fingers are so sensitive that he can detect quickly such signs of excitation as an increase in the beat of the pulse.

Many people are incapable of that complete disguise of expression which is necessary even to keep such a temporary secret. The fakir's trick is to make use of these signs which he is well trained to read.

For example, my friend the magician who performs this trick tells me that often people will hurry past the spot where they have hidden the article, or definitely avert their eyes from it. My friend watches, among other things, for the signs of this human impulse to avoid the place of concealment. He finds, too, that some people, apparently through the working of some subconscious faculty, push him, in spite of themselves, towards the spot, which seems to attract them.

A further point is that constant practice in this business of finding hidden things, develops in a man something that is a combination of knowledge and instinct. People, when forming part of a group, often act along lines well known to those accustomed to the atmosphere and situation. As children, when playing the game of " hide and seek," we used verbally to help by saying, " You are hot," or " You are cold," meaning, of course, that the searcher was either near or far from the object. The fakir or the trained performer does not need such verbal assistance. He gets it another way.

I think I have shown you that, although the fakir's thought-reading trick was clever, it involved nothing but quick observation, practice and a real knowledge of human nature. Houdini could perform feats of " thought-reading " at least as clever in their effect as that of the fakirs, but he always made it clear that his results were obtained by trickery only, and was annoyed by those who claimed to have supernatural powers. He insisted that all these things had a rational explanation.

CRYSTAL GAZING.—Playing the role of " clairvoyant," Houdini, not long before his death, hit upon a means of creating astonishment among the members of an audience. Boston was one of the last places where he performed this trick. The first display of these " powers " was given on a Tuesday night, following the opening of his engagement at the theatre. Producing a crystal on the stage he gazed into it, and said he saw strange things in the glass. He revealed, on this particular night, facts concerning members of the audience whom he certainly did not know, giving names, addresses and intimate details about complete strangers scattered about in various parts of the theatre. They were naturally astonished to hear from Houdini's lips facts about themselves and their domestic affairs.

Most of the revelations made by Houdini were of a humorous character, so that the performance created fun as well as mystery. For example, he would say, " Is Mr. Silas K. Turnbull in the house ? I mean Mr. Turnbull of Ohio Avenue."

Mr. Turnbull would indicate that he was present, and Houdini would say, gazing into the crystal, " Ah, Mr. Turnbull, I hope you had a good time at that birthday party last night. I am sorry to hear that you tripped over the mat on your return home." As this was true Mr. Turnbull was greatly surprised and the audience laughed loudly. Or perhaps Houdini would say, " If Mr. Thomas Smith of Twenty-Third Street is here, I want to tell him that he ought to buy a new alarm-clock because he was eighteen minutes late for work yesterday."

Without lifting his eyes from the crystal Houdini continued to throw light on the private affairs of scores of people in the theatre. At the end of the performance on this Tuesday night, he came before the curtain, and said, " Ladies and gentlemen, I am glad I have been able to mystify and amuse you as a ' clairvoyant.' Now, you have no doubt, I am sure, that I possess psychic powers. I shall demonstrate my wonderful gifts as ' clairvoyant ' again to-morrow night, but my psychic powers will not function without a little assistance from you. In other words, I expect you to urge your friends and relatives to

Houdini meeting Gloria Swanson, the famous movie star, while
both were appearing in films.

Houdini preparing to practise a hand balance on the head of a
stone lion at the Lasky Studio, Hollywood.

see my show, and then to leave a postcard for me at the stage door telling me something about their private affairs. In this way I shall get more material for my work as a mystic. Your friends have caught you, why not catch them ? "

Of course, the audience, particularly those whose names had figured in the "test," roared with laughter, and hundreds of people went home determined to induce at least one person to see the show, and to be caught in the trap into which they themselves had fallen. It was a splendid joke, and the theatre manager declared emphatically that it was the most wonderful trick in Houdini's repertoire ! The box-office manager, however, thought that the trick contained one serious defect—it could not be worked on the Monday night.

A friend of mine, concerning whom Houdini as a clairvoyant revealed an intriguing incident, tells me that he induced six people to see the show on the following night, and one of them was a man against whom he had harboured a secret grudge for years. He, too, visited the theatre again and had his revenge, he says, watching the surprise and embarrassment of the man he had lured into the range of Houdini's " psychic powers."

The trick was easy to work, because the postcards were hidden under the transparent crystal, and there was nothing for Houdini to do but to read them one by one, and to use their contents with appropriate showmanship.

Contrary to the generally held opinion, the magic and conjuring of the East is crude compared with that of the West. In Europe and America, stage magic and illusions have grown into a science to which some of the best brains have contributed. In the East, especially in India, magic has never advanced beyond the elementary stage. Not one idea of importance has come out of India where jugglers are still performing the simple tricks which their ancestors performed. There is no magician in India who would be given a week's engagement at Maskelyne's theatre in London in competition with the best Western illusionists. Yet in some curious way the conjurers and jugglers of the East have been invested in popular imagination with romantic glamour.

THE INDIAN ROPE TRICK.—Although the tricks actually produced by these men are poor, those they are said to perform are miraculous, the Indian rope trick being the best example of this. When Houdini was asked if he could explain how the Indian rope trick was done, he used to smile patiently and reply, " There is no such thing."

That was the correct answer. The Indian rope trick is nothing more than a legend passed vaguely from mouth to mouth, and gaining credence in the process. It is easier to believe in the sea-serpent than to accept the Indian rope trick as a fact. I have tried hard but I have failed to come into contact with any person who himself claimed to have witnessed the Indian rope trick.

The story is always the same—" I know a man who saw it."

It is reasonable to believe that, like other legends, the story of the Indian rope trick is a fantastic and picturesque version of a few simple facts unrelated to the miraculous. The origin of the legend, I think, is to be found in other tricks performed with ropes by Indians, but these are in no way startling or wonderful.

The plain truth about the Indian rope trick is that it is utterly beyond the power of mankind to achieve the effects claimed for it.

Briefly, the description of the Indian rope trick is as follows : in an open courtyard, while spectators stand around, a rope is thrown into the air by an Indian wonder-worker, and immediately becomes taut. An Indian boy climbs the rope and is followed by a man holding a knife. Both boy and man vanish into space at the top of the rope, and then the limbs of the boy fall separately from the sky. These are collected by the miracle-man into a sack which is closed and immediately afterwards opened again to allow the boy to emerge—restored to life !

The whole thing is grotesquely impossible, as any thinking person must realise. In the first place, there is no method in existence of making a rope thrown into the air in open space become taut enough for anyone to climb it, and, if it were possible, the disappearance of the boy at the top of the rope would be entirely beyond the powers of an illusionist.

It has been suggested that hypnotic influence exercised by the juggler might induce the crowd to believe that they had seen something which in fact had not happened. My plain answer to this suggestion is that it will not bear the test of a moment's thoughtful consideration. Hypnotic suggestion by one man to another might produce an optical illusion, although I have grave doubts even about that, but if asked to believe that a mixed crowd, with its varying temperaments and degrees of responsiveness, could be so controlled by one man, my reply would be that the suggestion was just nonsense.

In cases where, for medical or other reasons, hypnotic influence is brought to bear on an individual, the process is highly concentrated by the operator and has to be prolonged according to the susceptibilities of the patient or victim. Even when this is done, the precise extent of the hypnotic influence would, I believe, be extremely difficult to forecast. To assert that an Indian juggler could walk into a courtyard with a rope, sack and boy, and make a crowd, casually gathered, believe they had seen what I have described, is surely absurd. Houdini made a thorough investigation into the story of the rope trick and concluded that it was entirely without foundation.

I was once invited to see the Indian rope trick performed by native jugglers and eagerly accepted the invitation. It was disappointing to me to discover that the exhibition was to take place in a hall with iron girders as part of the structure, stretched across under the roof.

The motions of the legendary Indian rope trick were gone through, a clumsy attempt being made to conceal the fact that the rope was fastened to one of the iron girders, and that the boy, after climbing it, slid down another rope behind the curtain.

I have no doubt that the story of the trick being performed in the open air was superimposed upon the account of the trick done indoors, and that the legend grew in this way.

Several other tricks were performed by the Indian jugglers on that occasion, and, as we have also heard much of them, I shall describe and explain the simple secrets of these illusions.

One further word, however, on the Indian rope trick. Some years ago, an offer was made by the late Mr. J. N. Maskelyne, the famous illusionist, to pay £1000 per week to any Indian juggler, or in fact to anyone else, who could and would perform the trick. Mr. Maskelyne was prepared to hire Lord's Cricket Ground in London for the demonstration, and, I am sure, had his offer been accepted, he would have made a handsome profit. The offer remained open for years, and although representatives of Maskelyne's searched India they did not find anyone who could do the trick. The offer made by his father is still held out by Mr. Jasper Maskelyne, who maintains the high reputation of his famous family.

THE BASKET MYSTERY.—The jugglers who attempted to mystify us in the hall with the crude demonstration of the Indian rope trick showed us another example of renown in Indian magic—the basket trick. A juggler brought on to the stage a basket of small, peculiar shape, being considerably larger at the bottom than at the top. It was about three feet long, eighteen inches wide and two feet deep. The shape of the basket made it look much smaller than it really was.

One of the juggler's assistants came forward and was enveloped with a net which was tied securely together, and the man thus secured was laid across the mouth or top of the basket. A sheet was then placed by the juggler over the man and the basket, and a minute or two later we saw the net thrown out from under the sheet. In the net was the man's turban, suggesting that he had disappeared. To convince us that his assistant really had vanished, the juggler jumped on the sheet and into the basket, stamping all around it. He even sat in the basket to remove any doubt we may have had, and then, getting out, placed the lid on the basket and removed the sheet. The binding of the basket with rope was the next step, followed by the use of a sword, with which he pierced it in all directions through small holes in the top, with the idea of convincing his audience that the basket must be empty.

A minute or two later there were signs of movement in the basket, and it began to rock to and fro. The juggler unfastened the rope and removed the lid to reveal his assistant.

To those unacquainted with the principles of magic, this might seem wonderful, but it is old and easily explainable.

In the first place, the net, although ordinary looking, contained a trick which was that one of its cords running from top to bottom could be untied and unlaced, thus allowing the juggler's assistant to get out. When he had replaced the adjustable cord, he threw out the net from under the sheet with his turban inside, and then coiled himself around the bottom of the basket.

Some of the men lie with their back outward and legs bent against the body, but others lie with the back inward and the whole body in a circle. It was when such a position was gained by his assistant that the conjurer jumped into the basket, and followed up the movement with the replacing of the lid and the tying of the rope round the basket. The sword-thrusts were made in a certain way, although the audience thought that they were indiscriminate, but the man in the basket had to keep his eye on the sword, the movements of which were according to definite plan. This meant a little busy dodging, but nothing more.

Sometimes, instead of the man being produced from the basket, he is made to appear from out of the crowd. In this case a double is used.

Another method sometimes used by the Indian jugglers is that in which the man really vanishes from the basket, in the rear of which are assembled the five or six assistants of the conjurer or juggler, sitting on the ground close to the ring formed by the spectators.

After the conjurer has stamped around in the basket, standing at the rear of it, he takes hold of the sheet, and, lifting it up, draws it out and throws it over his assistants. At the same time, he gives the basket a strong kick, sending it bounding away from him towards the audience, who eagerly inspect it. In the act of drawing away the sheet, the man, under cover of it, has made his escape to his companions, the number of whom is never checked by the audience.

In a third method a small boy is used, as the baskets in this form of the trick have a trap in them. The vital move, when this method is used, is the tying of the rope around the basket by one of the conjurer's assistants who wears a loose robe. As he is tying the basket, the boy escapes through the tiny trap and clambers under the robe of the assistant.

A significant fact about the illusion is that the basket is never given out to the audience for examination before the trick. The stabbing of the basket with the sword in this trick requires some practice, both on the part of the conjurer using the weapon, and his assistant, who has to watch for its appearance through the basket. If a member of the audience were invited to stab the basket, the result would be fatal to the man inside it. The cleverness of the sword-movement lies in making it appear as though the sword were penetrating every inch of the basket, which is far from being the case.

I am puzzled to understand why this basket trick has gained such a reputation. It has little ingenuity and its fame, I think, has some relation to that of the Indian rope trick, because of the exaggerated descriptions of those who saw it originally. When our brilliant Indian jugglers had finished their performance with the basket, they proceeded to show us another famous example of their art—the mystery of the Mango Tree. One of them produced a large cloth and what we were told was a mango

seed, which he planted in some soil in a large flat box.
He placed the cloth over the soil and shortly afterwards
removed it, showing a small twig, apparently growing in
the earth. Once more the cloth was placed over the soil
and removed, exposing the twig which had reached a
height of about a foot. The operation was repeated until
the tree had grown to about five or six feet in height.

Here again the secret is simple. Twigs and small trees
of various sizes are concealed by means of a cloth, behind
which no one is allowed to peep. The manner of concealing
the largest tree, nearly six feet high, is by bending it so
that it occupies only half its height. The two ends are
tied together, one end a little lower than the other, this
end being planted in the ground. When the cloth is
finally removed the tree is untied and springs to its natural
height.

SAND AND WATER.—From the Mango Tree mystery
we were taken to the much cleverer trick with a bowl of
water and some coloured sand. This time the juggler did
give out his apparatus, or rather part of it, for examination.
The bowl he showed us was of metal and contained no
deception. On the stage, he poured water into it, and
produced on his table a bag of sand of various colours.
With bared arms, he took first of all from the bag blue-
coloured sand and poured it into the water. Red and
yellow sand followed, and the juggler churned them into a
multi-coloured mixture, which he showed by lifting out
of the bowl handfuls of muddy sand. Then suddenly,
he placed his hands in the water and produced dry sand
in blue, red and yellow colours. The bowl, water and
sand were unquestionably genuine, nor was there any
doubt that the sand was mixed with the water.

In the bag which contained the sand, there were concealed a number of small packets of sand encased in greased
waterproof paper. These were placed in the water among
the loose sand deposited there by the juggler. They could
not, of course, be seen by the audience, while the juggler
was able at any moment, by lifting out one of these packets
and breaking the paper, to produce dry sand. After the

trick, the bowl was hurried away for a good reason. The use of the greased paper meant that spots of grease would be floating on the water, and had any curious member of the audience noticed that fact he might have started to think too keenly.

The most interesting piece of apparatus used by the Indian jugglers during this performance was employed in a trick usually known as " The Fakir's Ordeal."

Two large blocks of wood in halves were shown to us. A powerful assistant came forward and drove two twenty-four-inch nails into the blocks, using a sledge-hammer for the work.

This was the prelude to the illusion, and was introduced to prove that the blocks were solid and to suggest that when nails were driven into them, they did pass through the centre of the blocks. The nails were then extracted with a large pair of pincers and the top halves of the blocks removed. The juggler came forward and reclined on the form, the two lower halves of the two blocks being under his back and waist. The two top halves of the blocks were placed over his chest and stomach, and we could see that the man was firmly encased in the two blocks.

The nails were placed in the top of the blocks and were apparently driven with the sledge-hammer through the juggler's body. Eventually the nails were removed and the juggler rose from his wooden couch without injury. The effect of the trick on the audience was heightened by the fact that the juggler was wearing nothing but a loin-cloth.

This was an illusion, the explanation of which is that, when the nails were first driven into the blocks, they passed right through the centre, but the same holes were not used for the actual performance when the juggler was on the blocks.

During the " ordeal," the nails were driven into two holes which were really the ends of two invisible iron pipes, bent in such a way that when the nails passed through them they went round the man's body. The nails were made of lead or other soft metal and so took the course of the guide when driven in by the hammer. When the nails were afterwards extracted in our view, they were straightened, because they had to pass up through a short vertical portion of the iron tubes.

This was distinctly a good trick, but I am afraid that the credit of its invention does not go to the East. It is the work of Western illusionists who, to obtain the atmosphere justifying the title, often employed a fakir or Indian to lie on the blocks.

In this case, the Indian jugglers were themselves presenting it and, I suppose, hoping that the audience would accept it as another example of their " mysterious powers." The illusion bears the stamp of Western inventiveness because it involves mechanical ingenuity. I cannot think of one trick of the Indian jugglers in which even the simplest use of universally known mechanics is introduced.

In the more important illusions of Houdini, mechanics played a definite part.

The making of water flow from a hole in a coco-nut at the command of the juggler was another trick with which we were entertained. The audience were not aware that the juggler had his finger in the hole in the coco-nut, and that by means of a certain simple arrangement, water was being forced from the coco-nut by atmospheric pressure. A piece of wood hollowed out into a tube was part of the apparatus used in the trick.

I agree with Houdini when he said that Indian magic is " so dull."

CHAPTER V

TO retain his reputation as one who could free himself from any handcuffs, Houdini had to exert himself and be constantly on the alert, watching for changes in types of handcuffs and for the activities of malicious rivals.

His career would have been at an end if, through some accident or other cause, he had been unable to free himself from manacles placed upon him, for example, one night at a music-hall in England or America.

Not many men would care to stake their reputation on their power to triumph over the locks and bolts of the world. Houdini pitted his courage and skill against the mechanical efficiency of locking devices, new and old, invented by the keenest brains.

The secret of his escape from handcuffs of all types was that he knew well that a fake key can be made for any lock, however ingenious. Even time-locks, with their intricate and wonderful mechanism, cannot defy the skill of the really expert lock-picker.

Houdini often knew beforehand which type of handcuffs he was going to tackle, and was equipped accordingly with his secret key. Handcuffs leave the fingers of the manacled man practically free and the strong fingers of Houdini found little difficulty in turning the lock with the key or fake which he had concealed about him.

Most locks have weak points and manufacturers con-

132

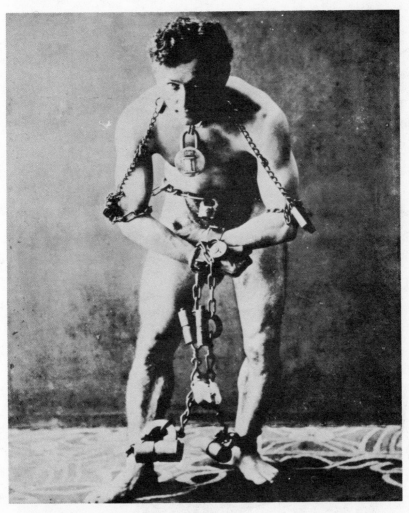

Houdini presenting his "Challenge Handcuff Act" under test conditions during his early career. Photograph supplied by the Houdini Magical Hall of Fame, Niagara Falls, Canada.

Houdini, handcuffed and wearing a ball and chain, about to plunge into a pool and escape under water.

centrate on this or that aspect of a lock, but there is always something which can be turned to advantage by the expert escaper.

The problem of escape confronting Houdini when several pairs of handcuffs were fastened on his wrists and arms was practically no greater than that of freeing himself from one pair. In such cases, he had merely to unlock each pair one after the other.

His ability to escape from handcuffs was one of the principal sources of publicity for Houdini and he exploited it to the utmost.

His greatest delight was to induce Scotland Yard, or the police of New York, or Berlin, to accept his challenges. They never caught him, although the German police at Cologne took certain action which resulted in a long legal case and ultimately in an appeal to the highest courts of Germany. The end of it was complete vindication of Houdini, although it involved, for him, a number of strenuous and exacting experiences.

IN OPEN COURT.—During these proceedings he had, in open court, to release himself from handcuffs and leg-irons which had been fastened upon him by police officers. He succeeded in doing so, and not only won his case, but obtained the widest publicity.

Following the case, Houdini was a popular figure in Germany, and always a great " box-office success."

In the German court Houdini did not, of course, show *how* he escaped from the manacles, as that was not the issue. The point was that he had to show that he *could* escape from them. When a pair of handcuffs had been locked on his wrists, Houdini would turn aside for a moment or two while his deft fingers were busy and then he would show the court that he had released himself from the 'cuffs. He had made an intensive study of the type of locks used by the German police, and constant practice enabled him to bring his concealed fake swiftly into action to operate the lock.

There were certain cases in which the magician found it advisable to use trick handcuffs of his own. An example of this is provided by his escape from a packing-case lowered into water. He could not afford to take the risk of being genuinely manacled by some member of the public because, had the lock, through stiff working or from other causes, given even the slightest trouble Houdini might have lost his life. The handcuffs he used looked real and no one but an expert would have suspected that they were otherwise, yet by a touch of the fingers in a certain part, these handcuffs could be made to open instantly.

Use of faked handcuffs was strictly confined by Houdini to those cases where definite personal danger for him would be involved by the use of the real thing. In all his challenges on the stage and elsewhere, the handcuffs brought to him were what they appeared to be. His mastery of locks was so great that there was no need to use prepared 'cuffs.

When performing in various countries Houdini could usually depend upon the standard type of handcuff used in that country being brought to him. Sometimes, however, when he was appearing in England, a challenger would produce a pair of American handcuffs of the newest type, but Houdini was always prepared to deal with them.

When in England, he usually insisted that English regulation handcuffs should be used, and when in America he made the same stipulation concerning the 'cuffs in that country. It was necessary for him to make this condition, because handcuffs which had been tampered with and altered ceased to be regulation 'cuffs—that is to say, of the type used by the police. Several times in the music-halls of England, America and Germany, challengers brought to Houdini handcuffs in which the springs had been altered or tightened by a locksmith. A simple test enabled Houdini to know at once when such alterations had been made, and he had constantly to be on the defensive against people who for one reason or another tried to embarrass him.

I do not say that Houdini was unable to escape from handcuffs altered in this way, but the test was more difficult and required a longer time for the escape to be accomplished. It was not fair to Houdini that altered 'cuffs should be presented to him, but he would sometimes accept the challenges thus offered if he were in the mood. He never failed, however, to let the public know that he was escaping from no ordinary pair of handcuffs.

There are a number of ways in which the mechanism of handcuffs can be tampered with. Houdini knew them all, as his professional career depended upon his knowledge.

A SIMPLE METHOD.—He used to say that of all handcuffs those of British regulation pattern were the easiest for his purpose as an escaper. He declared that he could

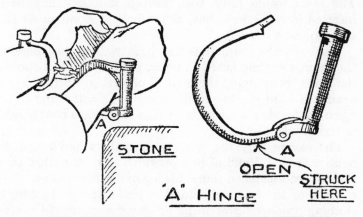

OPENING HANDCUFFS BY A SHARP BLOW ON THE RIGHT SPOT

open any pair of them in two seconds. He discovered more than one way of doing this. The first method was not normally applied by him for reasons which will be obvious, but it is distinctly interesting because it did not require even the use of a fake key.

After a close study of the British regulation handcuffs, during which he made a series of experiments with them, he found that by hitting the locked 'cuffs on the floor or against some hard substance he could make the lock fly open in an instant. The place where the blow was struck was a spot on the bend near the hinge.

Houdini made use of this little trick in a number of ways, with mystifying results. He gave to English journalists, during a visit to London, demonstrations of his ability to escape from the regulation British handcuffs without the use of a key of any sort.

After being searched Houdini would be handcuffed and locked in a room, usually in the theatre where he was performing. The journalists not only locked the handcuffs, but also placed sealing-wax or stamp paper over the lock, and Houdini would reappear in less than a minute holding the handcuffs still locked and with the seal intact. The fact that the 'cuffs could be opened without damaging the seals was a valuable, and mysterious, asset of the trick. The seals would have been broken if a key had been inserted into the lock, but, as the bolt shot out *under* the seal, no trace was left.

Although the journalists had been waiting just outside the room, they had heard no noise, yet Houdini had opened the 'cuffs by applying the method of striking them sharply against a hard object—a much more difficult thing to do when the handcuffs are on the wrists than when merely held in the hands.

The reason why the waiting journalists had heard no noise was that Houdini had provided himself with a thin strip of lead fastened round his leg under his clothes. The contact of the handcuffs and the lead through Houdini's clothing produced practically no sound because of the soft nature of the lead, which, nevertheless, was hard enough for the purpose of the trick.

This method of escape from British regulation handcuffs, leaving a sealed lock untampered with, had the effect of convincing those who saw it that Houdini had a knack of escaping from handcuffs by muscular contraction. They argued that the unbroken seal proved that the lock had certainly not been keyed open to enable Houdini to escape, and this drove them to the alternative conclusion that he had wriggled out. Houdini did not disillusion them.

A great deal of nonsense has been talked about muscular contraction. Although Houdini sometimes slipped handcuffs, he knew that it was a method which might fail him at any moment. There was only one way on which he

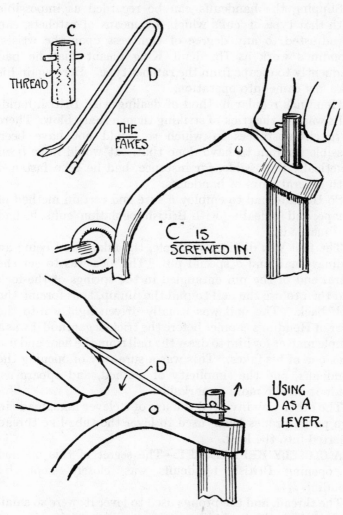

C

THREAD

D

THE
FAKES

'C' IS
SCREWED IN.

D

USING
D AS A
LEVER.

ANOTHER METHOD OF OPENING HANDCUFFS—WITH DIFFERENT
TYPE OF FAKES

could depend with certainty for his escape, and that was to reach the lock with his fingers.

Slipping the handcuffs can be regarded as impossible with that type of 'cuffs which, by means of ratchets, can be adjusted to any degree of tightness upon the wrists. Houdini's work as Handcuff King meant that he had frequently to escape from the ratchet type. Here again his fake key came into operation.

Houdini's regular method of dealing with British handcuffs was not the trick of striking them a sharp blow. There were circumstances in which it would not have been possible for him to have done that. It would have been practically impossible, for instance, had he been fastened with several pairs of handcuffs.

So Houdini had to employ a sure and certain method of escape, and in dealing with British regulation 'cuffs, he had two methods.

The first was distinctly simple, the fakes used being an ordinary nail and a special pin. The idea was to get the spiral end of the pin entangled in the springs of the lock and then to use the nail to pull the pin up, thus forcing the lock back. The nail was usually driven lightly into the floor of Houdini's cabinet before the trick began, and it was a simple matter for him to draw the nail from the floor and use it as one of his fakes. This was a sure way of opening the handcuffs, and the simplicity of method, and apparatus, made it all the more remarkable.

The other way involved the use of a clever fake, made in two parts, prongs being used to lever the tube-like thread inserted into the lock.

A CLOSELY KEPT SECRET.—The secret of this method of opening British handcuffs was closely kept by Houdini.

The thread, and the prongs used to lever it, were so small that they could be hidden quite easily, and it was not difficult for a manacled man to operate them on the lock of the handcuffs which held his wrists.

If one fake broke or failed for some reason, Houdini would apply the second method.

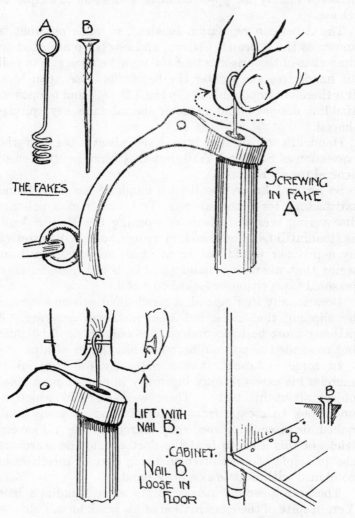

THE FAKES

SCREWING
IN FAKE
A

LIFT WITH
NAIL B.

.CABINET.

NAIL B.
LOOSE IN
FLOOR

OPENING HANDCUFFS WITH A SPECIAL PIN AND A NAIL

In the case of leg-irons used by the police, the type of lock is the same as that of the handcuff, and therefore involves merely an application of the same principle of release.

The American regulation handcuff is made on what is known as the " Bean " pattern, and can be so adjusted on the wrists of the prisoner that the more he struggles to pull his hands free the tighter the handcuffs close upon him. It is therefore impossible to slip the " Bean," and to open it, Houdini designed and made a special fake key, prong-shaped.

Handcuffs of similar type have always been in the possession of Scotland Yard, but they have never been in general use in England.

So far as I know, the British handcuff has been found satisfactory for practical use. The danger of a prisoner discovering secret methods of opening the British 'cuff, as Houdini did, is slight, and, moreover, such skill possessed by a prisoner would not be of much advantage to him, seeing that when he is handcuffed he is either under close personal supervision or locked in a cell.

Occasionally in England, a handcuffed prisoner escapes by slipping the 'cuffs, but such instances are rare. A prisoner must be lucky indeed, not only to slip his 'cuffs, but to evade the police officer who has charge of him.

In some instances, it was necessary for Houdini to exercise his extraordinary ingenuity in concealing a small object about his body. These were cases in which he undertook to escape from handcuffs and leg-irons while naked, or after being medically searched. He did several tricks of this kind to beat the doctors and the searchers, the principle of most of them being that of misdirection combined with a little sleight-of-hand.

The search would usually begin with Houdini's hair. Yet, in spite of the examination of his head, he was able, on a number of occasions, to conceal some small but useful fake there. From his head, the search would be directed next to his hands, then to the lower parts of his body, finishing at his feet.

One of his smartest tricks during a medical examination came immediately after his hands had been examined, when he would draw the attention of the doctors to a certain part of his body, momentarily touching it with a quick movement. The innocent-looking gesture was really Houdini's trick to recover some small fake placed there, usually stuck with a piece of wax.

The result was that the magician was then grasping some useful fake in his hands which had already been searched. Sometimes it was only a piece of wire, yet of great use to him when the doctors had retired and he was left alone to work out his own escape.

Although well skilled in searching, the doctors were no match for Houdini in the art of swift deception. They were dealing not only with an illusionist and escaper but with an expert conjurer as well. The nimble fingers essential to expert sleight-of-hand movements could also be most useful during such medical examinations. He was intimate, too, with the usual procedure in medical examinations of this kind, and never attempted to hide anything where he knew the doctors, by force of professional habit, would look. Occasionally, he made use of the soles of his feet to hide a piece of wire, as he had noticed a tendency on the part of searchers not to look there.

In cases where his escape involved not only freeing himself from handcuffs but finding a way out of the room in which he was imprisoned, Houdini used to employ a simple but effective little dodge. Before the medical examination began, he would look carefully at the door of the room on the pretext of examining the lock, but his real object was secretly to place a small piece of lock-picking wire under the case of the lock, which was an excellent hiding-place.

Houdini's examination of the lock and its frame before the test began seemed quite a natural proceeding, and no one suspected it. The wire was stuck to the lower part of the lock-case by means of wax. It is, in fact, impossible to see such a piece of wire placed in this position unless you bend down and look under the case of the lock, which no one ever thought of doing.

TAKEN IN WATER.—I know of a case in which Houdini obtained, through a clever ruse, access to the means of escape from a strongly locked room. As the fake-key he would have to employ was rather large, he did not risk having it concealed about him, but devised a means of obtaining it secretly.

When the usual examination of himself and the room had been carried out, and he was securely handcuffed, he requested, just before the committee retired from the room, a glass of water, as, he said, he felt hot. Naturally, this request was readily granted and he eagerly drank the water brought to him. Then the committee retired, and Houdini some time later escaped successfully from the room.

The key Houdini needed had been most cleverly conveyed to him in the glass of water which one of his friends standing by had kindly rushed to get when he asked for a drink. The key was slipped into the water by his friend whose natural hold of the glass as he handed it to Houdini hid the long but thin fake in the bottom.

When Houdini accepted the glass of water, the natural position of his fingers also hid the key. He drank the water in such a way that when the contents of the glass were nearly exhausted, the key slipped on to his tongue and was concealed in his mouth. It is not easy to slip a key into the mouth from a glass of water, but, of course, Houdini had practised well and was able to do it safely and without being noticed.

It is this curious lack of complete observation on the part of many people that makes tricks and illusions possible. In this case, the committee, including the doctors, made an intensive search of the room (which, incidentally, was quite bare of furniture), and of Houdini. I am sure that the members of the committee would afterwards quite conscientiously have sworn on oath that no one could have handed Houdini a key or any other article, yet in spite of all their earlier precautions they did permit in the last critical minutes someone to have contact with him and actually to hand him a glass.

The fact that most people can be misdirected in this way does not mean that the work of the illusionist or escaper is simple. It is not easy because, while at work, he is challenging the powers of observation not only of one man but of many. What A has failed to notice may be observed by B, and so with the committee of ten or twelve men the aggregate amount of efficient observation does, or should, increase.

THE BARRED PRISON VAN.—Several times Houdini made his escape from prison vans, and this was not so difficult as it sounds. His boast that he could get away from such vehicles resulted, while he was in Russia, in a serious challenge from the Russian police, who declared that he certainly could not get out of one of the vans used by them for the transport of prisoners.

Houdini accepted their challenge, and a condition he made, at first, was that the van should be normal in every way, that is, without additional locks. The Russian police, however, thought otherwise. They said that Houdini must escape from a van to be specially barred and bolted by them. At last, the magician, after a great many objections, which were really a part of his showmanship, agreed.

The test took place in the Courtyard of the old Russian capital and the most important police officers of the Czar took part in it. When Houdini entered the courtyard alone—he was not allowed to have an assistant near him— he saw a formidable-looking vehicle. A number of new locks and even chains had been fitted to the door in such a way that Houdini certainly could not have access to them when he was locked in the van. In addition to this the van was lined with zinc.

In the company of the police officers, Houdini made a close examination of the whole structure, and finally said he was prepared to start the attempt to escape.

The police officers did not object to his condition that they should retire from the courtyard to a place where they could not see the van. They were confident that it was impossible for anyone to escape from the specially strengthened prison on wheels. The handcuffing and locking of Houdini inside the van occupied some time, and when it was completed, the officers retired from the court-yard to a room in the police building, certain in their own minds that the magician would have to shout for their help to get out of the van. They did not conceal their surprise when, little more than an hour later, Houdini walked smilingly into the room. They sprang up and hurried into the courtyard to examine the van which was still locked exactly as they had left it. They were com-pletely mystified and could not discover the secret of Houdini's escape.

Houdini had no keys in his possession and could not, in any case, have used them, for the locks, being on the outside of the strong door, were beyond his reach.

It was in the first class as an example of escaping work, and once again Houdini had applied a fundamental principle of his art—that of misdirection. He had en-couraged the police officers to think that he was afraid of the extra locks and chains they wished to place on the door. As a matter of fact, he did not care how many locks and chains were there, for he had no intention of escaping by means of the door. He knew that it would be impossible, and turned his attention to another part of the van, the importance of which had been overlooked by the Russian police officers in their great anxiety to make the door doubly secure. It was upon the floor of the van that Houdini concentrated in carrying out his escape, in which there was a good deal of hard work and skill. He had in his possession a small cutter with which to cut through the zinc floor in such a way as afterwards to be able to smooth over the joint so that it would not be noticed. He had also to select the right spot at which to cut.

When he had neatly pierced the zinc, he pushed the edges back and reached the wooden floor of the van.

The next part of his task was to remove enough of the planking to enable him to squeeze through the floor,

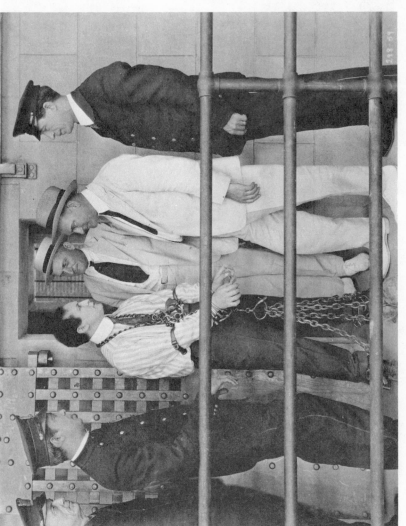

This scene from Houdini's movie *The Grim Game* is a reenactment of his famous "jail-break" which he performed under test conditions for many police chiefs.

Houdini about to be lowered and clamped within the water-filled "Chinese Torture Cell," one of his most famous escapes.

while he performed the task of readjusting the zinc so as to leave no trace of the fine, straight cut he had made at the point where the sides and floor of the van met. He selected this part of the van to do his cutting for the obvious reason that the signs of his work would be less noticeable there than anywhere else. The replacement of the floor planks was the simplest part of this remarkable escape.

It did not seem to occur to any of the police officers to eliminate the door in their attempts to solve the mystery of the escape. The door and its new locks obsessed them, and in all their discussions which followed, they kept on asking themselves how Houdini could have reached these locks from the inside of the van. They even made experiments themselves in the locked vehicle, and vainly tried a number of ways in which to get at the locks. It was impossible to do so and they gave up the problem, but whether they discovered the secret through subsequent and more minute examinations of the van, I cannot say.

The Czar heard of this and other episodes concerning Houdini and was interested. Later he made a valuable present to the magician.

Houdini toured a great deal in Russia and often said that the Russian lock-appliances were the worst in the world. He regarded the handcuffs, leg-irons and other apparatus of restraint used in Russian prisons and Siberia as being crude.

The price which Houdini paid for his expertness as a lock-picker was unceasing vigilance plus practice. While in Russia, he visited every locksmith's shop he came across and spent hours in examining and testing the stock.

When in Berlin, as a young man, he made the acquaintance of a locksmith and offered to work as his assistant for nothing. The offer was accepted and Houdini started on repair-work for him. The man discovered that his thirty years of experience as a locksmith were nothing compared with Houdini's tricks in opening locks, and soon a considerable number of people came to his shop to see the young man demonstrate his skill. He was often called to houses, the owners of which had lost their front-door keys.

At Houdini's request, the locksmith ordered a gross of the various locks used on police chains in Germany, later exchanging them for a gross of other patterns. Houdini practised on these for six and even ten hours a day, and with the assistance of his four favourite picks he could open any lock.

Houdini's experience with the Berlin locksmith proved of much benefit to him when he was compelled to justify himself at the German courts during his famous lawsuit.

The picks used by Houdini for opening lever locks were of a simple pattern. In Germany, he always carried with him a useful appliance in the form of a number of lock-pickers which folded into a handle like the blades of a pocket-knife. With these he opened many hundreds of ward locks in Germany. In the hands of a burglar such an implement would have had unpleasant results for house-holders.

During one visit to Berlin, Houdini came into possession of a most interesting implement. It was a multiple key or universal lock-picker which, by adjustment, could be made to fit many different types of locks. This lock-picker was the property of a clever German criminal who was later sent to a long term of imprisonment for housebreaking. Houdini was in Berlin at the time of his trial and had many interviews with him. The man had a notorious reputation as a lock-picker and finally he gave his ingenious imple-ment, which he had concealed from the police in spite of many searches, to Houdini. It was handed to the police by the magician but they later returned it to him.

It is sometimes hard to judge a lock from the outside. The simple encasement of some locks may hide the most intricate interiors.

Houdini found that, in France, the standard of lock-mechanism was good. In fact, he used to say that in no other country would be found so many expensive locks as in France.

Among Houdini's collection of lock-picks, were fourteen

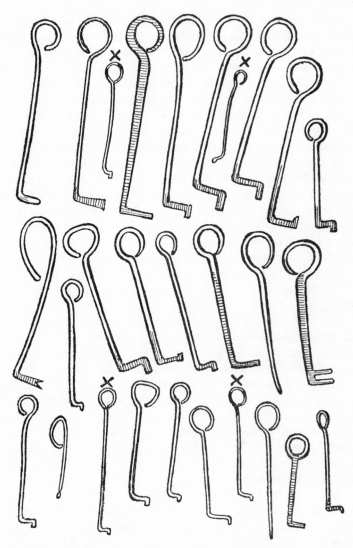

A COLLECTION OF HOUDINI'S LOCK-PICKS. THE FOUR MARKED "X"
WERE USED BY HIM IN HIS FAMOUS LEGAL ACTION AGAINST THE
GERMAN POLICE

with which, he said, he would undertake to open every door in England !

At Dortmund, Germany, the landlord of the hotel where Houdini was staying, told him that he had lost a key to the door of one of the bedrooms which he wished to prepare for a guest who was then due to arrive. Houdini not only picked the lock of the door but undertook to provide the landlord with a key, and his kindness resulted in an incident which caused him some annoyance. He went to an ironmonger's shop and purchased a blank key which he intended to cut to fit the lock of the bedroom door. The next morning he saw in the local paper headlines which read, " Houdini exposed. Buys up all the keys in the town." In the course of the article it was stated that the editor of the newspaper happened to be in the shop and saw Houdini " looking over all the blank keys and buying several thousands of them." From that time onwards, Houdini never entered an ironmonger's shop.

In releasing himself from what is known as the " Plug Eight " English handcuff, Houdini had to devise a means of removing the plug in the 'cuff. It was sometimes essential to use a small instrument for this purpose. Until the plug was removed from the 'cuff, the lock-opener could not be inserted and when the keyhole was face downward, the instrument had to be employed. The instrument was placed in Houdini's mouth so that his teeth held a small wooden wheel. Another part of the instrument was then pushed into two small holes on top of the plug of the 'cuff, and his tongue turned a tiny cog-wheel. This caused a small brass rod to revolve inside a cylinder, which in turn operated a wheel or catch at the end of the instrument, enabling Houdini to remove the plug from the handcuff.

A second instrument was used when Houdini's hands were fastened behind his back. In this case, the device was operated with the thumb, after the ends of the instrument had been inserted in the holes on the top of the plug.

The letter 'cuff is an interesting invention. It is so called because it cannot in the ordinary way be opened until the letters, arranged on a sort of revolving drum, form a secret word.

Houdini made a large number of experiments with 'cuffs of this type until he found the weak point which would enable him to release himself at any time. The finer the workmanship the harder is the lock to open, but Houdini never had a failure with the letter 'cuff.

A RIVAL OUTWITTED.—One of the most exciting and amusing incidents of the magician's career happened in connection with a 'cuff of this type. He was touring in Holland when a friend sent him a poster and a newspaper clipping announcing that an Italian rival of Houdini was boasting that he had beaten the American by placing upon him handcuffs from which he could not escape.

Houdini was angry, and asked the proprietor of the circus in which he was then appearing for leave to break his contract, so that he could go to Germany and deal with his rival. The circus proprietor refused to give this permission and there was a heated argument between the two. At last Houdini was granted five days' leave of absence and at once left for Dortmund where his rival was appearing—also at a circus. On his way to Dortmund he stopped at Essen, where he visited a barber, a friend of his, who glued a false moustache on his lip, and, by tampering with his hair, made Houdini look like an old man. Then with a handbag filled with what he called " Handcuff-King defeaters " he made for the circus at Dortmund.

Almost the first words of his rival when he made his appearance in the ring were to the effect that he had vanquished Houdini. In an instant the American rose to his feet and shouted " That is not true." Asked by his rival how he knew this, Houdini shouted " I am in the know," whereupon the performer offered to wager that he was right. With that, Houdini took a flying leap into the centre of the ring and, tearing off his disguise, cried, " You say I am not telling the truth ? Well, look, I am Houdini."

A wild scene followed and the audience looked on with delight at this unexpected episode. The manager hurried into the ring and there was an angry discussion. Houdini offered five thousand marks if his rival would allow himself to be handcuffed by him.

Houdini drew the attention of the manager of the circus to the advertisements in which a large sum of money was offered to anyone who could successfully handcuff his performer. The manager refused to make good this promise to back his man for the sum mentioned, and Houdini returned to his seat.

The next day the manager of the circus called at Houdini's hotel with a proposal that the American should engage himself for a night in a duel with his rival. Houdini was asked if he would handcuff the circus performer if challenged, and he replied that he would certainly do so.

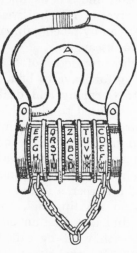

THE LETTER 'CUFF

The manager went away and the next day Houdini was surprised to see in the town huge posters announcing that his rival undertook to be handcuffed by him and to release himself. Houdini went home, polished his various hand-cuffs, oiled the mechanism, and waited.

A little later he was visited by the manager, who asked which 'cuffs he intended to lock on his performer. Houdini replied that the manager was at liberty to choose the 'cuffs to be used, and pointed to twelve pairs laid out. A pair of letter 'cuffs was chosen by the manager, who examined them carefully. As he did so, he asked in a peculiar tone, as though feigning indifference, "What word opens this 'cuff?" Houdini saw the trick at once, and after making the manager solemnly promise he would not tell his rival, said the secret word was "Clefs." When the manager requested permission to take the 'cuffs to show the proprietor of the circus, Houdini agreed, provided they were not shown to his rival. This promise was also given, and the man departed, not returning the 'cuffs until four hours later. Houdini knew that during that time his rival was making himself familiar with the 'cuffs, but the American still had a trick up his sleeve.

That night at the circus Houdini occupied a box-seat, and when his rival appeared, walked into the ring with his bag of 'cuffs. Houdini opened the bag and told his rival to make his choice of the twelve 'cuffs. As the American expected, the man instantly chose the letter 'cuffs and took them into the cabinet for examination. In a few minutes he came out shouting that he would undertake to escape from them.

Houdini locked the handcuffs on the man, who, in the centre of the ring, said to the audience, " After I have opened these handcuffs I will allow my wife to do so. She is very clever at this sort of work and she will open them in five seconds." Houdini then addressed the audience, saying that they might as well go home because his rival would never free himself. The circus performer went into his cabinet at nine o'clock. At eleven o'clock the entire audience had gone, and the man was still in the cabinet. The proprietor of the circus, angry and dismayed at the failure of his performer, instructed the attendants at the circus to throw him out of the ring. They knocked the cabinet over and the handcuffed man ran out of the ring and went to his dressing-room. About midnight, when Houdini was standing guard over the dressing-room door, the performer's wife came and asked his permission to join her husband, and the American allowed her to do so.

At 1 a.m., the manager of the circus asked his performer if he wished to give up. For answer, the man shouted to Houdini to come and release him, but this Houdini refused to do unless witnesses were present. A message was accordingly sent to the proprietor, who brought another man well known in the town and a representative of a local newspaper.

The unhappy circus performer, who was almost in a state

of collapse, was furious at his humiliation. Glancing at the handcuffs, Houdini smiled when he saw that his rival had arranged the letters to form the word " Clefs," and said, " You are wrong. The correct word is ' F-R-A-U-D.' That is what you are."

Forming this word, Houdini released the man from the handcuffs and went home happy. His rival's embarrassment had been due to the fact that, after the handcuffs had been tested by him for the word " Clefs," Houdini, in placing them on his wrists, was able swiftly and secretly to make a change so that the formation of another word was necessary to open the 'cuffs.

The next day his rival was impudent enough to issue handbills claiming that he had beaten Houdini and had won 5000 marks. The newspapers, however, told the true story and the exposure of the Italian rival was complete.

A handcuff in use in Ireland during Houdini's career as an escaper gave him more trouble than the English regulation handcuff. The reason for this was that when the Irish handcuffs were fastened on the wrists, it was difficult, owing to the structure of the manacles, to get the fingers into play so as to insert the fake key into the lock. Houdini overcame this difficulty by inventing a key which he could hold and operate between the teeth.

So that his teeth should not suffer injury when being used to open the Irish handcuffs, Houdini had part of the key made of rubber—the part actually held between the teeth.

For some of his minor tricks, Houdini sometimes used handcuffs which, though of regulation pattern, had been tampered with by him and could therefore be opened without the aid of any key.

A highly ingenious little device was used by Houdini in escaping from a pair of handcuffs by placing his manacled hands into a small bag which had previously been examined by the onlookers. The device was a false finger made of light metal with the appearance of a human finger, and so shaped at the bottom that it would remain securely between the fingers of the hand. No one appears to have noticed that there was an extra finger on Houdini's hand during this trick. Very few people have ever thought of the possibility of using an artificial finger in this way. As the fake-finger was hollow, it was an excellent place for concealing the small key he required to open the handcuffs inside the bag. When he had completed the task of releasing himself he would replace the key in the finger and the finger on his hand.

The same device was sometimes used by him to make a silk handkerchief vanish.

A little trick, more amusing than brilliant, was occasionally practised by Houdini in demonstrating an

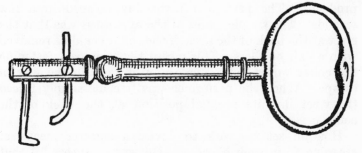

AN ADJUSTABLE LOCK-PICK

escape to one other person. He would remove all his clothing, submit to a search, and then offer his hands to be manacled. When handcuffed, Houdini would request his friend to turn his back on him for a few seconds while he released himself. In these circumstances, Houdini never failed to get free, although, in his nude state, nothing was concealed about him.

The trick lay in the fact that Houdini had managed to hang his fake-key by means of a tiny pin on the back of his friend. This little preliminary process would take place during a friendly conversation before Houdini started to demonstrate.

When his friend's back was turned, it was easy for the magician to remove the key attached by the pin, to open the handcuffs and afterwards to replace the key on his friend's back. To obtain possession of the key later was easy, and the magician's friend would never guess how he had been hoodwinked.

One of the simplest methods employed by Houdini to open handcuffs was of no use for the more modern and intricate 'cuffs. A shoe-lace was used, and Houdini found a way of forcing a loop of the lace into the lock, which could then be opened by a sharp pull.

IRON COLLAR SECRET.—One rival of Houdini's specialised in escaping from a neck-collar or iron collar which he provided for the inspection of his committees. He allowed anyone to place the iron collar round his neck, and to fasten it with any lock the challenger cared to produce. The performer invariably escaped in a few seconds. The simple secret of the apparatus was that the rivet at the back of the neck of the collar could be removed with a pair of pliers. This meant that the locks fastening the collar would not provide any obstacle in the way of escape. When the performer was free, he simply forced the rivet into its original position at the back of the collar.

Houdini set to work to devise a cleverer means of escaping from such a collar. He was so successful that even experienced magicians, who knew the trick of forcing out the rivet with the pliers, were mystified, and could not offer an explanation as to how the trick was done.

The collar invented by Houdini was made of light metal, and the faked part of it could not be moved either with the fingers or with an instrument. The secret was in the hinge, the rivet in which was hollow. Contained in the rivet was a steel pin which could be moved only by using a strong horseshoe magnet to draw it to the top and allow the hinge to open.

Houdini introduced this principle, not only into what he called the " spirit collar," but also into some of his faked handcuffs.

As the number of types of American handcuffs and locks is so great, Houdini's knowledge and skill were put to harder tests there than in any other country. There are dozens of different patterns in ratchet handcuffs, or 'cuffs adjustable to wrists of any size.

Houdini found that the majority of ratchet 'cuffs could be opened by using a strip of fine steel about three and a half inches long and a quarter of an inch wide, with a knob on the end. This was inserted into the handcuff where the lock snaps, but the method could not be used on the double-lock ratchets, a most difficult handcuff, for

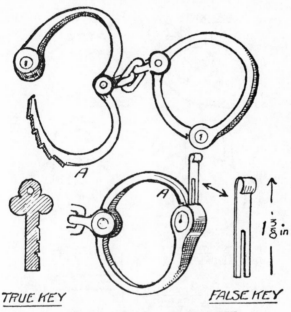

TRUE KEY   FALSE KEY

AMERICAN HANDCUFFS AND FAKE KEY

if the key or anything in the lock is broken, the 'cuff must be cut off the wrist and cannot be forced.

Houdini devised an excellent master-key which would open almost all double-lock ratchets.

A handcuff known as the " Berliner " was made in four styles. One of them involved the use of an attached belt, strapping the hands to the body. Houdini escaped from this type of handcuff by forcing his hands with the belt attached slowly down the legs and over the feet. The next step was to apply himself to the lock of the handcuff.

A device invented by Houdini himself was called the "Bell-lock," because a bell rang when the 'cuff was locked and when it was unlocked.

In extricating himself from the chain used by the German police for transporting prisoners, Houdini used nothing but physical force. He discovered, after some experiments, the right way in which to apply the force.

The German transport chain has two rings, one for each

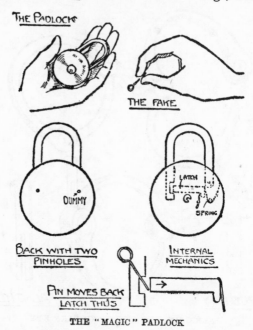

THE PADLOCK

THE FAKE

DUMMY

BACK WITH TWO
PINHOLES

LATCH

SPRING

INTERNAL
MECHANICS

PIN MOVES BACK
LATCH THUS

THE "MAGIC" PADLOCK

hand. One of the rings is located at the end of the chain and the other in the centre. The chain fastens both wrists, which rest one above the other, and, when in this position, the chain is locked on the wrists. The first movement in Houdini's method of escape was to bring the arms akimbo, thereby causing one hand to lie lengthwise on the other, the fingers of both hands pointing towards the elbows. Then the force was applied, the first hand being pulled out with the teeth as an aid.

A cleverly faked padlock was sometimes used by Houdini

for certain escapes. It had the advantage that it could be examined most carefully without much chance of the secret being found out.

In using this "magic padlock," as it is called, the performer declares that he has no duplicate key, which is true, for he does not need one. When his wrists are bound with chains and the hands fastened together with the padlock, a member of the audience locks it. Turning his back for a moment, the performer can free his hands by opening the padlock, without the assistance of a key. The trick in the padlock is that on its plain side there are two tiny, innocent-looking holes. One of them is a dummy, but through the other hole the performer inserts a tiny piece of fine wire, which can be pinned to his coat sleeve, and works the latch back.

The object of the dummy hole is to avoid any suspicion which may arise through the presence of one hole in the back of the lock. It has been found in practice that the *two* holes do not attract attention.

What was known as the " Houdini Challenge Handcuff " (Figs. 1 and 2) was another clever fake. He used to leave a pair of these 'cuffs in the vestibule of every music-hall where he was performing, so that anyone might examine them. To avoid the consequences that might have followed if some malicious person had tampered with the handcuffs so exhibited, Houdini performed with a duplicate pair.

At the end of the iron bar on which these 'cuffs were placed there was a large nut. To get out of the 'cuffs, Houdini inserted this nut in a space in an iron plate which was screwed on the floor of his cabinet. Thus the bar was held fast while the performer worked on the faked screw and levered off the top.

To enable him to do this, a peg was dropped into a hole at the top of the 'cuff to check the nut.

STRAIT-JACKET ESCAPE.—Escaping from a strait-jacket was a form of Houdini's activities which meant strenuous effort and much perspiration.

Houdini made his first escape from a strait-jacket when quite a young man at a theatre in Nova Scotia. Before presenting the escape on the stage he practised it intensively for a whole week. At first, the escape was made behind a curtain, but he found that when he emerged from the cabinet with his hair dishevelled, his face wet with perspiration, and his clothing torn, the spectators were sceptical and did not believe so much effort had been required. They thought that the whole thing was a fake, and so Houdini decided to show the audience how he effected his release, afterwards performing the escape in full view of everyone.

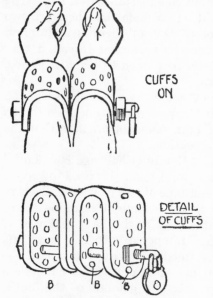

CUFFS ON

DETAIL OF CUFFS

B   B   B

FIG. 1. THE HOUDINI CHALLENGE 'CUFFS

There are various kinds of strait-jackets made from different materials. Some are made entirely of leather, and others of strong canvas or sail-cloth. The more inflexible the material the more difficult is the escape.

Once a police chief at Hanover had Houdini placed in a strait-jacket, from which it took him one hour and twenty-nine minutes to escape. He afterwards said that he would never forget the agony of the struggle.

A strait-jacket from which Houdini used often to release himself was made of strong brown canvas with a deep leather collar and cuffs sewn up at the ends, making a sort of bag into which each arm was placed. The seams were covered with leather bands, attached to which were leather straps and steel buckles which, when strapped upon a person, fasten at the back. The sleeves of this jacket were so long that when the arms of the wearer were placed

Houdini performing a spectacular strait-jacket escape in
New York City.

Houdini suspended upside-down from the cornice of a New York skyscraper, a feat which won for him a thousand-dollar bet.

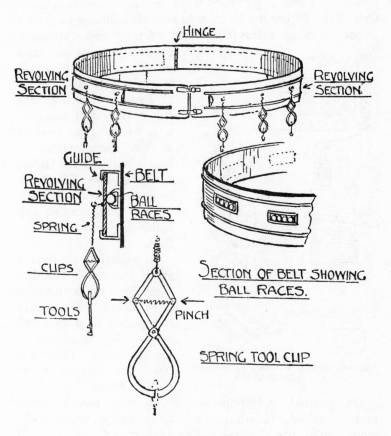

HOUDINI'S SECRET BELT

in them and folded across the chest, the leather cuffs of the sleeves, to which straps and buckles were attached, met at the back of the body, one overlapping the other.

There is no secret in Houdini's escape from strait-jackets. It meant just hard work directed on certain lines. One of the first steps he took to free himself was to get an elbow on some solid foundation and by sheer strength gradually force the arm up towards the head. When a certain measure of freedom for the arm was obtained, it was possible to undo the buckles at the back with the hands still encased in the canvas sleeves. The teeth were also used when the jacket was drawn up sufficiently near to the face.

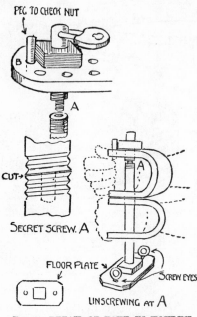

FIG. 2. DETAIL OF FAKE IN HOUDINI CHALLENGE 'CUFFS

In addition to honest strait-jackets, Houdini sometimes made use of a trick-jacket which could be opened in a moment or two by means of a secret lever. This was used for certain spectacular feats.

On normal occasions when he was not stripped and searched, Houdini used a specially made belt, worn under his clothing. The belt was so constructed that, with his manacled hands, he could slide a section of it round until a particular implement was near his fingers. Each of the fakes attached to the belt was detachable.

CHAPTER VI

HOUDINI had a great fondness for escapes from rope-ties, and was, of course, a brilliant expert in this art. He often used to say that escaping from rope-ties had the distinct advantage over other forms of escape that no suspicion could be attached to the ropes themselves. When a magician on the stage produces his own locks, chains, handcuffs or boxes, shrewd people in the audience are suspicious, but, generally speaking, a rope is an honest thing.

For the purposes of certain illusions, ropes can be tampered with in such a way as to make detection extremely difficult. It is possible to cut and re-join a piece of special rope without the joint being seen, though it is a somewhat elaborate business. Houdini did not use faked ropes in his escapes, though one such rope figured in his mock séances.

He had mastered the art of tying and untying knots and when being bound up, knew how to gain subtle advantages without the knowledge of those securing him. Six or seven members of a committee from the average music-hall audience were no match in this respect for Houdini, wily, resourceful and much experienced. For instance, he would try to find out by various means whether any member of the committee, through having been at sea or for some other reason, was familiar with knots.

The man with special knowledge usually likes to air it in such a situation, and so when the knot experts in his committee pressed forward to tie him up, Houdini would watch them closely and often use the man to his own advantage by diverting his attention in some smart way.

Travelling across the world as he did, Houdini had many tough encounters with men who did know a great deal about knot-tying. Sailors in particular loved to mount the stage and try to beat the magician by tying him up in a complicated manner. When appearing in English seaports or naval towns, he had lively experiences and, often, strenuous escapes.

Bluejackets tried hard to outwit "the great Houdini," but they never succeeded in doing so. None of them had his great experience, though some were experienced enough to make the situation somewhat difficult for him. On some occasions, he would, for the sake of showmanship, make a pretence of being in difficulties. In such cases there would be much excitement among the audience and often anxiety on the part of the management, but Houdini was never beaten. He loved to cause suspense or cause an argument among the audience. The more they talked when they got home, the better it would be for business at the theatre. If the impression were created in the town that Houdini had nearly been beaten on the previous night, many would flock to see the show in the hope of being in at the kill, so to speak.

Wherever possible, Houdini induced a local doctor to join the committee on the stage for his escapes from ropes. It added to the value of the magician's performance when the doctor examined his hands, wrists, arms and shoulders and afterwards informed the audience that Houdini could not have slipped out of the knots by contracting the muscles.

Houdini found that the best rope for general purposes was sash cord. For the escaper, new cord is in some cases the better; in others it is necessary that the rope should be soft and pliable Much depends upon the kind of knots to be tied.

During the last twenty years of his career, Houdini performed his rope-escapes on the open stage with all the lights upon him. He depended entirely on his skill to get free from the knots. In his earlier days he used often to be taken into the privacy of his cabinet to obtain his release and he is known, when in difficulty, to have cut the rope with a knife secreted in the cabinet and then emerge free holding another rope which he had hidden there. It was not difficult for him to dispose of the cut pieces of rope in the secret hiding-places of his cabinet, and afterwards to make the committee believe that the duplicate rope was the original one.

Houdini often demonstrated how to release the hands when they are securely tied behind the back Although the principle is simple, the procedure is not easy to carry out, as anyone who makes the experiment will discover.

To use Houdini's own words : " The escape is accomplished by bending the body forward and working the arms down over the hips until the hands are just behind the knees. This is most difficult when first tried but car be accomplished after some practice.

" When the hands are in this position at the back of the knees, sit down on the floor and cross the legs, the left above the right. Work the left arm down over the left knee and withdraw first the left foot and then the right from the looped arms. This will bring the bound wrists in front of the body, and the knots may then be untied with the teeth. New sash cord should be used for this escape because it is impossible to tie very tight knots with it. This cord has a smooth surface also, a fact which makes easier the slipping over the hips."

SPECTACULAR BUT EASIER.—It was constantly asserted by Houdini that the more spectacular the tying-up process to the eyes of the audience the less difficult the escape proved to be. The position, for example, in which Houdini was bound to a ladder seemed one from which escape was impossible, yet it was just a matter of slow, steady work.

Houdini was bound many times in this manner, and the

first thing he did when the committee had finished the tying, was to wriggle his arms and strain at the ropes. The effect of this was to bring one of his hands to the front of the ladder within reach of a section of the rope. By means of some hard work with the fingers, knot after knot was untied until one hand was free. The rest was merely a matter of time. For this escape, Houdini found it advisable to use short lengths of stiff, new sash cord, as the stiffer the cord the easier it unties.

Houdini used to pander to the public love for the spectacular, although he well knew that many unpretentious escapes were much more difficult—escaping from wet sheets or tarred rope, for example.

Among the spectacular escapes of this kind was that in which Houdini was tied in public to a huge wheel. Again it appeared that he could not possibly free himself from such a position. The principle of escaping from the big wheel was the same as that applied to the ladder. Thus bound, the average man would struggle wildly and without a definite method. The first object must be the liberation of one hand. After that it is just a question of untying knots, not an easy thing, but a form of skill in which the escape-artist must make himself expert before he begins performances in public. Houdini always encouraged his friends and assistants to bind him up with new knots and fastenings, in fact to make it as difficult for him as they could.

It must be remembered by those who would clearly understand how Houdini constantly escaped from these difficult rope-ties that he was a man of great strength and agility, with fingers of steel. To watch him effect his release from a series of complicated ties and knots was a pleasure to those who admired fitness and dexterity. As a rule, he undertook to escape from the rope-ties in less time than was occupied in binding him. He rarely failed to achieve this—a tribute to his mastery of the subject. Usually he had a large clock on the stage so that the audience could count the minutes and seconds during his fight to escape from the bonds.

Houdini strapped to a wheel.

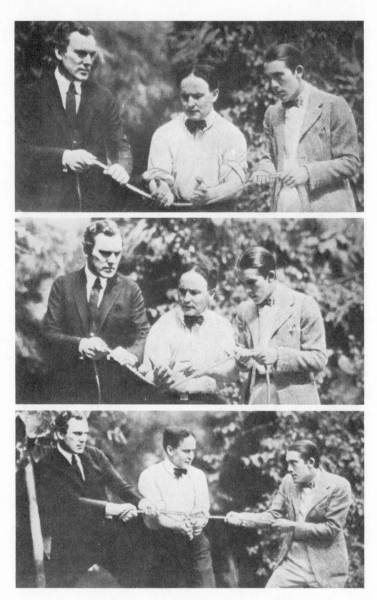

Houdini demonstrating his rope tricks.

One of the tricks of the escape-artist—indeed the most important—is secretly to secure a bit of " slack " as he is being tied up. Houdini was a master of this art.

THE JACOBY TIE.—One of the most effective ties is the Jacoby, the secret of which has been well kept.

Members of the audience are invited by the performer to bind his legs to the legs of a chair with cords, which can be tied in any way. The performer's waist also is tied to the back of the chair, and again those assisting have a free choice as to the method of tying.

As a matter of fact, these bonds have nothing to do with the experiment, but they serve three purposes. They help to make the feat appear to be more difficult than it really is and—more important, perhaps—they serve to tire the people who are binding the performer ; the process of tying, which is not done in a moment, also assists by making the audience a little impatient. So, when the assistants come to the bonds which really matter they will not be too careful about the tying or too critical of the way in which the performer submits to the process.

The magician tells the audience that his arms are going to be tied to the chair, and that when the tying is complete they will see that he is in the position of a man wearing a strait-jacket.

An assistant is directed to tie a piece of cord, about two yards long, round the performer's right wrist, and before he begins to comply with these directions the performer places the back of his wrist on the cord, at the centre, so that when it is tied the knot comes inside the wrist. (To make the position of the knot perfectly clear I add this further explanation : it should be in line with the palm of the hand.) The assistant may tie as many knots as he pleases, and, if he wishes to do so, can seal the knots—plasticine makes a useful seal. The performer then holds up his hand, showing the audience that the cord has been securely tied on the wrist ; the ends of the cord hang down.

When the other cord has been tied on the left wrist in the same way, the performer folds his arms and asks the assistant to bring the four ends of the two cords to the back

and tie them securely on his back.   The assistant can tie as
many knots as he likes and can seal them.   Finally the ends
of the cords are tied to the back of the chair, and all four
ends are tied together.

If the tying has been done properly and the performer is
a good showman he will appear to be in a helpless position.
He is firmly tied at the waist to the back of the chair;
his feet are tied to the legs of the chair;   his hands are

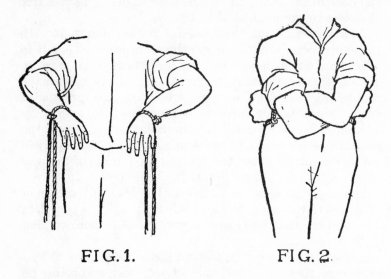

FIG. 1.   FIG. 2.

apparently tied so securely to his back that he cannot
possibly get either of them free.

A screen is now placed in front of the performer, and
directly it is in position the audience hear him clapping his
hands together and calling to the assistants to take the
screen away again.   The request is quickly obeyed, and the
audience see the performer still bound securely to the chair.
The committee from the audience can closely inspect the
knots and seals, as the performer has not tampered with
one of them.

The magician asks for the loan of a watch or a ring, and
when one is handed up to him he directs an assistant to put
it in his (the performer's) pocket.   The screen is again

drawn in front of him for a moment. When it is withdrawn, he invites the committee to find the watch and they discover it tied to two of the cords at the back of the performer. The committee—or any other members of the audience—can be safely challenged to remove the watch from its position. The screen is drawn in front of the performer for a moment ; presently the committee hear the performer telling them that they can now return the watch (or ring) to the owner. The screen is withdrawn and a member of the audience takes the watch (or ring) from the performer's pocket.

Any of the many " spirit manifestations " displayed by bogus mediums can be produced under the conditions of this tie. For example, the performer can have a bell placed on his knees, and directly he is hidden by the screen the audience hear the bell ringing. A tambourine can be " played," a musical-box set in motion, or nails hammered into a piece of wood— this being one of the most convincing of the many manifestations given by the famous Davenport

FIG. 3.

Brothers, who, however, did not use this particular tie.

The main secret is in the way in which the performer folds his arms before they are tied to his back. The left hand goes under the right arm-pit ; the right arm is then folded round the left elbow and the right hand should reach to the left arm-pit. The position of the arms is most important because if they are folded in any other way the performer will find that he is unable to release himself.

The excellence of this tie will be appreciated if the performer will stand in front of a glass and fold his arms in the ordinary, natural way, with the wrists crossed in front and the left hand under the right arm and the right hand under the left arm. Now the performer should fold his arms in the way directed for this tie, with the right arm outside the left elbow, and he will see if he looks at himself in the glass, that the position of the arms has a better appearance ; he seems to be well " trussed up." The performer seems to be more securely bound by the trick tie than he would be by an ordinary tie.

To release himself the performer pushes his left hand as far as he can under the right arm-pit. He then puts his right thumb under the two cords of the right wrist and lifts them right over his head with the right arm, which is then free. He can easily clap his hands together, put his arm back over his head and—there he is, in the original position.

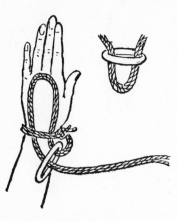

The performer's hair should not be too smooth when he is going to present this trick. It should be short and not brushed flat, because there is just the chance that when he is passing his arm over his head, he may ruffle his hair slightly and thus give some-one in the audience a clue to the mystery.

To give himself confidence during the first two or three presentations of this trick the magician should provide himself with duplicate cords and a sharp knife, so that in case of difficulty he can bring the trick to a conclusion by freeing himself from his bonds. The learner will find that his hardest task will be in getting his right arm back to its original position.

FIG. 4.

As the left arm is not really free at any time during the manifestations—it is not necessary that it should be—the performer will find that he gains a little by turning his body to the right when his arm is free ; in that way he lessens the strain on the cords of the left arm. He will also find that the task of getting the right arm over the head in the first place and then back again is best done when he is sitting forward on the chair—the tie at the waist prevents him from getting very far—and leaning back a little.

The trick with the watch or ring is simple, but it has a most convincing effect. The watch should be placed in the right-hand waistcoat pocket of the performer, who having got his right arm free, takes the watch from the pocket, gathers up a loop in the two cords hanging from the right wrist and passes them through the ring of the watch. The loop is then passed under the single cord round the right wrist, as shown in the drawing, over the right hand, under the cord round the wrist, and then back over the hand again. The loop should not be twisted. While he is doing this the performer should keep the watch as far as possible away from the right wrist. He will find, if he carries out these instructions, that when he puts his right arm back into position the watch is tied on the two cords behind him, and it will be impossible for anybody to remove the watch while the arms are in that position. To remove the watch the performer has only to get his right arm free again and reverse the tying process. This part of the performance should be practised with a single cord tied round the right wrist with both hands free.

The Jacoby tie is one of the finest " escapes " ever devised.

THE THUMB TIE.—The thumb tie came originally from Japan, being introduced into England by the Ten Ichi troupe, a company of clever conjurers.

The performer starts by inviting two members of the audience to come on the stage and tie his thumbs together. He gives each man a short piece of string and offers his hands for examination. When the voluntary assistants are satisfied that neither the two short pieces of string nor the performer's hands have been prepared in any way for the trick, the performer brings his hands together, crosses his thumbs, and asks one of his assistants to pass one of the pieces of string twice round his thumbs and then to tie the two ends together with the knot at the top, so that everybody can see it. The other assistant is asked to put the second string between the performer's thumbs, pass it twice round the first string and then tie the two ends together on the top thumb.

The performer holds up his hands so that the audience may see that the thumbs are securely tied.

One of the performer's professional assistants—a member of his company—hands out a number of small wooden hoops for examination. On receiving them back from the audience, the assistant stands a little distance away from the performer and throws the hoops to him, one at a time.

Immediately the performer catches one of the hoops, he contrives to get it on one of his arms, although his thumbs are still tied ; as each hoop is caught and passed on to an arm the performer holds his hands towards the audience, showing that his thumbs are still tied.

The illusionist then invites the two members of the audience who are assisting him to examine the hoops on his arms and satisfy themselves that there is no opening in any of the hoops. A little comedy can be introduced at this stage of the trick. After the assistant on the right has inspected some of the hoops the performer turns quickly to the other assistant and says :

" Perhaps you would like to examine the hoops ? "

With that the performer—his thumbs still tied—hands the man a few of the hoops ! The audience are quick to see that the performer has really repeated the trick right under the eyes of the man assisting him.

The trick is then varied in several ways. For example, the performer and his assistant link their hands together, and immediately they have done so the performer appears to pass his arms through those of his assistant, though his thumbs are still tied.

A pole is brought on the stage and while it is held perpendicularly, the performer passes his arms round it and again shows that his thumbs are still tied. Before the assistants have recovered from their surprise the performer has freed himself from the pole and is asking them to look at his thumbs once more ; they are still tied !

The performer concludes the trick by repeating it quickly two or three times.

The main secret of the trick lies in the way in which the performer holds his thumbs when they are being tied. No two pairs of thumbs are quite alike ; therefore, anyone who wishes to learn this trick may find that he can make it easier for himself by slightly altering the position of the thumbs. It may be necessary to put the thumbs farther apart or to bend them slightly so that the tips of the thumbs come under the hands. As a rule, the greater the distance between the tips of the thumbs the easier is the trick.

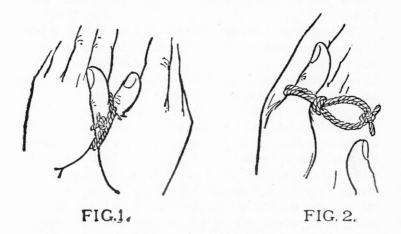

FIG. 1.   FIG. 2.

When the performer is being tied there is nothing to prevent him from pressing the lower thumb down, thus putting a slight strain on the string and preventing the assistant from tying the two thumbs too closely together.

The manner in which the second string is tied really helps the performer because it divides the first string into two loops.

If the learner will now have his thumbs tied together in the way described he will see at once that although the string is tightly tied when the thumbs are spread apart, the tying is not so tight when the thumbs are close together, one on the top of the other. Therefore, to release one hand the performer quickly brings his thumbs together, when he is able to slip the lower one out of the loop. (See Fig. 2.)

The learner may find that the feat comes easier to him if he slips the top thumb out of its loop, but most performers work in the other way because the released thumb is naturally hidden by the other.

It will be seen that the second string holds the loop out stiffly, so that the performer has little difficulty in getting his thumb back into the loop immediately he has caught a hoop and passed it on to his arm ; then he spreads his thumbs apart again, thus putting a strain on the strings, and he can at once show his thumbs securely and tightly tied.

The performer does not wait until he has caught a hoop before he releases one of his thumbs. He slips a thumb out of its loop, but keeps the hands close together. Then having caught the hoop he can instantly pass it on to his arm, and before the audience have recovered from their surprise he has got his thumb back into the loop.

When Ten Ichi did the trick he used string covered with Japanese paper, which probably made the performance of the trick a little easier for him, but an English magician will not take from the effect of the trick by using prepared string. The learner should start by using fairly thick stiff strings, and the first piece should be of such a length that when it is passed twice round the thumbs the ends are quite short ; then it will be impossible for anyone to tie them very tightly. Naturally, the thicker the string the easier the trick.

By the way, it is advisable to have a professional assistant to throw the hoops because he knows exactly how to throw them to suit the performer. Sometimes two or three hoops can be thrown by members of the audience, but it will generally be found that they will bungle the job, throw the hoops wide of the mark, and so spoil the effect of the trick. The performer cannot do the trick quickly and cleanly if he has to stoop down to the stage to pick up a hoop.

The above method, the usual one, demands a great deal of practice, but the trick is worth the effort. Some thumbs are much more suitable for the trick than others ; a

performer who has the misfortune to have large joints is
handicapped.

Here is a much easier method of performing the trick.
The thumbs are held side by side and a string is passed
under them. The hands are held up (Fig. 3) so that the
audience get a good view of the position of the thumbs
and the string. Then the hands are turned down in order
that the string may be tied on the tops of the thumbs and
immediately the hands are in that position the tip of the
first finger of the right hand is inserted in the string under
the thumbs (Fig. 4). If the fingers are curled in slightly
no one can see that the first finger has been employed in

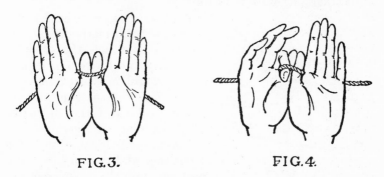

FIG. 3.   FIG. 4.

gathering up a little slack—only a little, but ample for the
performer's purpose. With the first finger secretly in
position, the performer can ask the man who is tying his
thumbs to pull hard and tie a tight knot. Directly the
knot has been tied the performer takes his finger out of
the loop. The slack is now under the thumbs, but the
performer must show the under side of his thumbs once
more to convince them that they have been tied tightly ;
therefore, he has to hide the slack and he does this by
working the string upwards with the sides of the first
fingers while he raises his hands. The job can be done in
the fraction of a second. Then the performer lowers his
hands again, working the slack back to its original position.

Here is another way of obtaining the necessary slack.
The performer, having submitted the strings and his hands

for examination, holds his hands together and asks the assistant on his right to put one of the strings under his thumbs. (See Fig. 5.) The performer then turns quickly round to the other assistant and asks him to tie the strings together, but during the moment occupied in turning from one assistant to the other the performer bends his fingers and locks them together. The performer also gets hold of the string with the middle finger of his right hand and draws it down for an inch into his closed hands, thus getting all the slack he wants. To the audience and to the assistant on the left the string still appears to pass straight under the thumbs, which can be crossed at this stage or held side by side.

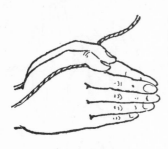

FIG.5.

When performed either by the second or third method only one string is used and the trick is fairly easy, but the performer has to be careful not to expose the slack. Either of these methods is quite good when the magician is performing to children or an audience which is not too sophisticated, but at a big public performance the first method should be used. If he can do so without creating suspicion, the performer should choose the two members of the audience whom he wishes to help him. If there is a man in the audience who is anxious to make things as difficult as possible for the performer he will probably get up at once when the performer asks for the assistance of two members of the audience, but if possible the performer should pretend not to see that man. Let him turn towards others who are not so eager to leave their seats for the stage. Most people are kind to the man who is entertaining them, but it is possible for two men who are determined to spoil the trick if they can possibly do so to carry out their evil intentions.

A BOW TIED IN A SECOND.—Can you tie a bow in a second ?

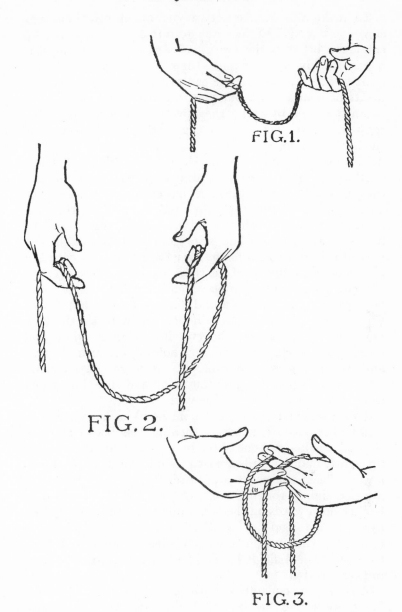

FIG.1.

FIG.2.

FIG.3.

To make the trick effective you apparently hold the cord—soft cord that does not go into kinks is the best—carelessly between the two hands, as shown. Bring the hands quickly together and—there is the bow ! You can tie it so quickly that no one can possibly follow the movements of your fingers, but you can demonstrate the trick to an audience by tying the bow as slowly as you like ; they will never get hold of the method until you show them what to do.

The left hand is held under the cord and the right hand over it (Fig. 1). In the second drawing the hands are nearer each other (Fig. 2), but the artist has exaggerated the size of the loops. In practice the right hand moves along the cord until there is only a short straight piece between the two hands. Then, when the hands are close together, you clip the part of the cord which hangs over the left fingers with the first and second fingers of the right hand ; at the same time you clip the part of the rope which is inside the right hand between the first and second fingers of the left hand. Fig. 3 shows what you have done. Now, to tie the bow you have only to pull the two hands apart while you retain those parts which you are holding between the first and second fingers of both hands. Here you have a little trick which seems very puzzling to an audience, but which is very simple—when you know it.

This particular knot—a double bow—is known as the Tomfool Knot. The hands (behind the body) are put through the loops of one of the bows, which are then drawn up tightly and the cords are tied with two or three ordinary knots. Then the cords are passed between the legs and are tied tightly round them. The victim is then asked to lie face downwards on the floor and the two feet are passed through the loops of another tomfool knot, which is tied up in the same manner, and finally the legs are tied to the hands. A single-handed performer would be helpless in that position.

Anyone unacquainted with the mysteries of knot-tying would be helpless if his hands were tied with one tomfool knot behind his back, but an experienced performer might be able to free himself from that position.

MAGIC KNOTS.—The trick in which the performer, having coiled up a long piece of rope on his left hand, throws it out straight and in doing so causes a number of knots to appear on it, is old and good. The trick is really taken, I believe, from the sailor's repertoire of knots, for I have been told that this little feat is always performed by a sailor when he is throwing a rope to a man overboard.

A man struggling in the sea would find it rather difficult to get a firm hold of a wet rope thrown to him, but if there are knots in the rope he is able to grasp it above a knot and so hang on to it. If the sailor waited to tie the knots in the ordinary way it is possible that the man overboard would be drowned before the task was finished, and therefore the sailor makes the knots tie themselves while he is throwing out the rope to the drowning man. And this is how he does it.

Hold the rope in the left hand as shown (Fig. 1). Pick up a piece of the rope about a yard away with the right hand, turn the hand towards you and then put the loop over the left hand. Keep on doing this until you have come to the end of the rope.

Now, if you were to drop the loops from the left hand you would find that there was not a knot in the rope, but if you clip the end of the rope between two fingers and then let all the loops slide off the hand you will find that you have as many knots as there are loops. The sailor throwing the rope to the drowning man, coils it up very quickly, but a magician can safely take his time over the job.

The best way to learn this trick is to take a short piece of soft string and tie one knot by passing a loop over the hand and then passing the final end of the string through it. If you cannot at first see how to do the trick, tie a knot loosely in the string and put your left hand in it ; that should show you exactly what you have to do if you would tie the knot magically.

Fig. 2 shows some of the loops on the hand and the right hand turning the next loop inwards before placing it on the left hand ; by the way, the loops should not be tight on the left hand because you want them to slide off easily. The knots tied on the rope are also illustrated. (Fig. 3.) Obviously, if you can tie knots on a rope in the way I have described you can as easily untie them by reversing the process.

Show the knotted rope to a member of your audience and ask him to satisfy himself that the knots are genuine.

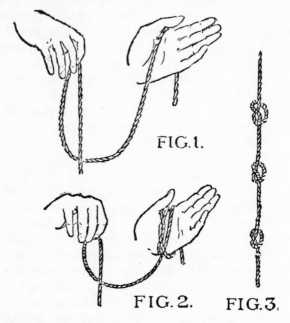

FIG. 1.

FIG. 2.   FIG. 3,

Then, holding one end of the rope, you throw it out and all the knots will have disappeared.

You partly did the trick when you asked a man to examine the knots because, apparently with the object of showing the knots, you opened out each one and as you did so you put the loops on your left hand. Unknown to the man you kept a tight hold of the end of the rope in the left hand by clipping it between the base of the thumb and first finger. When you have opened out all the loops on the left hand you have only to pass the end you have been holding in that hand right through all the loops and you have caused the lot to disappear.

Of course you must be careful when you are putting the loops on the left hand. Follow the direction of the rope from the end and you will see exactly how to bring about the effect. Try it, as a start, with a piece of string; it looks bewildering and wonderful, it is really quite easy.

IMITATION " TOMFOOL " KNOT.—To make an imitation " Tomfool " knot you fold the cord in half and

FIG. 1.   FIG. 2.

then tie a square knot at the loop, leaving a small loop above the knot. (See Fig 1.) You then tie two running knots in the cord a short distance away from the knot you have already tied and pass the ends of the cord through the loop, as shown in the drawing (Fig. 2). Of course the audience are not allowed to see the knot in that state.

The performer's hands or feet are passed through the big loops and the ends are drawn tightly, bringing the two running knots close to the other knot. The cords are drawn out a little way in order to allow the performer to pass his hands through the loops and then members of the audience can pull on the cords till they are tired, but the performer is not inconvenienced because the loops round his wrists are not really being drawn tightly. The ends of the cords can be tied to the performer's chair in any way that the audience please, but as he can always get his hands through the loops the method of tying does not trouble him.

This is a good knot to use if one has been tied in such a way that it is necessary—or at any rate advisable—to cut the cords round the legs. An expert performer will be able to wriggle himself out of almost any tie if he is given the time, but modern audiences are not so patient as those of bygone days.

The famous Davenport Brothers would take half an hour or more at times to free themselves ; a modern audience would not wait patiently—looking at a closed cabinet—for half that time. Therefore this knot is a handy one to know, because the performer can tie himself up with it. The loop is first tied in the way shown, the ends are passed through the loop, the legs are passed through the large loops, and the ends are drawn up to the chair and tied there. If the performer finds that he has given himself a little too much slack in the loops he can easily rectify the mistake by moving his legs a little from the chair.

The performer, addressing the audience on the subject of knots, tells them that there are various kinds of knots, and the most peculiar of all are known as watch knots, because they want watching.

" I'll show you a few," he says, picking up a piece of soft cord about a yard long. With this he ties a single knot, as in Fig. 1.

" There," says the performer, " that looks like an ordinary knot, but it is really a watch knot ; keep your eye on it. I'll tie another," he adds, and gets the cord into the position shown in Fig. 2. " Two more for luck," he continues, passing the cord first through the lower knot and then through the one at the top. " I hope you're watching these four watch knots," adds the magician,

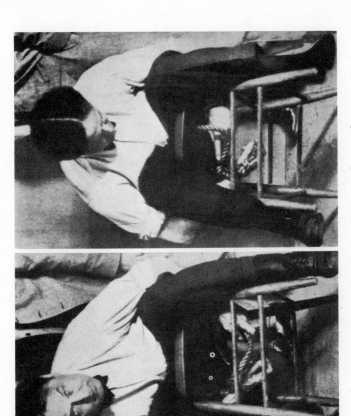

Houdini releasing himself after being tied to a chair.

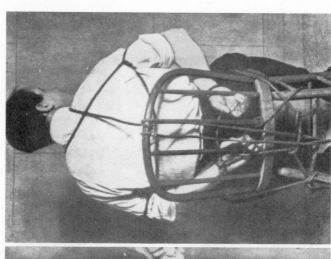

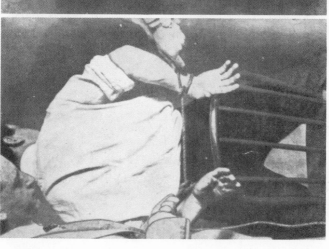

The back view of a series of rope ties from which Houdini escaped.

" because—there, they've gone ! You can't watch them now : I was afraid they'd do that."

All four knots have disappeared and the performer is left with the piece of cord in his hand.

If the reader will follow the diagrams he cannot go wrong. In tying the last two knots he must remember to pass the cord through the bottom knot and then through the top knot from the back.

MORE ABOUT SPIRITS.—Ties used by fraudulent spiritualist mediums may be exploited with advantage.

The performer invites members of the audience to come on the stage and inspect the " abode of the spirits "—a small enclosure made by two screens in which is a chair. One screen is removed for a moment so that the audience may see what goes on.

When everyone is satisfied that the chair is an ordinary one and that no one is concealed behind the screens the performer hands four ropes to the committee for examination. The performer then sits down on the chair and two members of the committee, acting on his instructions, tie him to the back of the chair with one of the ropes. They then tie his legs to the chair with two ropes and finally tie the last rope to one of his wrists. This rope is then passed under the chair, or round the back of it, and is tied to the other wrist. A tambourine, a bell and a musical-box are placed in the enclosure and the screen is put up in front of the performer.

Directly these preparations have been made the bell is rung, the tambourine played and the audience hear the musical-box in action. Finally the tambourine is thrown over the top of the screen, the assistant immediately takes the screen away and the audience see the performer still bound, hand and foot, to the chair.

This is a very convincing trick and yet a very easy one. There are three ways of doing it. If the performer has had his hands tied with the rope passed behind the chair he merely has to work the cord over his head—a very simple matter. Then, to all intents and purposes, his hands are free and he can cause the spirits to make their presence known !

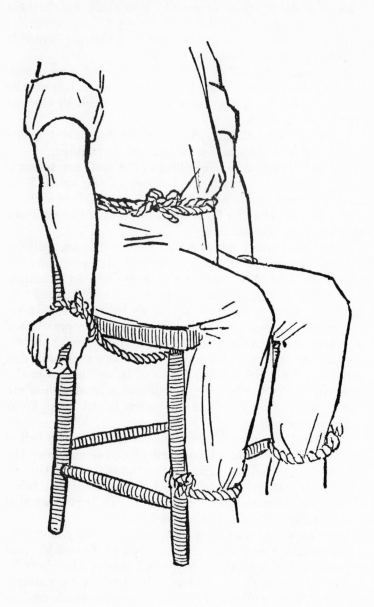

If the hands are tied with the rope under the chair, as in our illustration, the performer must watch the tying, and he will find that in ninety-nine cases out of a hundred one of the wrists will certainly be tied with a slip knot ; in fact, it is not easy to tie a man's wrists, in the way described, without tying slip knots. The performer is thus able to get one hand free ; directly the manifestations have occurred he puts his hand back in the loop and strains on the cord to make the knot slip back into position.

In either case there is no need to trouble about the rope that binds him to the back of the chair or the ropes which tie his legs to the chair.

The third method is easier still. Although the performer is bound to the chair there is nothing to prevent him from getting up, taking the chair with him, and, with his hands still tied, bending down and ringing the bell, banging the tambourine and setting the musical-box off.

A TRICK DONE BACKWARDS.—After a trick in which the performer has produced " spirit manifestations " under very difficult conditions—with his legs tied to a chair and his hands tied together—the performer suggests that he will repeat the trick by doing it backwards. (Fig. 3.)

The performer shows the audience two pieces of cord and then retires behind his screen. In a few moments the audience hear the trumpet played, the tambourine shaken and so on, and then the screen is quickly withdrawn and the audience see the performer tied to the chair and with his hands tied together. The screen is placed in front of the performer again and in a few moments he appears with the two cords in his hands.

To the audience the performer appears to have tied himself very rapidly in such a way that his hands and legs are securely bound, and then released himself in a few seconds.

The performer really ties his legs with one of the cords he has shown to the audience ; the other cord he hides in a pocket and uses in its place a cord already there. This cord is knotted in the way shown in the diagram. The performer ties the ends of the rope to his knees and,

bringing up the knots, puts his right hand through the loop
A and his left hand through the loop B. (Fig. 1.) By a
twist of the hands the loops are tightened on the wrist
and all four knots are brought together, when the loops
appear as in Fig. 2. The release is, of course, a simple
matter, as the other drawing shows.

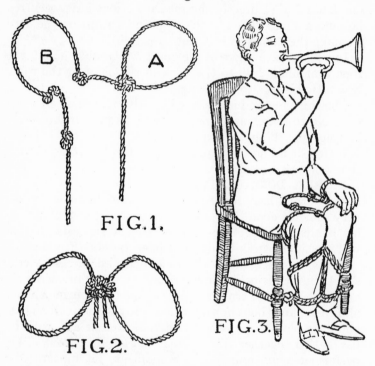

FIG.1.

FIG.2.

FIG.3.

THE GIRL ESCAPES.—The performer who is fortunate
enough to have a smart girl assistant can provide her with
a very simple escape trick.

A little platform, with a pole and a stool securely screwed
to it, is wheeled on to the stage, and the assistant sits down.

The performer, showing a number of short pieces of
muslin, invites members of the audience to come on the
stage, and examine the apparatus, and tie the young
woman's ankles to the legs of the stool. Her arms are also
tied separately with two pieces of muslin, and the four

ends are brought behind her and tied there. She is also tied at the neck by a piece of muslin passed through a ring on the pole and, finally, the performer ties his assistant's hands to the pole by means of another piece of muslin passed through the bandages already on the wrists ; this piece is then passed through a ring on the pole.

The usual appliances for a " spirit manifestation," a tambourine, bell and so on, are placed on the girl's lap, and a screen is drawn in front of her. The various " manifestations " take place immediately.

If the reader will turn back to the description of the way in which the assistant is tied he will note that the performer ties her hands to the pole. Her hands are not close together and the performer takes care not to draw the muslin which he ties close to the pole. There is therefore nothing to prevent the girl from pushing one arm through that loop and so getting one hand round to her lap, so that she can shake the tambourine and ring the bell, as seen in the drawing.

SPIRIT KNOTS.—To produce "spirit" knots, the performer shows a piece of cord, six or seven feet in length, and ties the two ends together. He then sits down and places a board on his knees. A member of the audience is asked to seal the cord, near the knot, to the board.

A screen is placed in front of the performer for a few moments. When the screen is removed the audience see the cord still sealed to the board but several knots have been tied on the cord.

This trick, which can be shown separately, or in a series of " spirit manifestations," is done very simply by means of a duplicate cord, with knots already tied in it, concealed in the performer's sleeve.

After the performer has placed the board on his knees he says to the person assisting him : " You will find a piece of sealing wax and a box of matches on the table."

For a moment the audience look at the person who is getting the sealing wax and during that moment the performer pulls the knotted end of the rope down his sleeve and holds it as it appears in the drawing, which shows the knot of the cord which was examined by the audience concealed in the hand. The diagram exposes the trick; of course the performer holds his hand in such a way that the audience do not see the cord coming from the sleeve. The loop of the cord hanging down convinces the audience that it is that cord which is sealed to the board.

When the screen is put in front of the performer he merely draws the cord right out of his sleeve and hides the other. The whole trick depends on the attention of the audience being misdirected at one moment.

A performer who specialises in escape tricks with ropes must be ready for any emergency. There may be times when he will find that his hands have been tied behind him a little too securely and that to get free he must use the open knife he has concealed on him.

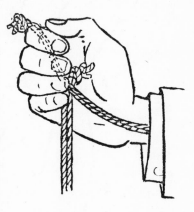

Obviously he cannot let the trick end there. Having performed the various feats expected of him while securely tied, that is to say, the bell is rung, the tambourine shaken and the rest of it, the performer must be ready to appear with his hands still tied behind him, and this is how he does it :

He has a length of rope concealed on him ; this rope is already tied in the way shown in the diagram. He gets this rope out, holds it in the left hand at the point marked with a cross, puts his left hand through it—still keeping the knot against the wrist—and then inserts his right hand. He then twists his hands round in opposite directions to tighten the circle of cord, and if the two knots at the side have been tied at the right places he finishes up with these two knots tightly wedged between his wrists. Then he can swing round (after the screen has been removed) and show that his hands are still tied tightly together. " Any port in a storm " is a good motto for the escape performer and this tie provides a very good one.

THE KELLAR TIE.—The knot known to the magical world as the Kellar tie received that name because of the splendid use to which Kellar, the famous American magician, put one of the devices—in fact, the principal secret—of the notorious Davenport Brothers. By the use

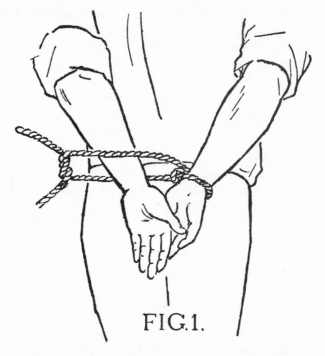

FIG. 1.

of this secret " tie " the performer, having had his wrists tied together, is able to slip one wrist free instantly and, as quickly, put it back in its original position.

The tie is generally used in the following manner. The performer brings forward a short piece of cord and asks for the assistance of a member of the audience. When the man comes on the stage the performer asks him to tie his right wrist, and suggests, as a matter of precaution, that the assistant should tie two more knots on the top of the first. The ends of the cord hang down from the wrist after the knots have been tied.

The performer then puts his hands behind his back, turns round, places the left wrist on the right and asks the assistant to tie the left as securely as he tied the right. When the performer is about to submit to this tying his hands appear to the audience as those drawn in Fig. 1. Afterwards the performer raises his hands—see illustration—so that the audience see the knots which have been tied. The performer then turns round, appears to be about to make a speech, but stops suddenly and says to his assistant from the audience :

" Excuse me, you have a hair on your collar," and he brings his left hand round and removes the imaginary hair. He then brings his left hand behind him again and turns round instantly, showing that his hands are still tied. He swings round again, facing the audience who, of course, are amused by what has happened, and says to his assistant :

" Don't pay any attention to them ; you tie knots very well," and he brings his left hand round again and pats the man approvingly on the shoulder. Once again the performer turns round and shows the audience that his hands are still tied.

The effect can be repeated as often as the performer wishes. Obviously, the performer must be able to get his left hand free instantly and must also be able to insert it in the loop and show his hands apparently still tightly tied.

There is more than one way of doing this. If the performer has had several knots tied on to his right wrist, he will get all the slack he needs by merely passing the rope round the knot before he has his left hand tied. The left wrist presses down on the right and holds the slack safely until the left hand is tied. Therefore, when the performer wishes to get his left hand free he merely has to slip it out of the loop.

But how is he to make it appear to be tightly tied afterwards ? The loop is large enough to allow him to take the left hand through it and if he merely put his hand back in the loop it would appear to the audience to be loose—

which is not what he wants. This is where the great secret of the Davenport Brothers comes in.

In replacing his left hand into the loop he does not put it in in the same direction but in the opposite direction ; then he twists his left hand round and in so doing gathers up the slack and his hand is in the original position.

The late Mr. J. N. Maskelyne, who discovered the

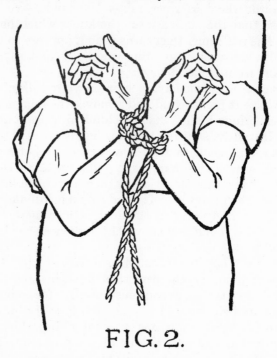

FIG. 2.

secret of the Davenport Brothers, was an adept at performing this particular trick and he liked demonstrating it to any magician who was interested in knot-tying.

To release the hand it is only necessary to untwist it in the opposite direction and the slack is obtained again and the hand is free.

Another method of obtaining the slack in the first place is by twisting one cord round the other twice when the right hand is placed behind the back and before the left hand is placed in position. The left wrist hides the twists in the rope, and the performer can safely have his left wrist tied tightly to the other. To release the left hand the performer merely turns it round on the other wrist twice and so takes out the twists in the rope and gets his slack. When he inserts the wrist in the loose loop again he turns the hand round twice and the slack is taken up.

Of course this knack is not mastered in a moment, but practice makes perfect. Still, if the performer wishes to make the trick much easier for himself he can do so by using two ropes. These are first tied round the right wrist and then the performer, in putting his right hand behind his back, so that the assistant may tie the left wrist to the right, secretly twists the cords as in Fig. 2. Naturally, when two ropes are twisted the performer gets far more slack with one twist than he would if only one rope were used. To the audience the effect is just the same, for, it is to be hoped, they know nothing of the performer's hunger for slack. By using two ropes the performer practically doubles the thickness of the rope, and a moment's thought will show the reader that the thicker the rope the easier the trick must be.

The reader, in practising this trick, must remember how his left wrist was tied on the right wrist. The natural position would be with the fingers pointing downwards. Therefore, when the left hand is free the reader must remember to put his wrist back in the loop with the fingers pointing upwards and then, after he has twisted his hand, to gather up the slack, the fingers will be pointing downwards—the original position. That is the main secret of the mystery.

THE ROPES AND RINGS.—This is one of the oldest tricks in the world and one of the best : the secret device which enables the conjurer to do it is described, in connection with a well-known little trick, in what is claimed to be the first book on conjuring in the English language—*Discoverie of Witchcraft*, published in 1584.

The trick must have been fairly well known at that time, so that we are safe in saying that it is at least four hundred years old—probably much older. The secret is very simple, and yet the effect is so good that the trick is still being performed by magicians all over the world. It is probably performed at hundreds of children's parties every Christmas, for it is a great favourite with the drawing-room conjurer and his audiences. Some magicians affect to despise it because it is old, but there are few modern tricks to equal it. It can be performed at very close quarters ; in fact, the audience may surround the performer.

It can be performed without any special preparation of the articles used in the trick and those articles cost only a few pence.

It would be difficult to find any modern trick for which so many good qualities can be fairly claimed.

Here is a good way of presenting the trick. The performer asks for the assistance of the best boy in the room. Perhaps no boy responds, so the performer continues : " Either the best boy or the worst—it doesn't matter which." Then, of course, there is a rush to the stage.

The performer selects two boys—" the best and the second best, or the worst and one a trifle better ; I leave you to decide."

One boy stands on the left of the performer, the other on his right. The magician shows the boys two long pieces of cord, and gives two ends to one boy and two ends to the other with instructions to have a little tug-of-war, just to convince themselves that the cords are strong. The performer says that he will take a hand in the game and he pulls on the middle of the cords.

When the boys and the audience are satisfied that the cords are sound the performer asks the boy on his left to take off his coat. While the boy is removing his coat the performer asks for the loan of two bangles of the " slave " kind, without a break in them.

" My friend on the right," says the performer, turning to the boy on his right, " will be responsible for their safe return." The boy is asked to hold the bangles for a moment. (In case he is unable to borrow bangles of the right kind the performer should provide himself with two metal or wooden rings, which he gives out for examination.)

While the bangles are being taken off the owners' arms and handed to the boy the performer threads the boy's coat on the cords by passing the cords through the sleeves ; the back of the coat faces the audience. The performer then ties a knot with the two cords. The boy holding the bangles is asked to hand one to " my friend on the left " and, acting on the performer's instructions, the boys themselves put the bangles on the ropes and pass them down to the knot which is lying on the back of the coat. The performer then ties another knot with the two cords. The boy on the right is asked to take off his coat and the performer passes the cords through the sleeves and drapes the coat over the bangles, the ends of the cords being handed back to the boys.

The performer then asks the boy on the left to hand him one of the cords and impresses on him that he can choose which he likes ; what is more, after he has handed a cord to the performer he can change his mind if he likes and the performer will use the other. The same request is made to the other boy.

The performer, holding the two cords in his hands, ties a single knot on the back of the coat and hands the cords back to the boys. He then reviews the situation, reminding the audience what he has done. First, he threaded a coat on the cords ; then he tied a knot ; then the bangles were put on the cords and they were tied ; finally the other coat was threaded on the cords and the coat was tied, " and," adds the performer, " there is the knot, and I am not going to cover it up."

After a little more patter the performer takes the first coat clear away from the cords (remember, please, that it was threaded on the cords in full view of the audience) ; then the performer removes the bangles and calls attention to the fact that there is still one coat left on the cords and one knot above the coat.

" We will take the coat away and dissolve the knot at the same time," says the performer. He tells the boys to pull on the cords and the audience see the performer with the coat in his hands and the two boys holding the cords, from which the knot has disappeared.

The secret is simple, but to get the best effect out of the trick the performer should be a good showman.

Before the trick begins the performer ties a piece of cotton round the centre of the cords. When the attention of the audience is engaged by the boy taking off his coat and the other boy receiving the borrowed bangles the performer divides the cords, keeping his right hand over the centre, so that the cords are in the position shown in Fig. 1. The cords are threaded through the sleeves of the coat and the join is concealed by the coat. Thus the boy on the left is really holding the two ends of one cord and the other boy is holding the two ends of the other cord.

The other manipulations are genuine, but when the performer is tying the last knot with the two single cords he must remember to tie a single knot and to give the cord from the boy on the left to the boy on the right and the cord from the boy on the right to the boy on the left.

If the reader has followed these directions with cords and two coats he will find that to remove the first coat all he has to do is to break the cotton, to remove the bangles he has to untie a knot and, for the final effect, he has to untie another knot ; the boys, pulling on the cords, do the rest for him !

If the performer wishes to show the cords separately in the first instance he can do so, but in that case he provides himself with a little piece of wire bent roughly in the form of a ring. (See Fig. 2.) The two ends of the wire are not brought close together, but a space is left between them so that the performer can close the ring over the centre of the cords ; then he squeezes the wire so that it holds the cords securely when he divides them. To remove the first coat he merely has to unbend the wire and hide it in his hand for a moment.

Two pieces of ribbon, or braid, or tape can be used in place of the cords ; they can be fastened in the centre with a pin while the boy is taking off his coat.

The trick can be varied in many ways. For example, instead of asking the first boy to take off his coat the performer can invite another boy to help him. This boy is asked to sit on a chair with his back to the audience; the cords, secretly divided in the way explained, are threaded through the boy's coat. A knot is tied and then the cords are passed through the back of the chair and tied. The back of the chair takes the place of the bangles.

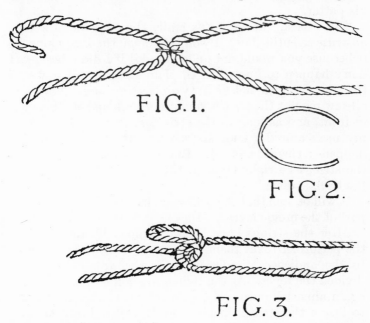

FIG.1.

FIG.2.

FIG.3.

Then a coat is borrowed, threaded on the cords and hung over the back of the chair and the single knot tied. The escape is managed in the same way.

Having done the trick the performer can safely take an encore and do the trick again in a different way; that is to say, the same secret is used but the trick has an entirely different " dress." The performer says that he will explain the trick, and so that everyone may be able to see exactly how to do it he will demonstrate the trick on himself.

The performer then brings forward two long pieces of soft string. These are handed out for inspection and returned to the performer who immediately places them behind his neck and then brings them round to the front of his body. He then ties a knot with one of the strings and brings the knot close up to his throat.

Having called attention to the knot the performer holds two strings in one hand and two in the other, and continues his patter.

" The trick," he says, " is really the outcome of a very abstruse scientific law. I won't give you the long name for it because you would not understand it if I did ; besides, I don't happen to know it. In plain English this law says that one thing cannot be in two places at once. Now, you all saw me put the strings round my neck and tie this knot in front, and as long as the strings remain at the back of my neck and the knot stays where it was tied nothing happens ; there is no trick. But if the knot disappears and the strings go right through the neck—well, that is how the trick is done."

It will be seen that the performer has merely done the last part of the previous trick—the one with the ropes and rings.

After the strings have been examined by the audience the performer takes them back again and, while pattering to the audience, divides them in the way in which he divided the ropes. As the strings are going to be separated again almost immediately the performer need not trouble to fasten the strings in the middle ; if he links one loop into the other, as in Fig. 3, and keeps his thumb on them they will hold together. In passing the strings round his neck he merely pushes the linked loops between his collar and his neck and holds them by pressing his neck against the collar.

The performer then brings the strings to the front of his body and ties a single knot with one string, taking care to pass the string in his left hand to his right hand and the string from the right to his left. One pull on the string brings them apparently through the neck and also causes the knot to disappear.

Houdini fastened in a strait-jacket and about to be suspended head down from the top of a skyscraper. The photo was taken a moment before he was pushed over.

Houdini.

ANOTHER ESCAPE.—Here are details of an escape performed openly as a trick. The performer hands out a piece of cord, fifteen to twenty feet in length, for examination. He then invites a member of the audience to bind his wrists together with a handkerchief. One end of the cord is then dropped between the handkerchief and the performer's body—that is to say, in the circle formed by the performer's arms—and the assistant is then asked to take hold of the two ends of the cord and pull the cord close to the handkerchief.

The performer is thus held by the cord pressing against the handkerchief tied round his wrists, and it seems impossible that he can escape from such a position. The performer moves his arms up and down once or twice and finally raises them clear of the cord ; the person who tied the handkerchief round the performer's wrists can examine his knots and assure himself that the performer has not tampered with them.

If the performer is right-handed he should stand with his left side towards the audience ; naturally, since the cord is long, the assistant must be at some little distance from him. To release himself the performer bends his right hand down behind the left hand, grips the cord with his second finger, drawing it up inside the hand, and then passes his right hand through the loop he has made ; with a twist of the wrist he can then free himself.

The object of moving the arms up and down is to cover the movement of the hand.

TWO SACK ESCAPES.—The sack used by a magician should be large enough to allow him to stand up in it when the mouth is closed ; black sateen is a suitable material.

After the sack has been examined by the audience the performer steps into it, draws it up round him, and has it bound by his assistant, who ties a large handkerchief round the bunched-up sack just below the mouth. Members of the audience can tie the last knots in the handkerchief which binds the sack if they so desire. A screen is drawn in front of the performer, who emerges almost immediately with the sack, still bound round tightly below the mouth, on his arm.

The assistant must rehearse his part of the trick carefully. The performer has a duplicate sack concealed under his coat. When he is in the sack which the audience have seen, the performer gets out the duplicate sack, grasping it just below the opening, and holds it over his head. The assistant, in gathering up the sack which the audience see, gets hold of the duplicate sack, pulls it out a little way and then holds his hand at the junction of the two sacks. The handkerchief is at once passed round the sacks at that point and tied ; then it is passed round again and more knots are tied. Thus the audience apparently see one sack with the performer in it and that sack is apparently bound with the tied handkerchief.

To release himself the performer merely has to draw down the sack in which he is standing, leaving the duplicate sack with the handkerchief tied tightly round it. He then folds up the loose sack and hides it under his coat and comes forward with the other sack on his arm.

The second method is, if anything, a little easier than the first and it is certainly more effective.

In this case the sack is fitted with a draw-string running round the hem at the top. The performer gets into the sack, and the assistant, holding the two ends of the draw-string, pulls on them and so closes the mouth of the sack. He then ties the strings together and invites members of the audience to tie any other knots they please on the top of the first knots and to seal them. Nevertheless, the performer has no difficulty in escaping.

There are two or three little gaps in the hem of the sack. When the performer is inside the sack he finds one of these gaps and pulls on the draw-string and keeps a firm hold on it. Thus, when the assistant draws the strings, closing the mouth of the sack, the performer is holding a large loop of the string inside the sack. The strings can then be tied and sealed outside the sack.

To release himself the performer drops the loop he is holding, widens the mouth of the sack, gets out, closes the mouth of the sack again by pulling on the loop he held, cuts it off, ties the two ends of the strings together and tucks the knot inside the hem. The sack is therefore tied tightly at the mouth, although the performer is outside it.

The assistant must be careful, when this method is used, not to allow anyone to bind the string *round* the sack, because if that is done the performer is fixed ; he cannot get out. The strings are merely drawn together, closing the sack, tied several times and sealed.

THE LADDER ESCAPE.—The magician is tied to a short ladder which is fixed in two holes in a platform wheeled on to the stage. A screen or curtain is drawn in front of the performer and in a few moments he emerges, with the ropes in his hands.

The feat is not as difficult as it appears to be. The reader will note in the picture that the performer is tied with his hands outside the posts of the ladder, but there is nothing to prevent him from working his arms round and so loosening the cords behind his neck. Thus he is soon able to get his head free, and as his hands are then free he can start to untie the knots !

CHAPTER VII

MISCELLANEOUS MAGIC—THE RING AND THE DOVE—THE
DISAPPEARING GLASS OF WINE—THE IVORY PILLARS—
CUT STRING RESTORED—THE COIN-FINDER—THE BOWL
OF INK—THE WATCH AND THE LOAF—THE PIERCED
HAND—VANISHING FROM A BOX AND CABINET—THE
MYSTERY OF THE CRYSTAL

AS Houdini performed a great number of miscellaneous tricks during his long career on the stage I give a selection of them here.

THE RING AND THE DOVE.—The conjurer borrows a ring from a member of the audience and asks another spectator to assist him in a " little experiment."

Having placed the ring on a tray, the magician asks his assistant to bend the ring a little, and, to help in this task, hands him a small mallet, telling him to give the ring " a little tap."

The assistant does so but, to the discomfiture of the owner of the ring, the " tap " proves to be too hard and the ring breaks in pieces.

The conjurer expresses surprise and suggests that the ring is taken back to its owner with an apology, and a glass of wine to " smooth matters over."

A professional assistant brings on a bottle of wine and pours out a glass, the conjurer then suggesting that his volunteer assistant should take the wine down to the owner of the ring and ask him to " help himself." The volunteer assistant does not care to do this, and the conjurer decides to finish the trick in another way. He wraps the broken ring in a small piece of tissue paper, and holds it over a lighted match. The paper and its contents vanish in flame.

" I am afraid you must ask the owner to accept the whole bottle now," says the conjurer. " I think the contents will interest him. Perhaps you would like to see them for yourself. Look ! "

The illusionist breaks the bottle (from which, it will be remembered, he has just poured a glass of wine), and out flies a tame dove with the ring, completely restored, tied round its neck.

The secret ? Well, fixed on the end of the mallet with which the volunteer is asked to break the ring is a kind of cap, held in its place by a simple bayonet catch. Inside the cap is a duplicate ring. In picking up the mallet, the conjurer presses on the cap and gives it a twist. This releases the cap, and allows the duplicate ring to fall into the hand. The conjurer puts the borrowed ring into the cap (under cover of pretending to examine the ring).

After the duplicate ring is broken, the conjurer's professional assistant takes away the tray with the mallet on it, and thus secretly takes the ring off the stage. The magician wraps the pieces of the duplicate ring in a little piece of flash paper, and substitutes the parcel for another piece of flash paper rolled into a ball. When a match is applied to this it goes off in a flame, and while all eyes are upon it, the conjurer has an opportunity of concealing the little parcel containing the pieces of the ring.

It is then that the professional assistant brings on the wine in a trick bottle. The upper part is of metal, and the wine is contained in that part only. The lower part of the bottle is really an inverted glass jar japanned black, and inside this jar is the dove. When the assistant took away the tray with the mallet on it, he extracted the borrowed ring from the cap on the mallet, tied the ring round the neck of a dove and put the dove into the jar, with its head uppermost.

THE BALL OF STRING.—The trick is done with a whole ball of string. This is what the performer does—or rather, appears to do. Borrowing a shilling, he has it marked. He wraps it in a piece of paper, burns the paper, and shows that the coin has vanished. From his pocket, he takes a ball of string. The string is unwound and the marked shilling found in the centre.

Unknown to the audience, the ball of string is prepared for the trick. It is wound round the end of a little flat tube of cardboard, which can easily be made by getting a strip of cardboard, making two creases in it, folding it down the creases, and sticking one end over the other. The tube should be wide enough to admit a shilling and long enough to stick out of a ball of string when all the string is wound on it. This ball the conjurer places in his right-hand trousers pocket.

After borrowing the shilling, the conjurer picks up a piece of thin paper which has been prepared beforehand by having two small cuts made at right angles in the centre. He keeps his thumb and first finger over these cuts, and is thus able to show the paper as an ordinary piece. He places the shilling directly over the cuts, and screws up the paper, which will hold the shilling quite securely until the conjurer presses slightly on the coin, when it passes through without altering the appearance of the screwed-up paper. The conjurer thus gets the shilling in his right hand and holds the paper in his left. He puts his hand into his trousers pocket to get a match, and in so doing drops the shilling down the tube. Up till now, the audience believe that the shilling is still in the paper.

The conjurer lights the paper, and when it is burnt away shows that there is nothing in his hands. He then puts his hand into his trousers pocket, pulls out the cardboard tube, leaves it in the pocket, and takes out the ball of string. The marked shilling is then found in the centre of the ball of string.

THE IVORY PILLARS.—Two small pillars of imitation ivory are used by the magician, who shows them fairly threaded on a piece of string. He can hold the string by the two ends and show the pillars, an inch or two apart, threaded on it.

The two pillars are placed together and the string is apparently cut. The knife is carried right down to the base of the pillars, which are then separated at the top, and the audience see the two ends of the string sticking through the pillars. Everyone will readily agree that the string has been fairly cut ; yet, when the performer places the pillars together again and pronounces his " magic word," he can pull the string backwards and forwards through the pillars, and, as a climax, can separate the pillars, showing them fairly threaded on the string and the string whole again.

The secret of the trick is in the pillars and in the knife used for cutting the string.

The blade of the knife is so blunt that it will not cut the string, and the two " inside sides " of the pillars are really sliding shutters. Thus, when the performer has put the two pillars close together he pretends to cut the string but he really pushes the string downwards and carries the " shutters " down with it. The shutters, of course, are flexible, and when they have been lowered by the string the first part of the trick is finished. The performer holds the lower part of the pillars together in his hands but separates the tops and shows the marks of the cut string. These marks are merely two dots resembling the ends of a piece of string.

Placing the pillars together again, the performer slowly pulls the string backwards and forwards through the pillars and this action draws the shutters up again. When they are finally in their original position the performer can separate the pillars and show them fairly threaded on the string and the string whole again.

DISAPPEARING TUMBLER OF WINE.—*Effect.*—The conjurer pours some wine from a bottle into a claret tumbler. He covers the tumbler with a handkerchief and holds it up for a moment. Then he suddenly flicks away the handkerchief ; the tumbler of wine has vanished.

Explanation.—The base of the bottle is removed and is fixed in about half-way up the bottle. Thus there is a compartment at the top of the bottle which will hold wine, but the lower part of the bottle is hollow.

Having poured out a little wine, the conjurer, still holding the bottle in his right hand, picks up a handkerchief with his left hand, and, with both hands, displays it to the

audience. The handkerchief is really a double one with a
disc of cardboard, of the same size as the top of the tumbler,
sewn into the centre. The handkerchief is placed over the
glass, and in doing this the conjurer takes care to get the
disc exactly over the top of the glass. Then he picks up the
covered tumbler (really only the handkerchief) with his left
hand and at the same time puts the bottle down on the
table. The bottle must come down on the table before the
edges of the handkerchief are clear of the table. Of course,
the bottle is really put down over the tumbler, and the
conjurer, holding the handkerchief in his hand, pauses for a
moment, and then flicks away the handkerchief. The
inventor of this excellent little trick is Mr. Elbert M. Morey.

THE MAGICAL BOWL OF INK.—The performer shows
a large glass bowl full of ink and places it on a skeleton
stand on the stage. A similar bowl, but empty, is on a
similar stand a few feet away from the bowl of ink.

Standing between the two bowls, the conjurer makes
some magical passes over them. The ink visibly disappears
from the first bowl and reappears in the empty bowl.

The first bowl is really provided with a celluloid lining, and
the ink in the bowl is that which is contained in the small
space between the lining and the glass. To any spectator,
however, the bowl appears to be full of ink.

In order to cause the gradual disappearance of the ink
the conjurer has to have a small plug withdrawn from the
celluloid lining. This movement is easily managed by
means of a thread pull, which passes to a hidden assistant
at the back of the stage. The moment the plug is pulled
out, the ink between the lining and the bowl begins to sink
and find its level at the bottom of the bowl.

The appearance of the ink in the second bowl is easily
managed by an assistant under the stage, as one of the legs
of the skeleton stand are hollow and is connected by a pipe
passing through the stage to an air-pressure pump below.

In order that the audience may not see the source from
which the ink flows, it is passed through the circular rim at
the top of the stand. This rim is perforated with small holes
so that the ink appears to be sprayed into the bowl by some

invisible agency overhead. It is thus impossible for the audience to see that the ink is really being forced upwards into the bowl.

THE DEVIL'S MIRROR.—Some visiting cards are borrowed by the conjurer from his audience. One of them is chosen and is signed by the owner; the performer places this card in an envelope and rests the envelope against a candlestick on the table.

The performer then shows a small photograph frame, and removes the back so that the audience can see through the glass in the front. Having replaced the back, the magician rests the frame, with its back to the audience, against another candlestick on his table. He then commands the card to leave the envelope and travel invisibly to the frame. Picking up the envelope he slits it open and shows that it is empty; then turning the frame round to the audience he shows that the card is now inside the frame. He takes the back off the frame, removes the card and has it identified by the owner.

The envelope is prepared by having a small slit cut in the flap side. When the conjurer is placing the chosen card in the envelope, he has the remainder of the visiting cards in his left hand, and he holds the envelope with the address side towards the audience in the same hand. Thus the chosen card really passes out through the slit in the envelope and is then on the top of the other cards, which are then placed on the table while the performer shows the frame.

The frame is really a sand-frame made with a back which can be removed. When the performer removes the back of the frame the sand is out of sight in the wooden structure. He places the back of the frame on the top of the cards on the table and as there is a small piece of soft wax on the back of the frame, the top card—which is the chosen one—naturally adheres to it.

Having shown the frame to the audience the performer picks up the back and, holding it with card toward him, replaces it in the frame. Then, turning the frame over, he causes the hidden sand to run down, making the frame appear to be empty. In resting the frame against the candlestick, the performer reverses it again, allowing the sand to run out of sight; then, when he turns the frame round, the card is seen. The back of the frame is removed in order that the card may be identified.

CUT STRING RESTORED.—The illusionist hands a piece of string and a yard measure to a member of the audience, and the string is seen to be exactly one yard in length. The performer, showing his hands empty, asks that the string may be folded exactly in half and handed back to him. He cuts the loop and asks two members of the audience to hold the two ends hanging down; the conjurer's closed hand holds the other two ends together. The hand is then opened, and the string is seen to be joined; the person who measured it in the first place is asked to measure it again. The length has not varied.

A small loop of string is concealed by the magician at the beginning of the trick between the first and second fingers of the left hand; the fingers completely hide the loop, and, therefore, the hands can be shown empty; with the fingers curved slightly the hands will then be in a natural position.

On receiving the folded string from the person assisting him the conjurer takes it in the left hand and in apparently pulling up the loop to the top of his hand really pulls up the concealed loop. Having cut through this loop, the performer at once passes his closed hand over the cut ends while he asks two members of the audience to hold the ends which are hanging down. In directing his assistants how to hold the string, he removes his right hand, thus palming away the two little pieces of string, and at once puts his left hand over the same place; thus, when the left hand is slowly opened and the string is seen restored the audience can see that the conjurer has nothing concealed in his hand. The two ends are dropped into a side pocket of the coat.

THE COIN-FINDER.—A small wooden box is placed on a couple of wine glasses. Three discs in a row are fitted to the top of the box. A member of the audience is invited to place a coin into one of the discs and to cover all three discs with three wooden caps. While this is being done, the performer's back is turned to the audience. When the coin has been hidden, the performer turns round, and to prove that he is not guided by anything he can see in the apparatus, he covers the box with a black handkerchief. In spite of the coin being covered by a cap and by the handkerchief, the performer is able to tell at once under which cap the coin will be found.

Two of the discs have terminal brass pegs which go right through the box and connect with a battery and lamp. The lamp lights at two points. If the coin is placed in the middle disc, the lamp does not light. The coin acts as a bridge between the two terminals and so completes the electrical current. Of course, the battery must be switched on before the trick can be performed, but the conjurer has no difficulty in doing this when he is covering the box with a handkerchief. For the fraction of a second the flash of the lamp is seen in one of the pin-holes in the box—unless the coin is in the middle disc.

SHOOTING AT A MATCH.—Two slits are cut at right angles in the end of a match ; this is done merely in order that the match will stand upright on the table. The match is placed at the extreme edge of the table, and, on the opposite side, in a line with the standing match, the conjurer lays down a match with the end just beyond the edge of the table. The feat consists of shooting at the standing match by flicking at the other match with the thumb and middle finger of the right hand.

The odds seem to be all against the marksman, and yet it is almost difficult to lose. The match which is flicked away turns in its flight, and by the time it reaches the standing match it is broadside on. Possibly the slight weight of the head of the match causes it to turn in this way, but whatever the cause the fact remains that the match certainly does turn. If the matches are in line with each other failure is practically impossible.

THE WATCH AND THE LOAF.—A watch is borrowed from a member of the audience. The magician wraps a handkerchief round the watch, and gives it to someone to hold, with the request that it may be held tightly in the handkerchief. Taking hold of one corner of the hand-kerchief, the conjurer whisks it out of the hand of the spectator. The watch has vanished.

The attention of the audience is then directed to a large paper parcel which has been standing on a side table. The performer carefully cuts the string from the parcel and pulls off the paper, only to disclose another paper covering. This is removed, but there are several others under it ; they are removed singly and, eventually, the conjurer holds up the contents of the parcel—a large loaf. He cuts the loaf in halves and discloses the missing watch in the centre.

The handkerchief is a double one, and it has a dummy watch sewn into one corner. In covering the borrowed watch with the handkerchief, the conjurer palms the borrowed watch and gives the dummy, sewn into the handkerchief, to the spectator to hold ; he, of course, believes he is holding the borrowed watch.

The performer, in picking up the parcel, manages to force the watch into the centre of the loaf, which is new and soft. The papers do not quite meet under the bottom of the parcel, and therefore the conjurer is able to push the watch into the loaf by inserting it into the little gap between the edges of the papers.

BROKEN COTTON.—About six feet of cotton is unwound from a spool by the magician who, giving one end to a spectator, requests him to break it up into little pieces. The magician takes the pieces, screws them into a little ball, and hands it to the spectator ; in doing this he allows the spectator to see that his hands are empty. Having satisfied his assistant on this point, the magician takes the little ball of pieces again, draws out an end, and hands the ball to the assistant, who is then requested to pull it slowly out of the magician's hand.

This request is obeyed, and the spectator is surprised to find that instead of drawing out one short piece of cotton all the pieces are joined together again.

This is effected by handing the spectator the pieces bunched up with the extra piece, which the performer previously concealed in his hand. The performer is thus able to show that his hands are empty and that there is apparently no " extra piece " of cotton.

Before commencing this trick the performer winds about twelve feet of cotton, having previously tied a knot in the middle of it, round a little piece of stick. Thus, when he casually unwinds the cotton in order to show the trick, he knows that he can go on unwinding it until he reaches the knot. He breaks the cotton just above the knot, thereby leaving the end with the knot on it in his hand. The piece broken off is given to a spectator with the request that he will break it into several small pieces ; while he is thus engaged the performer slips the little piece of stick out of the rest of the cotton and puts the stick into his pocket. The whole piece of cotton with the knot on the end is now in a position to be " palmed."

The magician takes the pieces from the spectator, rolls them up into a little ball, and adds to it the whole piece which he had concealed in his hand, to be able to show his hands empty. In taking back the ball of cotton, the conjurer merely has to find the end with the knot on it ; he holds this himself, and gives the remainder of the little coil to the spectator with the request that he will pull on it slowly. While he is doing this, the magician quietly tucks the ball of broken pieces into the fork of his thumb, where they can easily be concealed. When the spectator has pulled out the whole piece the conjurer can show once more that his hands are not holding the broken pieces. In gathering up the whole piece again the performer can include the ball of broken pieces.

THE PIERCED HAND.—The principal article used is a small box, oblong in shape, with a picture of a hand painted on the lid. A similar picture is painted on the inside of the bottom of the box, and a third picture is painted on the outside of the bottom of the box. A U-shaped hole, large enough to admit a woman's wrist, is cut out of one end of the box. The other end of the box and two sides are studded with small spikes. The lid and bottom of the box have a number of small holes pierced in them, and these holes, therefore, go through the fingers and back of the painted hands.

After the illusionist has shown the box to the audience, his assistant places her hand inside the box and shows that her hand exactly covers the picture of the hand in the box. The box is placed on a small skeleton stand on the table, and the performer shows a small stand on which rest half a dozen miniature swords with sharp points. These little weapons can be handed out for examination to prove to the audience that they are sharp and serviceable.

The woman then places her hand in the box, and the lid is closed and secured with spring clips. The performer drops a handkerchief over the woman's wrist, explaining that he does this in case of an accident.

Holding the miniature swords, the magician pushes them through the holes in the lid of the box and through the holes in the bottom of the box ; occasionally he turns the bottom of the box towards the audience, so that everyone can see that the points of the swords protrude. Apparently the swords have gone right through the assistant's hand ; this impression is increased by the fact that the swords pass through the pictures of the hand on the lid and on the bottom of the box.

The performer does not really begin the trick until he drops the handkerchief over his assistant's wrist. The handkerchief covers a slight movement of the wrist as the assistant draws it towards her, thus altering the position of the hand in the box. Immediately she has done this, she bends the second, third and little fingers under the hand. The first finger and thumb are extended in the box and serve as a guide to the assistant when the first sword is pushed through the box ; she knows that this sword should go through the hole near the root of the thumb, and that when the hand is in a position to allow this to be done, the remaining swords can be pushed through the other holes without meeting any obstruction.

After the hand has been apparently transfixed the swords

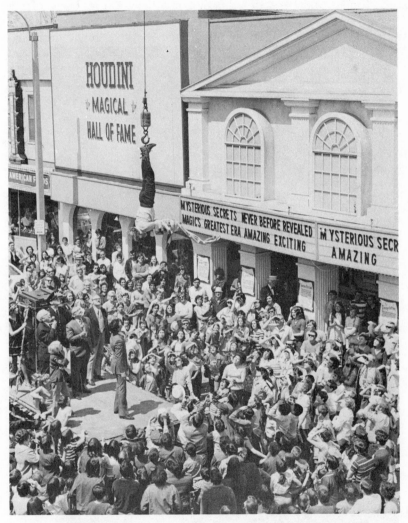

The Amazing Randi, a modern escape artist, duplicating Houdini's strait-jacket escape outside the Houdini Magical Hall of Fame in Niagara Falls, Ontario, Canada. Photograph supplied by the Houdini Magical Hall of Fame.

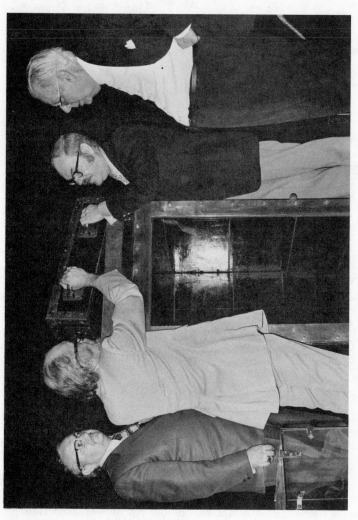

Houdini's original Water Torture Cell being installed at the Houdini Magical Hall of Fame in Niagara Falls, Ontario, Canada. Left to right: Henry Muller, proprietor of the Museum; James Randi, noted escape artist; Sidney H. Radner, owner of the Water Torture Cell; Walter B. Gibson, associate of Houdini and author of many magical books. Photograph supplied by the Houdini Magical Hall of Fame.

are slowly removed, the box is opened, and the hand is seen in its original position and, of course, uninjured.

AN ESCAPE FROM TWO BOXES.—The effect of this is as follows : the illusionist calls attention to two boxes, and invites any member of the audience to examine them. When they are satisfied that the boxes are " quite ordinary," the performer gets into one of the boxes, and his assistants lock and strap it. The box with the performer inside is then lifted up and placed in the other box, which, in turn, is also locked and strapped. If the members of the audience wish to take all precautions against trickery, they are at liberty to lock the boxes and strap them, or, if they wish, they can bring padlocks and chains and fasten the boxes in any way they please. In spite of all these precautions against escape, the performer manages— behind a screen—to get out of both boxes, and immediately afterwards the boxes can be examined.

To heighten the effect, the performer can have both boxes placed into canvas bags, and the bags may be laced up and tied.

Now for the secret, which is ingenious. The planking of the backs of both boxes is divided into three parts. The middle part is fastened to the lower by means of two stout rods which pass through the centre of the middle plank, and the holes for the rods are so large that, but for the upper plank, the middle plank could be easily lifted off the rods.

The middle plank is held up against the top plank by means of three spring catches connected by one rod in the centre of the plank. Just beneath the centre catch is a large air-hole. (There are several similar air-holes in the boxes.)

When the performer takes a special key and pushes this upwards in the air-hole of the box, he is able to depress the springs of all three catches, because they are connected with a rod. When the springs are depressed, the performer pulls out the plank towards him, and so gets it quite free from the upper plank. The conjurer then slides the middle plank upwards and inside the box, and so makes a space at the back of the box sufficiently large to enable him to escape. If the boxes have been placed in canvas bags, the conjurer unfastens the laces and replaces them after he has closed the trap-door.

The magician is provided with two keys, a short one for the inner box and a longer one for the outer box. Directly the first box is in the second, the performer gets to work, and has the middle plank of the inner box removed before the outer box is closed. He is therefore able to make his escape within a few seconds of the screen being placed in front of the boxes.

The two trick air-holes of the two boxes are flush with one another. Directly the performer is out of the boxes he draws down the two middle planks, and then closes the boxes. The planks, being fitted with spring catches and running on rods, are held quite firmly, and there is absolutely no clue at the end of the performance—nothing that the most inquisitive individual can fasten on to as being " something to do with it." Houdini performed this trick with great speed and skill.

THE RING ON THE CORD.—There is nothing to lead the audience to believe that two pieces of string shown by the conjurer are held in an unusual way, but, as a matter of fact, one of the pieces has a ring threaded on it, and the ring is palmed. The other piece, folded in half, is held between the first finger and thumb with the two ends projecting upwards. A wedding ring—a duplicate of the one palmed—is passed over the end of the string above the thumb and first finger and someone is asked to tie a knot. The performer covers the knot with his other hand, and after a little manipulation shows the string with the ring on it, but the knot has disappeared.

When the magician covered the tied-up ring with his hand, he also secured from his sleeve a spring hook attached to an elastic pull in his sleeve. He then snapped the hook on the loop of string on which the ring was threaded and released the hook, which carried the ring and loop up his sleeve. In due course the other string is shown with the ring on it, and this convinces the audience that the knot which fastened the two pieces of string together has, in some " magical " way, been dissolved.

A BOX AND A BASKET.—A large wooden box, something like a packing case, the lid of which is provided with hinges at the back, and hasps and staples at the front, is brought on the stage, and a committee, appointed by the audience, is invited to examine it. After the box has undergone the severest scrutiny, the committee proceed to tie it up with rope in any way they see fit. When tied, the knots of the rope are covered with sealing-wax, and stamped with the private seal of some member of the committee.

On the top of this box is placed a board about as wide as the lid of the box, but not so long, somewhat like a mason's mortar-board, on two opposite sides of which are heavy plate staples. A man stands on this board, and is covered with a conical shaped basket. This basket has a heavy iron ring running around and woven about its mouth and to the ring are forged, at opposite sides to each other, two staples. When the basket is placed over the young man, the staples in its ring fit directly over those on the board ; padlocks are passed through these staples and locked, the key is held by one of the committee, and, if it is desired, the keyholes are sealed with wax.

It would seem impossible for the man to get out of the basket.

A screen is placed around the box to shut it out from the sight of the audience, and in a short space of time the man not only gets from under the basket without removing the padlock or breaking the seals, but gets into the corded box without apparently tampering in any way with the ropes.

The explanation is that the simple-looking packing-case is in reality a trick-box. Along the edges of the front, back and ends are fastened stout battens. These battens are screwed to the boards which form the upper part of the box ; the boards at front and back and at both ends are simply sliding panels. The parts of these panels which come directly behind the battens are fitted with iron plates, pierced with holes. The screws on the lower parts of the batten are dummies—that is, they go partly through the battens, but do not reach the panels. On the inner side of the battens are iron plates, each carrying a stud. When parts of the panel plates are directly opposite the studs of the battens, the panels can easily be pressed in, and will fall inside the box; but if the studs be pressed and the panels pushed along so that the shanks of the studs slide through the slotted parts, the panels will be securely locked.

In order to slide these panels when in place, they are pierced with small holes, ostensibly to admit air, in reality to allow of a short piece of iron rod, of about the diameter of an ordinary lead pencil, to be inserted.

When the screen is placed about the box, the performer gets out of the basket, as will be shortly explained, slides a panel, separates the ropes, which are more or less elastic, and, creeping inside the box, closes the panel.

Of course, only one panel is needed for the trick, but it often happens that the ropes are so closely woven about one part of the box that it would be very difficult for the performer to creep through them, and in such cases the panels in some other part are used.

The construction of the board on which the basket rests is much more complicated. The whole mechanism lies in the so-called plate-staples, which are made so as to be released at the option of the performer. The staples proper are not of a piece with the plates, but are separate; they are made with a shoulder, and in each of the ends, which fit tightly into holes drilled in and through the plates, there is an oval-shaped hole. Inside the board are two double bolts, which pass through these holes and keep the staples in place. When the performer is under the basket, he passes a thin steel blade between the boards and slides back the bolts at one end. The mere operation of rising lifts the basket, carrying with it the staples. When outside, he replaces the basket, adjusts the staples in the plate and pushes it down, the rounded ends acting sufficiently on the bolts to force them back, and the light spiral springs through which the latter are run causing them to go through the holes of the staple, which in this way is again locked.

THE MYSTERIOUS COINS.—The necessary preparations for this trick are made in full view of the audience. Two pieces of string, knotted together in three places, are first shown. Then the conjurer produces a number of Chinese coins, or English coins that have been defaced by having a hole made in them ; these too can be examined. Seven of the coins are passed on to one end of the double string and six coins on the other, and anyone in the audience may assist in doing this. Two more of the examined coins are tied on to the ends of the string, and the knots are sealed.

The performer takes the string in the centre and holds the centre coin, leaving six coins on either side supported by the two coins that have been tied and sealed on the string. It is obvious, therefore, that the six coins on either side cannot pass the tied coins.

A large dark handkerchief with a hole cut in the centre is now thrown over the coins and string, and the performer passes the centre coin through a hole in the handkerchief and slips a buttonhook into the hole in the coin. He hands the buttonhook to someone in the audience.

Next, he puts his hand under the handkerchief and removes all twelve coins, leaving the centre coin still held by a member of the audience and the two coins on the end of the string.

Actually, one of the lower knots in the string is a fake. This end is really a short loop of string fastened to the other. When this knot is pulled tightly, it looks just like a real knot. If the string is fairly stiff, the magician will have no difficulty in unfastening the fake knot at the right time under cover of the handkerchief.

The preliminary preparations for the trick are all fairly made, but a little deception is practised by the performer when he covers the string and apparently pushes up the centre coin through the hole in the handkerchief. Shielded by the handkerchief, he secretly pushes six coins from one end on to the top of the six coins on the other end, but before he does this he holds the centre coin and so makes people believe that it is this coin which he passes through the hole in the handkerchief. The real coin which is passed through the handkerchief is the lowest one of the stack. Thus twelve coins are all on the faked end of the string.

The performer merely unfastens the knot, allows the coins to rest in his hand, and quickly fastens the loop of string on the main piece again. He then produces all twelve coins, and makes a show of drawing them off both ends of the string.

The audience are always so intent on examining the coins that they never give a thought to the string, and even if they were to do so it is extremely unlikely that they would discover the secret of the trick.

ESCAPE FROM A BOX AND CABINET.—This illusion may well be performed in two parts. After the box and the cabinet have been examined by members of the audience, the performer gets into the box, which is fastened with three padlocks. The box is then lifted into the cabinet and the doors are closed. Almost immediately afterwards the performer looks out at a small hole in one of the doors and greets his audience.

The conjurer withdraws into the cabinet, and when the doors are opened he has vanished.

The secret of the box is very simple. One end of the box fits into the body of the box by means of a mortice joint. The performer merely pushes out the top of the joint and carries it away with him while he gets out of the box. Then he replaces the end and looks through the hole in the door of the cabinet.

The cabinet is a much more elaborate affair. To begin with, it is lined with boards, and there is a line of screws all the way round. It is also divided up into partitions by means of wooden railings. The right-hand side of the back and the left-hand side of the cabinet are fitted with two secret " mirror doors." When the cabinet is first opened these are shut, and therefore appear to be the part of the back and side, respectively.

Of course, the magician has to open these doors, because

he never really escapes from the cabinet at all. He is concealed inside at the conclusion of the illusion. The door at the back opens out to the middle, and the mirror on the right side of it then reflects the side of the cabinet. The audience believe they are seeing the back of the cabinet, but what they really see is the reflection of the side.

This would not be sufficient " cover " for the performer, and therefore the second secret " mirror door " has to be used. It opens out from the side to the centre of the cabinet, and so reflects the side of the cabinet, but again the audience are led to believe that they are seeing the back of the cabinet, and that therefore the cabinet must be empty, whereas the man is really concealed in the space enclosed by the two mirror doors and the left-hand half of the back of the cabinet.

It remains only to show how these secret " mirror doors " are pulled out from their places, where, by the way, they are held securely by means of springs in the doors. There is a line of screws all round the cabinet. Two of these screws—one in each of the doors—are dummy screws. Their heads are flush with the wood but they can be pulled out easily by means of a special little claw instrument. The performer does not need to take these dummy screws away from the wood. They merely help him to get a good hold on each of the two doors, and pull it into the right position. When the screws are once more pushed home the panels are locked and the cabinet appears to be in the same condition as it was when it was examined.

RING AND STRING.—A piece of string, about a yard and a half long, is tied tightly round the wrists of the magician. He borrows a ring, turns round for a moment, and shows that he has managed to get the ring on the string and to tie it there, although the two ends of the string are still tied tightly round his wrists. This is how it is done. The performer takes up a loop in the centre of the string and pushes it through the ring, he then passes the loop under the string tied round his left wrist, over the hand, through the string again on the other side of the wrist, and then over the hand again. The ring is then tied on the string.

THE CRYSTAL OF DAMASCUS.—A wooden pedestal with a large crystal upon it stands on a table. The "medium" makes "passes" over the crystal, and then anyone looking in it sees a living hand, in miniature, writing a message. Presently the vision changes to that of a woman's head. The face smiles and the lips move as though the woman were speaking ; other movements are made to prove that the vision is "real"—that is to say, the woman in the crystal is a living being, although only a small fraction of the size of a woman. Other messages and visions can be shown.

The crystal is really a hollow ball of glass with a mirror fixed at an angle across its diameter.

Beneath the stage is a series of mirrors. One of these is the reducer, which converts the scene to the size of the mirror in the crystal. The image is conveyed by means of a kind of telescope projector through the leg of the table and the pedestal of the crystal.

When the hand writes a message, a supplementary mirror is necessary in order that the writing may be corrected from the reverse when it reaches the crystal mirror, but this can be dispensed with when the vision is being shown. The reducing mirror can reflect the girl's face directly on to the mirror which is in the position to transmit it through the projector.

THE MAGIC KNOT.—Twisting a handkerchief into a rope and, holding one corner, the performer snaps the other in the air, but no knot appears. This is merely preliminary play. He quickly gathers the loose end into his hand, shakes one end free, and the knot is at the extreme end of it, although the fingers have apparently played no part in the trick at all.

The secret is the tying of a one-handed knot in the end of the handkerchief when first shaking it out and keeping the knot concealed in the hand. The twisted handkerchief is passed over the little and third fingers, under the first and second, and so round into the hand. The thumb pushes the end round until it can be clipped between the first and second fingers. Then the handkerchief is slipped off the hand and the knot is tied. This is done quickly, but the knot is kept concealed in the hand. The other hand gathers up the free end and the right hand then holds both ends. The conjurer in shaking out the handkerchief for the second time, merely releases the end with the knot in it.

CHAPTER VIII

ILLUSIONS AND DISILLUSION—DISAPPEARING MAN—THE
VEILED WOMAN—AN ESCAPE IN MID-AIR—THE CAGED
WOMAN—THE GIRL AND THE DOMINOES—FIRE AND
WATER—ILLUSIONS WITH MIRRORS—THE COUNTRY GIRL
—THE HAMMOCK—THE ARBOUR

GENERAL stage illusions figured in Houdini's
programme. He did not himself invent such
illusions, but he presented them with great skill.

The reader will, I hope, understand the underlying
principles of stage illusions after reading the descriptions
of the few examples I give here.

A man lies on a small table, the magician covers him
with a small cloth, and the body rises in the air. Suddenly
the performer snatches away the cover and the man has
gone.

The secret is that the top of the table is fitted with a
number of small strips of rubber, which are tightened up
by means of a screw and beam. The weight of the man
is supported by a kind of scissors apparatus, but immediately the two " blades " are shut against the sides, the
man sinks through the table to a canvas " bed " below
the table. This movement is masked by the sheet which
the performer throws over the man.

The dummy which rises in the air is made of fine invisible wire and is concealed at the commencement of the
illusion behind the table. An assistant is in the wings
controlling the working of the illusion. The invisible
supporting wires are carried up to the flies over two fixed
pulleys, and thence to a handle in the wings. There are
also wires passing from the dummy through the stage,
over pulleys under the stage, and up again to the same

A Houdini lobby display, replete with lithographs and featuring two challenge devices.

CHALLENGE

HOUDINI.
Orpheum Theatre.
St. Paul, Minn.

Dear Sir:

Hearing that you escaped from a packing case in Minneapolis, we, the undersigned employes of the Raymer Hardware Company challenge you to escape from a heavy packing case which we will construct from heavy timber, and we defy you to escape from it after we have securely nailed up the box and thoroughly roped same.

If you accept our challenge, we will send the box along when finished, but demand the right to renail all the boards before you enter to prevent preparation on your part.

Yours very truly

SHIPPING DEPARTMENT OF
THE RAYMER HARDWARE COMPANY

Arnold Reibestein   M. J. Dunn
Louis Kosanke   Herman J. Dunn

HOUDINI

ACCEPTS ABOVE

CHALLENGE

Test to take place on the Stage of the Orpheum Theatre

Friday Night, Feb. 16th, 1923

Under the condition that the box must not be airtight

One of the many challenges successfully undertaken by Houdini.

handle at the wings. It will be seen that the assistant can make the dummy rise and fall by merely raising or depressing this handle. Directly the cloth is pulled away, the assistant jerks the dummy down to the stage, where, being behind the table, it is not seen.

THE VEILED WOMAN.—In this case a girl can be made to vanish.

Having taken up her place on the table, under which the audience can see, the girl, heavily veiled, remains motionless while the magician proceeds to cover her with a large sheet. Several times he places the sheet over her, and then snatches it away again as though he were anxious that the audience should have " one last look." Finally he covers her with the sheet, and attaches it to a rope hanging from the flies. Having stepped down from the table, the conjurer picks up a revolver, fires it, and the woman vanishes.

Several ideas are contained in this illusion. To begin with, the veiled girl has a wire frame over the top of her head, and her veil and dress are in one piece. After the conjurer has placed the sheet over her and removed it a few times, the audience do not perceive that anything unusual has happened, but, unknown to them, she has slipped away through a trap in the stage.

Her manner of departure was arranged in this way : for a few seconds, while taking the sheet from the girl, the conjurer allowed it to drop down and hide the table. In that moment the woman slipped out of her dress and veil, and, being in tights, had no difficulty in passing downwards, being assisted in her descent by an elevator trap. The veil and dress were prevented from falling because, a moment before, the conjurer held them in position by means of a small catch attached to his elbow. The wire frame under the veil kept it in place, and the audience were therefore unable to see that the woman had really gone.

The rope to which the conjurer apparently attached the sheet was a faked rope, being hollow, and fitted inside with a spring terminating in a hook. The conjurer placed this hook in the wire frame forming the head-piece, a hole in the top of the veil permitting this.

The sheet was wrapped round the figure, but the audience were led to believe that it was fastened to the rope. Attached to the hook in the rope was a thread, which, being pulled by an assistant off the stage, released the hook, which thus drew up the wire frame into the hollow rope. The dress and the veil then fell on the table and were hidden by the sheet, and in this way the disappearance of the girl was effected.

AN ESCAPE IN MID-AIR.—In another illusion a girl is seen in the cage which imprisons her after the cage has been hoisted into mid-air.

The cage is merely a metal skeleton-frame fitted with four blinds, and when the young woman steps in, the blinds are drawn.

After the cage has been drawn up well away from the stage, the girl puts out her hands as though to arrange the front curtain. A moment afterwards, either as the result of the firing of a pistol or the shouting of the word " Go ! " the cage is found to be empty.

The cage was really empty before it was hoisted up clear of the stage. Directly the front blind and the two side blinds were drawn, the assistant disappeared down a trap. The hands which apparently arranged the curtains were really dummies. One of the assistants in arranging the curtains pulled down two catches, which caused the dummy fingers to come through slots in the front pillars of the cage, and open out in front of the curtain. When the catches were released the hands were returned to their places, being carried there by means of springs.

THE CAGED WOMAN.—A small square stand with a post at each corner is shown by the illusionist. The stand does not reach to the floor of the stage. After he has shown the stand the magician draws the curtains and in a second is able to draw them again and to show a large cage swinging in the centre of the cabinet, with a living woman in the centre of it.

The cage is really a large form of the old-fashioned

folding bird-cage. The slides and bottom of the cage fold up and are fastened to the top, and the cage, in its collapsed condition, is concealed in the top of the cabinet. The girl who is to appear in the cage is hidden under the floor of the cabinet and comes up through a trap in the floor and so into the cage.

The presence of the girl is never suspected because the bottom of the cabinet is of thin board with only a narrow ornamental fringe around it.

THE GIRL AND THE DOMINOES.—The effect of the dominoes illusion is as follows : the conjurer stacks a number of solid dominoes of a giant size on the table, and his assistant comes on and steps into a large box on the stage. The magician has a large square tube lowered over the dominoes, and when it is lifted the woman is seen on the table. Going to the box, the magician shows it full of dominoes.

The dominoes on the table are solid pieces of wood. The lower part of the table is made of wickerwork, and the audience can see through it. To prove this fact, the conjurer can hold a light behind the table.

A large crescent-shaped piece is cut out of the back of the table, and the tube that covers the dominoes is fitted with a flap door. After the light has been shown behind the table, black blinds are drawn down by an assistant beneath the stage, thus forming a complete " cover " from the top of the table to the stage. Behind the table, in the space left by the piece cut out of the table, is a trap. After the tube is placed over the dominoes, the assistant gets up through the trap, removes the dominoes by taking them through the flap door in the tube, and then allows the girl to step into the empty tube.

The young woman gets clear of the box on the table because there is a hole in the bottom of the box and another in the stage. The box is arranged on the principle of the well-known drawer box, which can be shown either empty or full at the will of the conjurer. The dominoes shown at the end of the trick in the box are dummy ones, made of canvas and springs. All the dominoes, in a compressed condition, were kept at the top of the box when the girl first got into it. After the young woman has been shown on the table, the conjurer pulls out the drawer of the box in such a way that he also draws out the dominoes which have been concealed in the box.

One turn of the knob in the drawer of the box operates a small catch, which enables the conjurer to do this, and the drawer is then shown apparently full of dominoes.

FIRE AND WATER.—From a cabinet on fire to a tank of water, the girl goes in this case.

A small cabinet, with sides of wire network, stands at the side of the stage. The performer's assistant, dressed in tights, gets into this cabinet and covers herself with a silk sheet.

Then the performer directs the attention of the audience to a large glass tank of water suspended by four chains from four rods fixed to a wooden floor, which is raised from the stage. These rods are connected by other rods, making a very substantial structure. Heavy curtains are fixed to the rods.

The performer draws the curtains, but the other cabinet with the fire in it is not covered. Suddenly flames burst out from the interior of this cabinet, and when they die down the assistant is not visible. The performer draws the curtains of the other cabinet, and discloses the young woman in the centre of the tank of water.

I will deal first with the working of the apparatus in the wire-enclosed cabinet. When the woman enters this cabinet she holds a large silk sheet in front of her, and, at the same time, an assistant beneath the stage pulls a cord which causes some lazy-tongs (or scissors) to shoot up from a trap in the base of the cabinet. The top of the lazy-scissors is crowned with a small wire shape to resemble the girl's head.

The girl gets out of the cabinet under cover of the sheet and hides herself in some steps. The steps were previously used to enable her to get into the cabinet.

Round the sides of the base of the cabinet is a narrow trough containing red fire ; this is ignited at the right time by means of flash-cotton and an electric wire which passes down the leg of the stand.

When the fire is well alight the assistant pulls the cord which brings the lazy-scissors down again.

The steps are used, of course, to enable the girl to get secretly into the tank, the top of which is closed with a sliding lid of glass. When one of the performer's assistants is drawing the curtains round the cabinet he pulls out the lid, and so enables the young woman to get from the steps on to the lid and so into the tank. The assistant then pushes the lid back into its place.

THE WOMAN IN THE CASE.—The case in question is of glass, is completely isolated from the stage, and is demonstrated by the performer to be empty beyond all doubt. There is apparently no possible place of concealment and no covering of the case is involved.

In the first place, the woman is actually concealed in the apparatus itself, ready to make her appearance at the right moment.

The glass case, octagonally constructed, is mounted strongly in a metal frame, which, for appearance's sake, is " bowed " over on top to give a look of " finish " to the design. These canopy bars are mainly responsible for the mystery, as they serve to mask the presence of two mirrors, behind which the woman has room to conceal herself. The rear top of the case behind the mirrors is formed into a triangular trap, opening with a spring hinge in a downward direction. The woman, therefore, has merely to drop feet first through the trap, which automatically closes back after her descent. To mask the woman's entrance, the case magically fills itself with flowers, which are really four screens fastened to the inside top of the case and weighted with an octagonal base. When the screens are folded, the false bottom is suspended in position at the top of the case by four catches, which are automatically released, when desired, by a pull on four joined threads which pass through one of the rear standards of the frame into the hands of an assistant stationed behind the back cloth.

THE COUNTRY GIRL.—The " scene " is the verandah of a house, and in the centre of the stage, a small garden table is standing, a circular frame supporting a curtain attached to it. The curtain is drawn around for a second. When it is pulled apart, a little " country girl " is seen on the table.

The girl stands behind the " house " on the stage. As the audience can see under the table, under the verandah and through the windows of the house, it does not seem possible that the girl can get to the table without being seen.

As a matter of fact, however, the audience do not see through the centre window, because that is partly a reflection of the two side windows, double-sided mirrors being placed between the pillars and the wall of the house. Before the curtain on the table is drawn, the audience in the centre of the hall see the centre window and its reflections on the " inside " of the mirrors, but they take these reflections to be the side windows of the house. The audience on the left and right of the hall see the side windows and they think they also see the centre window, but what they really see are the reflections of the side windows. Thus there is a space closed at the sides with two mirrors, and closed in front by the curtains on the table. The girl is able to come through the centre window without being seen either at the sides or in front. When she is on the verandah, the girl raises a small plank, and places it between the table and the verandah. Using this as a bridge, she steps on to the table, and then pushes the plank back on to the verandah. Being padded, the plank falls noiselessly.

THE HAMMOCK ILLUSION.—Dressed in a flannel suit, the magician walks on the stage and sits down on a small curtained platform in the centre of the stage. The curtains are pulled back to the corners, and the audience can see plainly under the platform.

For a few seconds, the platform is concealed by drawing the curtains. Then a garden scene is revealed. Two large palms in pots stand on the platform ; a fountain is playing, and a girl is reclining in a hammock slung to the top of the platform.

The solution of the mystery is that at the beginning of the performance the girl is hidden behind one of the drawn curtains. The " palms " are made of feathers, the pots for the palms and the " stone " fountain are really flat, and are fastened by spring hinges to the floor of the platform. A piece of thin linoleum covers the " garden " at the beginning of the performance. When the curtains are drawn, the girl steps on the platform, rolls up the linoleum and hides it behind one of the curtains, or she can pack it into the ceiling.

The connection for the fountain is a rubber pipe passing under the floor of the platform, and through one of the legs, to the assistant below.

The " ceiling " is in two parts, each being attached by spring hinges to a side of the platform ; the two parts meet in the centre and are held in place with a simple catch. There is space between this ceiling and the top of the structure for the storage of the hammock, which has a loop in the centre so that with one pull the girl can get it into position.

The performer gives the signal for the fountain to begin and, the girl having climbed into the hammock, the illusion is ready. The whole process does not take more than a few seconds.

THE ARBOUR ILLUSION.—At the back of the stage is an arbour which the audience can see is not occupied. A hammock is slung near the arbour ; the performer wraps himself in a cloak, gets into the hammock and falls asleep. Gradually the figure of a woman appears in the arbour. She steps out, sings a song, and then returns to the arbour, fading away as mysteriously as she came, but while her figure is becoming indistinct, the audience sees it change slowly into the figure of the performer. When the figure is quite plain to all, the performer steps out of the arbour, and an assistant comes in and draws away the cloak from the hammock.

The first thing to be explained is the manner in which

the performer disappears from the hammock. He wraps himself in a cloak, but in doing so manages to raise a " strut," and this gives the appearance of his arms being under the cloak. The performer is behind the cloak, which hangs down to the floor and so enables him to escape through the back cloth.

The appearance and disappearance of the woman are caused by a sliding mirror, which passes diagonally across the arbour. At the commencement of the illusion, this mirror is in position across one corner of the arbour, and the woman is hidden behind it. The mirror reflects part of the side of the arbour which thus appears to be empty. The silvering of the mirror is etched away toward the edge, and so, when it is drawn slowly away, the woman is made to appear gradually. She comes out, sings her song, and returns to the arbour. When the mirror is being pushed back into its original position, to cause the disappearance of the woman, the performer's " double " stands in one corner of the wings, and his reflection in the mirror is taken to be the figure of the performer himself. The mirror is not pushed right across, but only far enough to allow the woman to escape from the back and for the performer to take her place. Then the " double " leaves his position, and the glass, being pulled back, shows the performer, who steps out. The lighting is that of the usual stage moon, with a little blue tint in it, to hide the movement caused by the sliding of the glass.

THE DIE BOX.—In this mystery, two large boxes are shown on a raised platform which is so small that no one could hide behind the boxes. Having wheeled the platform round to prove this, the conjurer opens one of the boxes and closes it again. He opens the second box and closes the door. Both boxes have thus been shown to be empty, but as the boxes are so close together it seems possible that someone hidden in one of them might move from one box to the other. Therefore, a member of the audience is sure to invite the conjurer to " open the other box." The conjurer immediately does so, but takes care to close the first box before doing so. " Open both boxes, both at once," comes the cry. Though at first pretending to be embarrassed by the request, the magician ultimately flings both doors wide open to show that both boxes are unmistakably empty.

The smaller of the two boxes is then hoisted up and lowered into the other. During this operation the audience can see the bottom of the smaller box. There does not seem to be any chance for deception, but when the doors of both outer and inner boxes are opened, the assistant is seen.

The larger of the two boxes is fitted with a mirror placed across one corner. This mirror reflects the side of the box, which therefore appears to be empty, but the assistant is concealed in the space behind the mirror. The other box is normal, except that in place of a wooden floor there is a black spring blind. When this box is raised the audience see the " bottom of the box," but in the act of steadying it, the performer releases the spring and the blind is drawn back, thus making a bottomless box of it.

While this is being done the assistant emerges from her hiding-place, pushes back the mirror so that it is flush with one side of the box and then stands in the centre of the box. Thus, when the smaller box is lowered into the larger one it comes directly over the assistant, who merely has to stand there until the two doors are opened.

A MYSTERY CABINET.—The distinguishing feature of this illusion is the fact that the cabinet is built up on the stage. After it has been put together, the performer opens the two front doors and shows that it is empty. He closes the doors, and a tapping noise is immediately heard. The doors are flung open and the performer's assistant is seen.

Once more the doors are closed, and the next time they are opened the assistant has vanished. At any time during the progress of the illusion the performer may have the cabinet turned round and round on the stage, thus showing that no one is concealed at the back of it.

The assistant is hidden, in the first place, in a pedestal supporting a plant. One side of this pedestal is fitted with spring doors. When the doors of the cabinet are opened, the assistant comes out of the pedestal, and steps behind one of the doors on to a shelf at the back of the cabinet. He then gets inside the cabinet by means of a spring door working on a pivot. Directly he is inside, and this secret door is released, it is held in place by the springs, and thus appears to be the panel of the back of the cabinet. When the cabinet is to be shown empty, the assistant steps through to the back again, and when the cabinet is to be turned round, he steps through the door and remains inside for a few moments.

Another illusion is known as " The Lady-Bird." The performer has a large hollow cylinder suspended over a small raised platform on the stage. He holds this horizontally and thus displays the interior to the audience. Next, he calls attention to a large wire cage on the stage. Having lowered the cylinder until it stands upright on the platform, the conjurer takes the cage and places it in the cylinder. The cage fits exactly, and the conjurer places a lid on the top of the cylinder and awaits " results."

The lid of the cylinder is raised and with it the top of the cage, and the conjurer's assistant appears inside the cylinder.

About half-way up the cylinder, there is a kind of partition, and in the space above, the girl assistant is concealed. As the interior of the cylinder is painted black, this partition is not seen. The partition is of peculiar construction ; it does not reach quite to the edge of the cylinder, and it is supported on a smaller cylinder. The bottom of the cage is covered with black paper, and when it is lowered into the cylinder, it comes directly over the girl, the lower half of the cage fitting nicely between the outer cylinder and the inner one. The top of the cage is fitted with a bayonet catch and therefore can easily be removed by one turn.

A MAGIC WARDROBE.—Much amusement is caused by the magic wardrobe. In the centre of the stage stands a large double wardrobe with big doors right and left, and a cupboard with drawers under it in the centre.

Casual photograph of Houdini near the height of his career.

Houdini and his wife Bessie visiting the famous Chinese magician Chung Ling Foo and Madame Foo, during their American tour. At the right is Theo Bamberg, noted magician also known as "Okito."

The performer opens one of the small drawers and takes out two sets of pyjamas. He hangs one set in the compartment on the right and one in the other compartment. The audience can see that with the exception of the pyjamas, the compartments are empty. The doors are then closed for a moment. When they are reopened, a man and a woman, dressed in the pyjamas which the performer had placed in the two compartments, step out on to the stage. They stand looking at each other for a few seconds. Then the centre cupboard and the drawers suddenly fall away in front, revealing a bed. The two assistants run off at different exits.

The two assistants are, of course, already dressed in pyjamas similar to those which the performer is going to produce. The backs of the two large compartments in the wardrobe turn on two pivots, and at the opening of the performance the two assistants are standing on little ledges behind the backs of the compartments. Therefore, in order to make their appearance the two assistants merely have to turn the backs of the compartments round—an easy matter.

The centre cupboard and drawers in the wardrobe conceal the folding bed ; the drawers are very short dummies with just room enough in the top drawer to hold a couple of suits of pyjamas. A catch at the top of the wardrobe holds the folding bed in place until the performer wishes it to be released, when an assistant behind the scenes pulls on the cord attached to the catch and the bed drops down by its own weight ; it is hinged to the base of the wardrobe.

To make another mystery cabinet, four frames with canvas stretched on them are screwed to a wooden base, and a fifth canvas is put on the top and screwed down.

Before the cabinet is finally closed the conjurer's assistant gets inside. A net is dropped over the cabinet and a rope tied round it. A small screen is then placed in front of the cabinet for a second or two ; when it is removed the assistant is outside the cabinet, which can again be examined.

The canvas on the lower half of one side is not really tacked down to the frame; the tacks are dummies, or, rather, they attach the canvas to a frame which fits in tightly to the visible frame. A hidden ball-catch at the bottom holds this part of the canvas securely. The inner frame is hinged, and when the net is placed over the cabinet the performer takes care to see that the two ends of the net are on the trap side of the cabinet so that when the trap is opened to allow his assistant to escape, the net will yield to the trap.

The assistant carries a small fake, which she inserts in a hole at the bottom of the frame and so pushes out the inner frame, taking the canvas with it.

Here is a packing-case illusion which can be presented in two ways.

In the first method, the case is screwed and roped up, and the performer, screened from the view of the audience, gets into it in a few seconds.

Another form of presentation is that in which the performer escapes from the case after it is screwed and roped.

The edges of the case are bound, and the trick is in the binding. All the screws, with the exception of two, are dummies, and therefore the removal of two screws enables the performer to slide a panel and so get in or out of the box. If the performer is to be inside at the close of the trick, he replaces the screws from that position. He should provide himself with a small electric torch to enable him to work quickly.

The escape from the box is worked in the reverse way. The performer loosens two screws and forces the panel with his screw-driver. Then he quickly replaces the screws when he is out of the box.

The box will stand examination, both at the beginning and close of the trick.

AN ESCAPE FROM AN IRON CAGE.—The iron cage used in this illusion can be thoroughly examined, both before and after the performance. After the preliminary examination, the performer's assistant gets into the cage and the door is padlocked. The escape is effected in a few seconds.

One of the bars is held in place by a tapering pin which the assistant easily removes with the help of a little tool made for the purpose. After this pin is removed the bar can easily be pushed upwards. When the performer's assistant is outside, he pushes down the bar and replaces the pin.

To make the trick still more interesting an additional effect is introduced. As soon as the assistant has been secured inside the cage, the performer covers it with a case made of stout canvas on a wooden frame. The case, however, does not really add to the difficulties of the trick, because the top of it is made in such a way that the canvas can be drawn back from the frame, thus allowing room for the bar of the cage to pass upwards. The top edge of the canvas is not really fastened to the wooden frame, but is held taut by means of a flat spring, which can be pulled back easily, thus opening the top of the case. The two sides of the case are faked. A piece about eight inches in length on both sides is fitted with a hinge, so that when a spring is drawn back the two sides move with it. A touch on the spring, after the performer's assistant has got out of the case, sends the spring back into its place, and it then holds the canvas taut and the two hinged portions of the sides close against the rest of the frame of the case.

THE VICTORY ILLUSION.—The performer commences this illusion by drawing attention to a small table with a decorated box, octagonal in shape, upon it. There is a drawer in the table. The performer opens the drawer and shows it to be empty ; he also opens the front of the box, demonstrating that it contains nothing except three small electric lamps which illuminate the bare interior.

The front of the box is then closed again and a circular curtain, stiffened at the top with a hoop of metal, dropped down over the box. The curtain does not reach beyond the table.

Having fired a pistol, the performer directs the attention

of the audience to the transformation scene. The circular curtain suddenly opens and is immediately converted into a large banner, decorated with flags. A woman, representing the Spirit of Victory, is standing on top of the box.

At the outset the woman was concealed, partly in the table, partly in the box. Two mirrors arranged in the box in the form of a wide " V," permit the performer to show that the box is empty—that is to say, that it is apparently empty. The woman is hidden behind the mirrors, and the lower part of her body extends into the drawer of the table. This drawer is made on the principle of the well-known drawer box, and thus the performer can pull out the drawer and show it empty, the " load " being in position all the time. The top of the box has two little trap-doors cut into it to enable the woman to make her exit through the top of the box directly the curtain is let down.

Concealed at the top of the curtain is a large wreath ; it is merely hung on wires so that the woman can take it off and place it on her head. Having done that, she releases a catch in the metal hoop at the top of the curtain. This hoop is made of spring steel and when the catch is released the steel band opens out flat, revealing the flags and the woman standing on the top of the box.

THE HOUDINI PILLORY ILLUSION.—A kind of pillory is placed on the stage, and the performer secured in it, the top being raised to allow the performer to place his head and hands in the holes made for them. The top of the pillory is then closed and padlocked. In a moment, after a screen has been placed in front of the pillory, the performer is free and the pillory is in the same state as when the audience last saw it.

The pillory is strengthened with straps of metal both at the back and front. These pieces of metal are really to hide a false joint in the woodwork, which allows the lower half of the woodwork to drop from a hinge concealed in the opposite corner. The performer merely has to kick the left post. In so doing he shifts the joint which is on a loose tenon. This allows the lower half of the top of the

pillory to drop down, and the performer escapes, closing
the joint again immediately afterwards. The rivets on the
metal bands are only dummies—the heads of rivets.

THE DREAM OF WEALTH.—A roll of bank-notes is held
by the magician and then dropped one at a time into a
large brazier standing on one side of the stage. He sets
a light to them, and a great volume of smoke arises from
the brazier. Suddenly a huge bank-note appears stretched
across the stage.

The performer looks up " in surprise," and shows, by
pantomime, that he is anxious to possess the note, but as
he approaches it the note vanishes, and in its place a
large bright star is seen.

Presently coins begin to flow from the points of the star.
Then other points of the star open, and more streams of
money pour on to the stage. Lastly, the centre of the
star opens, and a woman appears, holding a large cornucopia in her hand. She pours a large stream of coins
from the cornucopia, and the act is brought to a conclusion
with the appearance of several children on brackets at
the wings. Each child holds a large cornucopia full of coins.

These effects are produced as follows : to begin with,
the large bank-note or flag is hidden behind the brazier,
and is drawn up at a given signal by lines passed over
pulleys in the wings. The star is attached by wires to a
trolly with wheels, which runs on a taut cable stretched
across the flies. It is an easy matter for the men in the
flies or grid to pull this trolly backwards or forwards.

The woman concealed behind the star controls the working of the points. Behind the star is a large tube, ending
in a kind of funnel, which is in the centre of the star.
A cord with a spring hook attached is passed down this
tube, and when the star is close to the flag the woman
attaches the cord, by means of the hook, to the centre ring
in the flag. When the flag has been pulled up out of sight,
the woman, still concealed behind the star, takes off the
funnel and hangs it up behind the star. A cornucopia
hanging behind the star is in readiness for the finish of the
act.

The star, when it first appears, is a plain five-pointed star. Afterwards five more points open, and, finally, the centre ten points. When all the points are opened, the woman appears with the cornucopia.

Several different devices are used for the production of the coins. The two lower ones are simple, being nothing more than the usual coin-droppers which some conjurers use. The coin-droppers are of the kind that can be placed under the waistcoat and operated with a slight pressure of the hand, releasing the coins one at a time. In the present case the droppers are much larger than those usually used, but the principle of their working is exactly the same. By merely pulling a thread the woman behind the star releases the coins one at a time.

The coins produced from the upper points of the star have to be lifted from their places, and this action is accomplished in each case by means of a sliding plug in a flat tube. A thread is attached to the plug, and passed upwards and over a little pulley at the top. The pulling of the thread causes the coins to rise out of the tube.

The coins concealed in the minor points of the star are produced in a different way. A pile of coins, arranged on their edges, is forced out of flat tubes. A continuous cord is used. This cord is passed through little eyes in the star up the side of each tube, down the tube, under the bottom coin in the tube, and up again. Thus one pull on the cord causes the coin in the tube to fall out.

Sitting behind the star the woman has control of the various threads used in the performance, and, as they are all arranged on a little " control board," she has no difficulty in producing the various effects. The only pull needed off the stage is that which causes the flag to vanish.

There is no attempt at illusion in the appearance of the children with cornucopias at the wings. The children merely take up their places on brackets, which are pushed out from the wings towards the conclusion of the act.

THE IRON CHEST PRODUCTION.—A small raised platform, with the floor made of glass, is placed on the stage. The assistants show three large tapestry screens, back and front, and place them in positions at the back and sides of the platform, where they form a kind of cabinet. A rod and curtain are fixed in front, and the curtain is drawn for a second. When it is pulled back the audience see a large iron chest on the glass-topped platform. The conjurer opens a little flap in the front of the chest, and shows his assistant there. Then he unlocks the chest, and assists the woman to get out of it.

The chest is of the collapsible kind, and is packed into the back screen. The sides collapse inward, and the whole box is then concealed by a blind similar in material to that of the screen. The woman enters the box and the cabinet by means of a small plank which is pushed out from the back cloth. It rests for a moment on the back of the platform, and, when the woman is safely there, is quietly withdrawn. The woman gets through by pulling up a flap at the back of the screen and then pushing the front of the box forward. She is able to do this, because at the back of the box there is a small curtain. When the box is expanded, she gets inside by pushing up the curtain at the back of the box. A piece of black silk stretches out across the bottom of the box as the front is pushed forward. The box is fitted with small rubber-covered rollers, which run on ball-bearings, and thus the box can be opened easily and noiselessly.

The padlocks in this device, which is the invention of Will Goldston, are " dummies," fixed on to the hasps on the lid.

CHAPTER IX

CARD TRICKS—EXAMPLES OF THOUGHT-READING—A CODE
—THE JUMPING CARDS—MAGNETIC ACES—THE CHANGE-
OVER—A FEAT OF STRENGTH—THE BOOMERANG CARD
—CUTTING THE CARDS—THE TORN CARD—VANISHING
CARDS BY PISTOL—THE FOUR ACES—THE HERSCHELL
CARD-STABBING TRICK

AS Houdini in the early part of his career was known as the " Card King," this book would be incomplete if it did not contain some of his tricks with cards. I have had to select from some hundreds, but I have given in simple language those which can be understood by the ordinary reader. With the exception of one or two which involve the " pass " of the expert, most of these tricks can be reproduced by the competent amateur.

Reasonably simple tricks are here given, together with those of an advanced type. Here is one in which a telephone figures :

Show six cards and ask someone in your audience to think of any one of the six and to name the card. Next request him to go to the telephone and ring up a number which you give him, to ask for a Mr. ——. " What card have I just selected, Mr. —— ? " is the question to be asked. The person thus rung up will reply correctly to the question.

And this is how it is done. The man at the other end of the telephone is an accomplice, of course. The names of the six cards to be used in the trick have been written down by him, and against each one is written the name of a person. Thus, against the first card is written a name beginning with " A." Against the second card is written a name beginning with " B," and so on with the remaining four cards. The conjurer remembers the names and the cards.

238

All he has to do, therefore, when he knows the card which his assistant has selected, is to ask him to ring up the number and ask for Mr. ——, filling in the name given to that particular card.

His accomplice knows, directly he hears the name, which card is being thought of.

A medium or confederate is necessary in the method here described.

The conjurer asks someone to take three consecutive cards from a pack, which has really been prearranged in a certain order, and to place them in a row on the table. He says it is quite impossible for him to know the cards, but he will look at them, think of them, and then " transfer his thoughts " to the medium sitting at the other end of the room beyond and behind the audience. So that the medium will not be suspected of looking for signals he turns his back on the performer during the process of " thought-transference." The medium names the cards correctly.

This is the explanation : directly the chosen cards are taken away the magician holds quite casually the top half of the pack, from the bottom of which the cards have been selected, with its face towards the audience, and the medium sees the bottom card. Knowing the order of the cards, the medium can then tell at once which three cards are on the table. By that time, as the medium has memorised the pack by means of a code, he knows which cards must follow the bottom one shown to him by the performer. Those are the three cards taken away by the member of the audience. Here is the code-sentence which enables the pack to be memorised—Eight kings threatened to save nine fair ladies for one sick knave.

The pack should be arranged in the order : diamonds, spades, hearts, clubs.

The interpretation of the code is—Eight (eight)—kings (King)—threatened (three, ten)—to (two)—save (seven)—nine (nine)—fair (five)—ladies (Queen)—for (four)—one (Ace)—sick (six)—knave (Jack).

By memorising this sentence, and remembering the

order of the different suits in the pack, the code is made easy, if the cards are previously arranged in their correct positions.

Many tricks can be done by means of this code.

Taking six cards from the pack, the magician asks someone to think of one of them and then to replace the cards.

Dealing the cards in small lots of five or six the conjurer asks the spectator, as he does so, if he can see the card of which he is thinking. Directly the answer " Yes " is given the conjurer names the card.

In this case, when the six cards are returned to the pack the conjurer slips his little finger under all of them, and, by means of the pass, brings the lot to the bottom of the pack. He then shuffles the cards, taking care not to disturb those at the bottom of the pack, and immediately afterwards deals a few cards and includes in the lot one of those from the bottom of the pack. Thus, in each lot he exposes there will always be one of the six cards which the spectator took, and this one will be the bottom card. Therefore, directly the conjurer is told that the card of which the spectator is thinking is visible he knows at once which card it is, and names it.

In this " thought-reading " trick, the conjurer comes forward with a new pack of cards. He calls attention to the fact that the Government stamp is on the wrapper before he breaks open the pack, and holds out the cards, first to one spectator and then another, until about a dozen cards have been chosen. When the required number of cards have been selected, the conjurer hands the pack to each person who has taken a card, and asks him to return it himself and to shuffle the cards. When all the cards have been returned to the pack, the magician asks those who took cards to think of them, and then he tells them of what cards they are thinking.

Let me point out again that the pack of cards is a new one, and that it is not tampered with in any way before it is opened.

The secret is that cards belonging to one particular

" brand " are packed in the same way. Open any pack
of Steamboats—these are made especially for conjuring,
though they look like ordinary cards—and you will find
that the cards are packed in this order : Spades 2–10 ;
Diamonds 2–10 ; Hearts 2–7, and Ace, King, Queen,
Jack ; Diamonds, King, Queen, Jack, Ace ; Spades, Ace,
King, Queen, Jack ; Clubs, King, Queen Jack, Ace ;
Hearts 8–10 ; Clubs 2–10.

This order must be committed to memory, but it is not
a difficult task to do this.

To discover the chosen card one must, while walking
away to another member of the audience, turn up with the
left thumb the corner of the card immediately above that
which was taken.

It will be noted that the magician does not have each
card returned immediately after it has been taken away.

If the man selecting a card were given the opportunity
to replace it at once, he might upset the order of the cards.

The services of a confederate are required for this card
trick which will baffle most people.

In the temporary absence of the performer, a card is
selected from a pack and shown to the members of the
audience. When he returns to the room, he names the
chosen card.

And this is how it's done : before the trick starts the
confederate lights a cigarette and stands behind the
others, apparently engaged only in watching and smoking,
but is actually giving signals to the performer.

The performer should place his hand to his forehead as
if " to control his thoughts," but really to get a chance of
observing his confederate's signals.

The code is as follows : if the card is an ace, the cigarette
is held in the right hand by the thumb and first finger.
If a two, it is held in the same hand by the thumb and
second finger ; if a three, the same hand and third finger ;
if a four, the same hand by thumb and little finger ; if a
five, the same hand by thumb and first two fingers ; if a
six, the same hand by thumb and two middle fingers ; if
a seven, the same hand by thumb, third and little finger ;

if eight, the same hand by thumb and all the fingers ; if a nine, it is held left hand by thumb and first finger ; if a ten, in the left hand by thumb and second finger ; if a knave, in the left hand by thumb and third finger ; if a queen, in the left hand by thumb and first two fingers ; if a king, in the left hand by thumb and all the fingers. To give the different suits, the cigarette is placed or held as follows : clubs, put the cigarette in the right-hand corner of the mouth ; hearts, place the cigarette in the left-hand corner of the mouth ; spades, have the cigarette in the middle of the mouth ; diamonds, hold it away from the mouth.

To perform the trick of making a card " jump," show the top card of the pack and place it in the centre. Command it to jump back to its former place on the top, and ask anyone to prove that it has not obeyed your command.

This is how it is done :   the top card of the pack is the eight of clubs ; the second card is the seven of clubs. Take off these two cards and show them as one ; then put them back on top of the pack. Take off the top card (the eight of clubs) and place it slowly in the centre of the pack. When it is half-way into the pack show the face of it to the audience, who, seeing the top half, believe that it is really the seven of clubs. But you must be sure and keep your hand over the index number in the corner.

MAGNETIC ACES.—It is easy to mystify an audience with this trick. The conjurer takes the ace of diamonds, the ace of clubs and the ace of spades from the pack and holds them towards the audience with the ace of diamonds in the centre and the other two cards diagonally across it, so that only the top of the red ace is seen. The conjurer then takes one of the black aces and openly places it at the bottom of the pack. The other black ace is laid on the top of the pack, and then the conjurer takes the remaining ace and puts it in the centre of the pack. To convince the audience that everything so far has been quite fair he shows the top and bottom cards once more. Everyone sees that they are the two black aces.

" Now," says the conjurer, " we will place one black
ace in the centre of the pack and another a few cards away."
He puts both aces in the centre of the pack.   Then he
continues, " We have all three aces—the ace of clubs, the
ace of spades and the ace of diamonds—in the centre of
the pack.   Ace of diamonds—jump ! "

He taps the top of the pack and asks someone to take
off the top card.   It is the ace of diamonds.   Someone is
sure to suggest that there must be more than one ace of
diamonds in the pack, whereupon the conjurer hands the
pack out for inspection and anyone can prove to the
satisfaction of the audience that the pack contains only
the usual number of aces.

It is so easily explained.   The trick is brought about
solely by the manner in which the cards are held in the
first place, and by a little subterfuge.   In running through
the cards with the object of taking out the three aces the
conjurer secretly pushes the ace of diamonds on to the
top of the pack and takes from it the ace of hearts and
the two black aces.   He places the two black aces over the
ace of hearts so that only the point of the heart is visible.
The ace of hearts then appears to be the ace of diamonds.
After the conjurer has put the two black aces in the centre
of the pack he has really finished the trick, and the rest
is showmanship.

THE CHANGE OVER.—In this trick, the ability to palm
cards is necessary.   The performer takes the two red
cards of any number, say the ten of hearts and ten of
diamonds, and places them under a handkerchief on the
table.   He puts the two black tens under another handkerchief.   He then commands them to change places, and
lifting the handkerchief, shows that his " command " has
been " obeyed."

It is done in this way.   The conjurer has two extra
black tens in his right-hand trousers pocket.   In taking
out the two handkerchiefs to be used in the trick he palms
these cards.   Picking up the two red tens, he covers them
with the palmed black ones and shows the two red ones.
The audience are unaware of the presence of the two black

ones behind the red ones. In covering these with a large handkerchief the conjurer palms away the two red ones, but as the audience see the shape of the remaining two cards under the handkerchief they believe they are the same two cards they have just seen—the red ones. In picking up the two black tens, the magician palms the two red ones on top of them and squaring the cards shows the face of the front black ten. The audience believe that only the two black cards are there. In covering these with the second handkerchief the conjurer palms away the two black tens and leaves the two red ones under the handkerchief. He slips the two palmed cards into a pocket and commands the cards to " change over."

Here is another trick in which the conjurer has three or four cards selected and returned to the pack. Taking the pack in his left hand, and showing his right hand empty, he throws the cards into the air, and while they are falling catches at some of them with his right hand. When the other cards have dropped the conjurer is seen to be holding the cards that were selected and returned to the pack.

It will require practice to do this. When the cards are returned the conjurer brings them to the top of the pack by means of the pass, and turning a little to his right, palms them off the pack and then back-palms them. The selected cards are now at the back of the right hand, which can then be shown with the palm towards the audience. The conjurer throws up the pack with his left hand and in putting his right hand among the falling cards brings those which were palmed to view again.

Another variation of the trick is that the magician has two cards selected and returned to the pack. He then throws the whole pack into the air, quickly plunges his hand among the falling cards, and catches two cards, which are found to be the two cards which were selected.

In this case, the two cards were brought to the top of the pack by means of the pass and then one of them was shuffled to the bottom of the pack. The conjurer held the pack with his thumb in the middle of one side and his

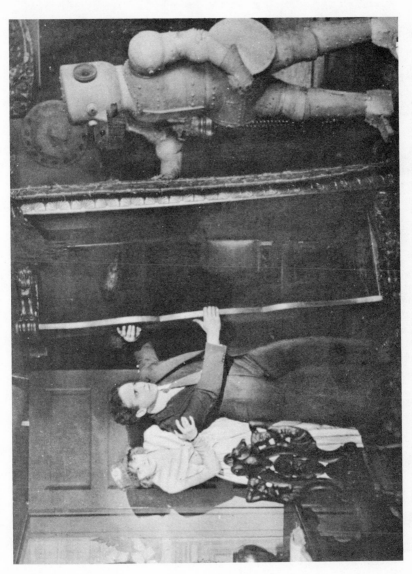

Houdini, as Quentin Locke the inventor, is confronted by a formidable robot in an episode from the serial movie, *The Master Mystery*.

A dramatic scene from one of Houdini's movie thrillers, produced during the days of silent films.

fingers in the middle of the other. In throwing up the pack the top and bottom cards were thus drawn away from the rest and all that the conjurer had to do was to grip them tightly while he placed his hand among the falling cards.

A FEAT OF STRENGTH.—To tear a pack of cards in half hold them by putting the right hand over one end of the pack and the left hand under the opposite end with the fingers on the opposite side.

Now the pack can be held tightly between the two hands and by suddenly twisting the two hands—the right hand towards him and the left hand away from him—the conjurer contrives to tear the pack. Cheap cards are the easiest to tear.

Here is the boomerang trick : the conjurer throws a card away from him and causes it to return to his hand ; as it comes back he picks up a pair of scissors and, catching the card with them, cuts it in halves.

To do this the magician holds the card between the second finger and thumb, with the first finger curled over the top corner. He then bends the hand inwards so that the card nearly touches the wrist, and in throwing the card away from him jerks it back by means of the first finger on the corner. The card is thrown away, but is revolving on its own axis all the time, and this motion causes it to return to the thrower.

To indicate red or black cards as requested by his audience, the magician begins by having all the black cards at the top of the pack and all the red ones together underneath. Slipping his little finger in the pack between the two sets, he is able to insert his middle finger. Then, using the right hand, he bends all the cards below the middle finger in the opposite direction. The cards can then be shuffled, but when they are spread on the table all the black ones will be slightly convex and all the red ones slightly concave. A new pack should be used, and only a very slight bend in the cards is necessary.

IN THE DARK.—The performer requests the person taking a card to show it to someone else, so there may be no doubt afterwards as to which card was taken. He then explains that he is going to perform the trick in the dark, that is to say, the cards are going to be in the " dark."

He squares up the pack and asks the person who has taken the card to place it in the centre of the pack. The conjurer then puts the cards in the " dark " by covering them with a handkerchief and placing them on the table. Directly he has done so he asks the person who took the card to think of it, and the conjurer at once names the card.

This is the secret : when the card is being shown to the second person, the conjurer has ample time to make the necessary move for the accomplishment of the trick. He turns over the bottom card of the pack so that when he squares up the cards and holds them with the bottom card upwards, the cards appear to be all face downwards in the usual way. When the card is returned all that the conjurer has to do is to turn over the pack once more and spread out the cards on the table while he is covering them with a handkerchief. He is then able to see the chosen card through the handkerchief because that card is facing him.

Having asked someone to cut the pack and to remember the card at which he made the cut, the performer picks up the cards and, running them over, at once names the card at which the person looked.

How is it done ? Well, few persons ever replace the cards properly. It will be found that most people replace the portion they lift off in such a way that the cards are not quite level. In other words, they leave what is known as a " step." In picking up the cards the conjurer presses down on the pack with his first finger so as not to shift the cards at the step, and he is then able to discover exactly where the pack was cut.

A TORN CARD TRICK.—A woman in the audience is asked to name any card she likes, and upon her doing so the performer finds it in the pack and gives it to her with a request to tear it up. This being done, one corner is retained and the remaining pieces " vanished " or burnt, and upon the card being reproduced minus one corner the retained piece exactly fits.

The following apparatus is needed : a " magic " pistol, a plate, three packs of thin cards, exactly alike, a small frame, and a small cap of stiff black paper to fit over one corner of a card giving the appearance of the corner being missing when held against a black coat.

The pistol, frame and plate are on the table and the corner fake in a convenient pocket. One pack is arranged in a known order so that a given card may be instantly found. This packet is concealed in a small pocket behind the left hip with one end protruding so as to be easily pulled out. The other two packs are arranged as one big pack in regular order, each suit separately, and every duplicate card together, i.e. 2, 2 ; 3, 3 ; 4, 4 ; 5, 5 ; 6, 6 ; 7, 7 ; 8, 8 ; 9, 9 ; 10, 10 ; Kn, Kn ; Q, Q ; K, K ; Ace, Ace. The performer comes forward with a double pack in his hand, taking care to hold it so that the extra thickness is not noticeable. The thinnest cards are, of course, the best for this trick.

Supposing the woman selects the four of diamonds, he runs through the pack until he comes to the two cards of that name. He then takes one out and hands it to her, slipping his little finger under the other one (cards are face upwards) ; the " pass " is then made and the pack turned back upwards, this bringing the duplicate four of diamonds to the top, and while instructing the woman how to tear up the card she has, he tears one of the lower corners off the top card and palms it in the right hand. This is a simple move, as all eyes are on the woman's card. The fingers of the hand holding the pack must close over it so as to hide the missing corner. The performer picks up the plate from the table with the left hand (which holds the pack) and asks the woman to place the pieces on it. He then selects one corner (really the palmed one) and gives it to her and carries the plate back to the table in his right hand. Under cover of putting the plate down (right side to audience) he drops the double pack (except the top card, the four of diamonds) into his " profonde " and obtains the other arranged pack, which he places on the table, retaining the four of diamonds with the corner off in his palm. This sounds difficult, but will be understood better if the performer palms the card off before changing the packs. The palmed card does not interfere with the change.

He then picks up the frame and takes the back out, handing the whole thing for examination. While this is being done he obtains the loan of a handkerchief, and asking permission of the woman who selected the card originally, he spreads it on her lap. Then obtaining possession of the frame he puts the back on, at the same time slipping the palmed card in, and placing it face downwards on the handkerchief, asks the woman to wrap it up by folding the four corners inward. The performer loads the pieces of card into his pistol from the plate and fires in the air, and the woman finds the card in the frame, testifying to the corner fitting exactly. While attention is fixed on the woman, the performer picks up the pack from the table, and in accordance with his memorised system, makes the pass at the nearest point and gets the four of diamonds to the top. Dropping his hand to his pocket, he obtains the black corner, slips it on the card and keeps it concealed with his fingers. By this time the woman will have finished her part of the trick by seeing that the corner fits. It is now that the card is changed for the duplicate with the fake. Taking the card in his right hand, he also picks up the handkerchief with the same hand and places the latter in his left, which holds the pack. At the moment the hands are together, the card is changed for the one on the pack, keeping the black corner concealed by the fingers. The handkerchief is then handed to the owner. Turning again to the woman, the performer asks for the missing corner, holding out a card as a kind of tray for her to put it on. Holding them at arm's length he walks back to the table ostensibly to place the pack down, but really to get sufficiently far from the spectators to show the card (with the fake) against his coat, which, of course, everyone takes to be the same card as the woman had. All he has to do now is to palm the loose corner and fake under pretence of running the card and piece together and getting rid of them into his "profonde" as he advances to have the card examined.

VANISHING CARDS BY PISTOL.—The effect is that three envelopes are sealed by the audience, one inside the other, the outer one being strung upon a tape, which is tied between two brass pillars, fitted into the table. A small silk handkerchief is now covered over the envelope. A card selected from the pack is deprived of one corner, which is retained by the audience ; the card is placed on top of the pistol in full view of the audience, yet it vanishes immediately upon the pistol being fired, and the effect of the shot is not only to vanish the card, but the handkerchief over the envelope.

The envelope is next cut down and slit open, and the second one taken out ; this is in turn opened, and the smaller one given, still sealed, to the audience, who, upon opening it, discover the card minus the corner inside. On the corner which was retained being fitted to the card, it proves to be an exact fit.

The explanation lies firstly in the pistol, which, although apparently quite innocent, has really a coiled spring fitted inside the barrel around the centre tube ; this is in turn enclosed in another split barrel, which has a cogged end. This tube has four steel pins brazed in the open split pointing towards the opposite direction in which the spring is wound.

To set the pistol, the barrel is twisted to its full extent, and a lever pushed down to keep it from revolving. When the hammer is cocked all is ready, as it follows that if a card is placed in the slit, the hammer, upon the pistol being fired, strikes the lever which releases the cogs, causing the inside barrel to revolve rapidly, the pins catching the card and rolling it round inside the outer case. So much for the vanishing of the card.

The next things to be considered are the envelopes. These are unprepared and are really fastened by the audience, but unknown to them, the tablecloth has a small slit large enough to take an envelope the same size as the smaller of the three, and contains a card similar to that selected by the audience, but minus a corner. Upon receiving the envelopes back, the performer lays them on the table casually over the slit ; this enables him to pick up the concealed one with the three, a small piece of wax causing it to adhere to the back of the envelopes. He hangs the collection up by the tape after exhibiting the pillars, and covers over the lot with a handkerchief which is fastened by a thread to the centre, and is vanished down the table leg by means of a thread and weight.

To open the envelopes it is necessary only to cut the tapes, and with the scissors slip open the first envelope along the top, the forefinger and thumb withdrawing the envelope inside and at the same time the one outside. The second envelope is now opened in the same way, but this time, instead of drawing out the inside envelope, the duplicate containing the card is apparently taken out and handed to the audience to open, the other envelope being left inside. No one ever thinks of asking to look into the second envelope, or suspects that the exhibited one does not really come from inside. The " corner trick " is performed when replacing the cards upon the table after the selection.

THE DEVO CARD TRICK.—For this the performer has the assistance of two men from the audience.

They are handed an ordinary pack of cards, with a request to remove the four aces and four kings from the pack, and, if they desire, privately to mark them with a pencil. Two ordinary envelopes are also examined, and on one they write " Aces," on the other " Kings." The performer calls for the envelope on which " Aces " has been written, placing the aces in full view inside the envelope, and giving it in charge of one of the men. In like manner, he places the kings in the other envelope, which is held by the second man.

The marked aces and kings change places from one envelope to the other !

Take a duplicate ace of hearts and a duplicate king of diamonds, fake these cards by colouring their backs the same as your table-top, preferably a dead black. Have these faked cards lying face downwards on the table-top, where they will be invisible by reason of the faked backs. You are also provided with an ordinary pack of cards, two ordinary envelopes and a lead pencil. Obtain the assistance of two men ; hand them the pack with a request to remove the four aces and kings and mark them as already indicated.

While the examination of the envelopes is in progress, take back the aces first by showing the cards, then shuffle, and toy with them. If the ace of hearts is not already in front bring it there. In the same manner take back kings ; see that the king of diamonds is in front. Place the packet of four aces down over your fake king of diamonds and your packet of kings over the fake ace of hearts, showing your hands entirely empty. Now call for the envelope on which " Aces " is written ; take up from table apparently the four aces, really the kings, with fake ace in front ; the audience seeing the front card unchanged do not suspect a change has been made. Take the envelope and, turning cards with backs to spectators (after showing them) appear to place them in it. In reality the four kings go inside the envelope, the fake ace is allowed to slide down behind it, held by thumb of hand holding envelope ; in the act of raising the envelope to lips to seal flap (a natural movement) the fake ace is palmed in left hand. Give envelope back to the men, getting rid of the palmed fake card meanwhile. Now pick up (apparently) the packet of kings (really aces with faked king in front) and repeat the movements as above.

ANOTHER CARD TRICK.—Requisites : spirit-writing slate ; plain frame with clear glass front and loose back fastened in with cross-bar ; forcing pack ; photographs of three statesmen pasted on back of three cards to match forcing pack ; and paper bag made double—really two bags fastened together.

Effect.—The freely selected cards leave a marked envelope held by one of the audience, and appear in the empty frame. The names of three cards are found written on two slates. In place of the cards, the envelope contains three photographs of statesmen, whose names are found written on a piece of paper which has been freely selected out of a dozen or more collected from the audience, after they have written on them the names of any three statesmen.

Secret.—Arrange forcing pack as follows : suppose it is composed of ace, ten and three, put a ten, then a three, then an ace and so on through the pack. Offer the pack to be cut, and have the three top cards taken, when they are bound to take the three cards you wish to force. Have them shown to the audience and put in the envelope. Take the envelope, and, in walking back to the stage, change it ; then, as if you had forgotten, say you will have it marked (they will then, of course, mark the changed envelope, which contains the three photos). Leave it with the audience. Next give out a number of slips of paper for them to write on the names of the three statesmen. Collect them in bag, double bag, one side containing several slips, all having written on them the names of the three statesmen you have in the envelope. In walking back, turn bag around, and ask someone freely to select any paper he chooses—all being alike he cannot take the wrong one—and retain it. Now show slate, on which you have beforehand written the names of the three cards you forced, and covered up with loose flap—blank at both sides—and put it down on the table. Next call attention to the frame, which you take to pieces. Take out the back, then the brown paper, which now has the cards underneath, without turning it over (cards will now face the glass), and put in the back. Fasten all up in the handkerchief, without letting the audience see the front of the frame, or they will see the cards there, and give it to someone to hold. Command the changes to take place, and show the slate with the names of the cards written on frame, with the three cards in, and the envelope will contain the three photos of the statesmen whose names are written on the slip of paper.

THE THOUGHT-READER'S BOX.—Having shuffled a pack of cards, the conjurer places it in a little wooden

box, into which it exactly fits, and closes the lid. He asks
someone to mention a small number under 10. Suppose
the number is " five."

" Very well," says the conjurer, " we shall deal with the
five top cards of the pack in the box. Will you please take
the box from the table and give it to me ? "

The performer then names the five top cards and
removes them one at a time, as he names them. The box
can be thoroughly examined, and the cards are, of course,
above suspicion.

The trick is done in the following manner : the lid of
the box is almost as deep as the box itself and is ornamented
with a small black disc of wood in the centre. This little
black disc is there for a purpose. When the conjurer opens
the box, the audience see that the disc in the lid goes right
through it—or apparently goes right through it. As a
matter of fact the disc seen in the inside of the lid is not
the one in the lid itself. It is the disc in a thin wooden
flap fitting snugly, but not tightly, in the lid. Behind
that flap are ten cards, with their faces towards the flap.
Therefore, when the box is closed and the flap falls down
on to the pack, the ten cards fall with it, and as the side
of the flap which is then uppermost is covered with the
back of a card, it passes as a card. The pack with the fake
in it can be taken out of the box and the box can be given
for examination. Of course, the conjurer must know the
top ten cards by heart and in their right order.

THE TWEEZERS TRICK.—Having shuffled a pack of
cards, the magician lifts off about half of them and gives
the cards to a member of the audience. Requesting that
he will select three of the cards and return the remainder,
the conjurer turns his back on the audience while the
person holds up the three selected cards. The conjurer
then turns round, hands back the remainder of the pack
to the person who chose the three cards, and asks him to
shuffle the cards. The performer calls attention to the
fact that during the whole progress of the trick he does
not once touch the selected cards himself.

The cards are spread out, face upwards, on a tray, and

the conjurer, holding a pair of small tweezers, asks the person who selected the cards to touch his wrist. He then picks up the selected cards, one at a time, with the tweezers.

It is done in this way. The shuffle is a false one. The conjurer does not disturb the top half of the pack. After three of these cards have been selected the conjurer turns his back on the audience (for the reason given above) and quietly drops the cards into his " profonde " and takes out some other cards, all of which are different from those first shown. Thus, when the cards are spread out on a tray no duplicates are visible. These cards have the white portion of their faces slightly tinged with yellow.

To get them this colour, spread the cards out to the light for a day or two. The rest is easy, because the conjurer can distinguish the chosen cards by the fact that they are slightly different in colour from the rest, being a dead white.

FOUR-ACE TRICK.—The four aces are shown and laid on the table. Three cards are dealt out behind each ace. The aces are placed on the packets of three cards. A packet is chosen by the audience and placed on one side. The other three packets are turned over and the cards dealt out. The aces have disappeared. All four aces are found together in the packet chosen by the audience.

This is the way in which it is done : the first three packets of three cards are in reality packets of four cards. This is easily managed. The top two cards are taken off the pack together and shown as one card. As each card is dealt, its face is shown to the audience. When three packets have been dealt, the conjurer deals three cards which, unknown to the audience, are three duplicate aces ; that is to say, these aces and the one behind which they are placed make up the four aces. These duplicate aces are, of course, dealt face downwards, but as the audience have seen the faces of the cards in the first three packets they are not likely to question this move. In squaring up each of the first three packets the conjurer contrives to get a little bit of wax from under his finger-nail on to the tops of the cards. He then covers each packet with an ace, and in doing so presses down on the first three aces. The fourth packet is then forced on the audience. The other three packets are dealt out face downwards, and as the aces adhere to the cards over which they were placed, they are "missing." The other packet is then turned over.

SEEING THE CARD.—*Effect.*—A spectator takes a card, returns it and shuffles the pack. The conjurer spreads the cards out in a line on the table and announces that the spectator is unable to see his card. The spectator admits that he cannot see it. The conjurer picks up the cards, shuffles them, and spreads them out again. " Now," says he, " you can see your card, can't you ? " The spectator admits that he can. The conjurer immediately gathers up the cards, squares up the pack, tells the spectator the name of his card and the position of it in the pack, counting from the top. The spectator is invited to count the cards and to see if the statement is correct.

Explanation.—The conjurer brings the card to the top of the pack and pushing it down with his thumb gets a glimpse at the index. He then knows the card. In spreading out the cards in a line so that they overlap one another, he takes care to hide the top card under the others. In picking up the cards and shuffling them, the magician takes off the bottom half, and in the act of shuffling some of them on the top of the others counts the cards he shuffles on the top by drawing them off one at a time with his left thumb. Then when he exposes the cards again, he can easily reckon which was the chosen one and he knows its position in the pack.

ANOTHER CHOICE.—A new pack of cards is taken by the conjurer, who breaks open the wrapper, gives out the cards for examination, and asks anyone to shuffle them.

Having had the cards shuffled by the audience, the performer invites someone to take a card and to replace it in the pack. He then shuffles the pack, and shows that the card chosen is neither at the top nor at the bottom of the pack. He produces the chosen card in any way he pleases. Perhaps the most effective way of doing this is to spread out the cards in the hands, and ask the person who chooses a card to think of it directly he sees it. After a few moments the conjurer immediately names the card.

The secret for the trick consists in one faked card. It has a small crescent-shaped piece cut out of one end. This card can easily be added to the others when the conjurer receives the pack back from the audience. The faked card is kept at first at the bottom of the pack. After a card has been chosen, the conjurer gets it to the middle of the pack, and has the chosen card placed on the top of it. The pack is then squared up.

A FAKED CARD.—Holding the pack in the left hand, and lightly covering it with his right, the conjurer " riffles " the left-hand corner with his thumb, while asking the chooser of the card to think of it. The conjurer then " riffles " the end of the pack with his right thumb, and he knows that the pack will " break " at the faked card. This card will travel past the thumb, and the next card to it is the chosen card. The conjurer bends the pack slightly and gets a glimpse of it.

A second secret is a faked card made up in such a way that the whole pack, with the faked card in it, can be handed out to anyone to shuffle without the slightest fear of the discovery that one of the cards has been tampered with.

The faked card is easily made. The white edge of a card is first trimmed away, and the centre which is left is gummed on to the centre of another card. Thus the faked card will be slightly thicker in the centre than any other card, and the chosen card, replaced upon it, can be discovered quite easily by running the thumb along either end of the pack.

This secret also affords an excellent method of doing the blindfold trick. The conjurer can have the cards replaced on the faked card, and the pack immediately squared up. If he pleases, he can shuffle the cards, so long as he takes care not to disturb those immediately above the faked card. (If only one card has been chosen, either when this or the other faked card is used, there is little fear of the two cards being disturbed by an ordinary shuffle.) Having had the cards squared up, and having shown, after the shuffle, that the cards chosen are neither at the top nor at the bottom of the pack, the conjurer asks someone to blindfold him, and as he is not dependent upon the slightest speck of light for accomplishing the trick, he can even have his eyes covered with pads of cotton-wool before the hand-kerchief is placed over his eyes.   He takes a small knife in his hand and spreads out the pack on the table.   The chosen cards are above the faked card.   The position of the faked card is discovered by the touch of the fingers, and the cards immediately above it are pulled out to the edge of the table.   The rest requires no explanation.

With regard to the use of the first faked pack, I may say that this gives anyone an easy way of producing any chosen cards from the pocket after the chosen cards have been returned to the pack, the pack has been returned to the conjurer and placed in his pocket.   He can shuffle the pack casually before putting it in his pocket, and then asks the choosers of the cards if their cards are at the top or bottom of the pack.   When the pack is in his pocket the conjurer merely has to run his thumb along the end, and the cards above the faked card will be the chosen cards.   He turns this portion of the pack over and produces them one by one, or, if he pleases, he can leave the chosen cards in his pocket after he has removed the first card, and offer the pack to anyone to shuffle, and then put it back in his pocket.   When the last chosen card has been taken out of his pocket, the conjurer takes out all the cards except the faked card, and goes on to the next trick.   The use of a faked card is then not suspected.

DISCOVERING A CHOSEN CARD.—A few cards—about half the pack—are held out by the performer, and he asks someone to select a card, look at it and replace it.   The conjurer immediately gives out the pack to be shuffled, and directly he takes it back again he is able to pick out the chosen card.

It will be understood, of course, that this is not a trick, but a method by which a trick can be performed.   No conjurer would be content merely to find the card; he would want to produce it in an effective manner. This merely shows how the card is discovered under these conditions. There are countless ways of producing the chosen card afterwards.

The conjurer should take the pack of cards in his hand, and draw from it the ace, three, five, six, seven, eight and nine of spades, clubs and hearts.

It will be seen that the cards with the odd numbers can be arranged so that single pips on the cards point in one direction. The aces' pips are obvious. In the three, the centre pip gives the clue; the same with the five. In the seven and nine the single pip in the centre of the card gives the clue, and in the six and eight the two centre pips on either side give the clue.

Now arrange the cards so that the pips giving the clue point all in one direction. If one card is chosen, and while the chooser is looking at it, the conjurer quietly reverses the cards he holds. It will be obvious that when the conjurer looks at the cards again, after they have been shuffled by a member of the audience, he can easily pick out the chosen card, because the pip giving the clue will point in the opposite direction to that of all the " clue pips " in all other cards.

THE FOUR ACES.—*Effect.*—The conjurer places the four aces, face upwards, in a row on the table. He then puts them back on top of the pack and makes a sharp clicking noise with the pack (technically known as a " riffle "). A man who has been asked to assist in the trick is then invited to say where the aces are. Having heard the noise of the " riffle," he will probably believe that the aces have been brought by sleight-of-hand to the middle of the pack, and will probably say so. If he does say so, the conjurer at once shows that the aces are still on the top of the pack. If, on the other hand, the man says that the cards are still on top of the pack, the conjurer quickly makes the pass and brings them to the middle and shows them there. Then he says he will begin the trick again, and once more he puts the aces down on the table, and then on the top of the pack. The same little piece of by-play is carried out, and the aces are put down on the table for the third time, and for the third time, also, put on the top of the pack. This time the conjurer does the latter part of the work very slowly, and then asks : " Now, you are quite convinced that the aces are on the top of the pack ? " There can be no doubt about this, and the man questioned is sure to say " Yes." The conjurer says he will get on with the trick, and this time deals the four aces face downwards on the table and then deals three cards on each ace. The assistant is asked to choose two of the packets and then one of the packets, so that finally there is only one packet on the table. The conjurer announces that he will try and make the three aces which have been returned to the pack change places with the three indifferent cards which are on the top of the fourth ace on the table. He riffles the cards three times, and then turns over the four cards on the table. They are the four aces.

Explanation.—Before showing this trick the conjurer secretly places three indifferent cards in his right-hand trousers pocket. He is then ready to perform the trick. To make the " riffle," he holds the cards in the left hand with the first finger pressed against the back of them. By pressing on one corner of the pack with the thumb and releasing the cards in that corner quickly, the conjurer makes a snapping noise with them. After the performer has put the cards on the table he stands for a second with his hands in his trousers pocket. It is as well for him to take up this attitude, a perfectly natural one, all through the trick, because when he wants to make use of the three cards in his pocket no one is likely to suspect him of using his pockets for the purpose of the trick.

The first two attempts at hoodwinking the assistant in regard to the position of the aces are of no consequence. There is no trickery required beyond the making of the pass, and even that is not always necessary, because often the assistant will help the conjurer by affirming that the aces are in the centre of the pack or at the bottom, in which case all that the conjurer has to do is to turn up the aces on the top and show that they have not moved from that position.

At the third attempt, the aces are placed slowly on the top of the pack, and once more the conjurer puts his hands into his pockets as he stands with an expectant attitude, and says, " Now, you're quite convinced that the aces are there ? " This time he quietly palms the three indifferent cards from his pocket and secretly places them, in the act of squaring up the pack, on to the top of the aces. He then deals out the four top cards which the audience believe to be the four aces. On No. 4 card he places the next three cards, which, unknown to the audience, are the four aces. Three cards are dealt on each of the three remaining cards.

Looking at the packets of four cards from left to right, the conjurer knows that he has to force his assistant to choose No. 4 packet, on the right. He begins by asking the assistant to choose two of the packets, and then proceeds to influence his choice (without it being known) by means of " heads I win, tails you lose " principle. If the person chooses the first two packets the conjurer immediately takes them away, leaving No. 3 and No. 4 on the table. If, on the other hand, the assistant chooses No. 3 and No. 4, the conjurer says, " Very well, we will use one of those. Please choose another." If the choice falls on No. 4, the conjurer makes a great hit by pointing out that the packet which the person has freely chosen himself shall be used in the trick. If the person chooses No. 3, the conjurer takes it away and says, " That leaves us with one packet left. You could have had this one taken away if you had liked, couldn't you ? " The way in which No. 4 packet, containing the four aces, is forced on the person who thinks all the time he has a free choice in the matter will now be quite clear. The audience never know, until the choice is actually made, whether the conjurer is going to take the chosen packet away from the table or leave it there. The rest of the trick explains itself.

THE "SYMPATHETIC" CARDS.—To perform this trick, a pack of thirty-two cards is used. On the top are four queens in the following order : heart, spade, diamond, club ; the queen of clubs on top. Bring, by means of the " pass," the queen of clubs to the middle of the pack, and force it on somebody. Now place the pack on the table, divide it into two heaps and place the top half, on which the three queens are, at the right side of the bottom half. Ask another spectator to choose one of the two heaps. In case the heap is chosen on which are the three queens, the performer picks it up, places it in his left hand and palms with the right the three queens, and gives heap to spectator to hold. The performer picks up other heap and places the palmed cards on the top of it and places the heap in the left hand. Now he asks the person who keeps the other half to take at random three cards from it one by one without looking at them. The performer places them on the heap he has himself, and as soon as all three are placed on top he passes them to the bottom. The three queens will thus remain on the top. Place carefully on a tray or plate the three top cards and hand them to a third person with request to place his other hand on the three cards. (It will be understood that it would facilitate matters in case the first spectator had chosen the bottom on the left-hand heap.)

The performer now makes the following remarks : " Ladies and gentlemen, when doing magical experiments, I occasionally remark that some of them depend entirely on the sympathy existing between the ladies and gentlemen of the company. The same can be said of cards, and in some cases the success depends on this, which I will try to prove by a little experiment."

The three cards chosen " sympathise " not only amongst themselves, but also with the three cards selected by the first gentleman, so that when, for instance, the first person has selected a knave, ace, seven or ten, the cards selected by the second person ought to be the same. Addressing the first person, the performer requests him to be so kind as to tell which card he selected. Queen of clubs will, of course, be the answer. Request the person who has his hand lying on the three cards to be so kind as to tell you what they are. They will prove to be queens also.

Show the four queens, and place them under the other half of the pack, after which the remaining heap must be placed again at the top. Now take secretly from the " profonde " four cards, which are prepared in such a way that on one side they show the four queens and the other side they show four spot cards. Place them secretly under the real four queens, picture side downwards. Seem to change your mind, and place the four bottom cards in a row on the table, with the queen side exposed. Request somebody to choose any one of the four queens, not to touch it, but by calling it out. By the way, the four queens at the bottom of the pack must lie in the same order as the four prepared queens lying on the table. Suppose the queen of hearts is chosen. The performer at once passes to the top of the pack the four bottom cards, and quickly slips the queen of hearts to the bottom of the three other queens lying at the top of pack. After this is done, place on each queen lying on the table three ordinary cards, taken one by one from the bottom of the pack. Place them face downwards and be careful that they cover the queens entirely. There are now lying on the table four heaps, each of four cards. Pick up the heap in which is the chosen queen of hearts, change this heap quietly with the four queens lying on top of pack, and, advancing to the person who selected the queen of hearts, give to him the four queens to hold. To the spectators, it will appear that they are the four cards taken from the table, namely the queen of hearts, with three other cards on top. Be careful that only the backs of the cards are visible. Now touch with your wand three heaps on the table, and also the heap kept by the spectator. Pick up separately each heap from the table, turn them around, spread them out and show that the queens have departed. Request spectator to show his card, and the audience will see the four queens.

THE CIGARETTE TRICK.—A card is selected from the pack, torn in pieces, one piece given back for the purpose of identifying the card later. A piece of paper is shown to the audience and the paper is folded into a square to resemble an envelope. The pieces of card are dropped into the paper, and all sides folded down, the paper being given to one of the company to hold. The pistol is fired, the paper torn open, and the card is found restored, except the small piece which was given back to the company. The card and the small piece are placed in a card-box. You tell the audience that you are going to restore the card to its original condition. As it will take a few seconds to go through the process, if the company do not mind, you will " enjoy a smoke " while waiting. Borrow a cigarette, attempt to light it, say it is strange it will not light; then tear it open, and instead of tobacco, the chosen card is inside, the box being opened is found empty.

The card is forced; the supposed piece of paper is really two pieces pasted together, with a duplicate of chosen card, corner torn off, in centre. The envelope being formed round the card, when torn open it is slit along the front edge with a penknife. The cigarette is changed for a faked one, and the card rolled up and enclosed in cigarette paper. The card box is normal.

THE MEXICAN TURN OVER.—*Effect.*—The queen and two other cards are placed in a row on the table, and the performer moving them about as though he would confuse his audience, asks someone to " find the lady." The person choosing is told at once that he is wrong. The conjurer picks up one of the other cards and slipping it under the chosen card, turns it over and shows that it is not the queen. He then turns over the other card in the same way, and finally throws the card he is holding on the table.

Explanation.—Let us suppose that the person who is asked to " find the lady " points to the card which the conjurer knows is the queen. He picks up one of the other cards, face downwards, and slips it under the queen and a little in advance of it so that the top of the card in his hand is about half an inch beyond the top of the queen on the table. The card in the hand is held at the tips of the first finger and thumb. When this card is well underneath the queen, the conjurer moves his thumb to the corner of the queen card, and thus holds that card face downwards while he turns over the other card with the tip of his first finger. The effect to the audience is that the conjurer merely turned over one card with another.

The reason for turning over the other card on the table is this : after the conjurer has turned over the first card, he is holding the queen in his hand. By turning over the second card and using this queen, he is able to show that it was the second card that was the queen. If he merely showed that the card in his hand was the queen the audience might suspect some kind of change, although if the trick is done neatly and quickly it is quite impossible for anyone to detect it.

THE MISSING CARD.—*Effect.*—A card having been chosen and returned to the pack the conjurer shuffles the cards, removes three, and places them on the table. He announces that the chosen card is one of the three and says that by means of his own will power he will cause the person who drew the card to touch the actual card that he chose. The person is invited to touch one of the three cards. He does so. The card is turned over and is not the chosen card. The conjurer then pretends that he has made a mistake and asks the person to look at the other two cards on the table. Neither of them is the chosen card. " Some mistake," says the conjurer, looking through the pack. " By the way, which card did you take ? The six of clubs (or whatever card is named). I'm sorry, but I think you have made a mistake ; there is no such card here." He then runs through the pack and shows that the six of clubs is undoubtedly missing. A search is made for the the card and eventually the person who chose it is asked to get up, when the audience see that he has been sitting on the card all the time.

Explanation.—After the card is returned and brought to the top of the pack the conjurer takes any three cards and places them on the table well away from the person assisting him so that when the person is asked to touch one of the cards he has to rise from his chair to do so. The conjurer stands close to him while he gets up and holds the pack in his right hand. When the person is well away from his chair and while all eyes are on the cards on the table the conjurer quietly pushes off the top card with his right thumb, so that when the person sits down again he covers the card.

THE RISING CARD.—A large frame is standing on the table. At the base of the frame is a receptacle for holding a pack of cards, and at the top of the frame is a tiny ornamental arch. Having had a card chosen by the audience and returned to the pack, the conjurer hands the pack to another member of the audience with a request that he will shuffle it thoroughly. The conjurer then places the pack in the receptacle and asks what card was chosen. Suppose it was the two of hearts. Commanding the card to show itself, the conjurer makes some passes towards the frame, and the card rises slowly to the top of the ornamental arch above the frame.

Explanation.—The card is forced. The houlette or receptacle is provided with an extra space at the back, and in this is placed a card similar to the one which is to be forced. This card has a thread attached to it. The thread is drawn up to the arch, passed through a little hole there, and then brought down and fastened to a little weight concealed in one of the sides of the frame. This weight rests on the top of some sand in the sides of the frame. When the conjurer wishes the card to rise he releases a little catch at the bottom of the side of the frame and the sand runs into the bottom of the frame. This action causes the little weight to drop down into the side of the frame, and in doing this it naturally draws down the thread and so causes the card to rise. The conjurer stands away from the apparatus while the card is rising, to prove that he is " not operating the trick in any way. "

THE MYSTIC CARD-BOX.—The performer hands out a small flat box for inspection. Someone in the audience is invited to take any card from a pack and place it in the box. The conjurer, holding the box to his forehead, immediately names the card in the box.

Here is the explanation. One of the screws at the back of the box is a dummy. In holding up the box the conjurer pulls out this dummy nail a little way. This enables the conjurer to slide the front panel a little to one side with his thumb. At the lower right-hand corner there is a small hole in the panel, and through this the conjurer is able to read the index corner of the card. The frame can be immediately restored to its original condition and handed out for inspection.

THE WATCH AND THE CARD.—Someone in the audience is invited to shuffle the pack, take a card, replace it in the pack, and shuffle the pack again. The conjurer wraps the pack in a handkerchief and places it on the table. He then takes out his watch and asks someone to tell him the time ; he shows that person that his watch is in good going order and is very nearly " on time." The watch is placed on the covered pack of cards.

The conjurer tells his audience that the watch will help him in the trick by telling him what card was taken.

He immediately names the card and then shows the audience how he gained the information from the watch. The watch is of an unusual kind ; the usual figures from the face have vanished and their places have been taken by some miniature cards. The hand of the watch is pointing to a card similar to that which was chosen.

The climax of the trick is reached when the conjurer uncovers the pack, and, riffling it, shows that the chosen card has disappeared from the pack.

After a member of the audience has shuffled the pack the conjurer forces a card ; this card is slightly shorter than the remaining cards in the pack. After the card is returned to the pack, anyone may shuffle the cards.

The object of the conjurer in asking the time is merely to give him a chance of showing his watch in a natural way. If he took the watch from his pocket and called attention to the fact that he was going to use the watch in the trick, somebody would probably want to look too closely at the watch. The watch is really only a dummy with small cards and a hand on the face. Over the face of the watch there is a false dial, similar to that of an ordinary watch. After the conjurer has called attention to the watch, he places it on the covered pack of cards and in doing so palms off the false dial which is attached to the body of the watch by means of a small bayonet catch. A slight turn releases the dial and the watch is placed on the packet.

As the forced card was slightly shorter than the rest of the cards there is no difficulty in causing it to vanish when the cards are riffled, for its face cannot be seen when the cards are " sprung " by the riffle.

THINK OF A CARD.—Having invited someone to shuffle the pack the conjurer deals off three cards, asks the person assisting to think of one of them and not to give him any clue as to the card chosen.

The performer then puts the three cards in his pocket and repeats his request to his assistant to think intently of the chosen card. The conjurer takes two of the cards from his pocket and throws them on the table. He then asks his assistant to name the card of which he is thinking, and immediately takes that card from his pocket, thus showing that he had " read " the person's thoughts.

The explanation is as follows. The conjurer prepares for the trick by slipping two cards into his pocket; these cards can be hidden by means of the old trick of pushing them to the top of the pocket. No two pockets are quite alike and it may be necessary to bend the cards in order to fix them in their right position. When he deals the cards on the table the conjurer memorises them, or, alternatively, he can see that the cards are arranged in numerical order; he need not trouble to remember the suits.

With the order of the three cards clearly fixed in his mind, the conjurer puts them in his pocket, and after some little pretence at thought reading takes from his pocket the two cards which he hid in his pocket before the beginning of the trick. It is not advisable to show the faces of these cards, because it is just possible that the assistant may have remembered all three cards which were shown to him, and in that case he would at once notice that the conjurer was using two extra cards.

Having thrown the two cards on the table the conjurer asks his assistant to name the card of which he has been thinking.

The conjurer, remembering the order of the three cards in his pocket, has no difficulty in drawing the particular card required from his pocket.

CARDS, COINS, AND GLASS.—The performer introduces an ordinary pack of playing cards and a glass tumbler; they may be examined if necessary. He then borrows a number of coins (say three). The tumbler is placed on the table, cards on top of it, and, at the command of the conjurer, the coins leave his hand, and are distinctly seen and heard to fall into the tumbler.

A fake, made as follows, is needed Cut an ordinary playing card in two. Take one half and paint black both sides. Glue a piece of black linen on one side at about half an inch from the end (oblong). Attach fake to long thread with loop at end and fasten to vest button, put wand under left arm, take coins in left hand, stand away the length of the thread, make pass from left to right, take wand in right hand. Give thread a downward blow with wand, when the fake flies out and coins fall into the glass. Now break thread off vest button, and let it fall on carpet.

Anyone can then take up coins, cards and glass for examination. When performing this trick, stand well behind the table.

FIVE CARDS TO VANISH AND REAPPEAR.—*Effect.*— One card is picked up by the magician, who makes it disappear. He picks up another card with his left hand, places it in the right hand and makes that one disappear. He continues in the same way with five cards. Then, raising his right hand in the air, with a quick movement, he brings the cards back one at a time.

Explanation.—The effect is produced by what is known as the " back and front palm." The first card is held in the centre of one end between the second finger and thumb of the right hand. The conjurer waves his hand up and down, and that movement covers the movements of the fingers which are necessary to get the card to the back of the hand, where it is concealed.

These are the movements of the fingers : the card is held between the tips of the second finger and thumb. Now the little finger and first finger come up at the sides of the card. The second finger is bent towards the palm, and the thumb is released while the card is gripped between the first and second fingers and little and third fingers. To make the card disappear all that is now necessary is to straighten the hand.

To " back palm " the other cards, each is brought up by the left hand to the right, and dealt with in the same manner, each card sliding on to those at the back of the hand.

To cause the reappearance of the cards one at a time, the conjurer proceeds in the following manner : turning his hand round from the wrist and in such a way that the cards cannot be seen by the audience (the exact angle at which the hand should be held can be determined by doing the trick before a looking-glass), the conjurer bends his fingers and then slides the top card of the packet upwards with his thumb ; the little finger releases it, but grips the remaining cards.

The conjurer then extends his first finger and slides it under the card and straightens his hand. This brings one card to view, and keeps the remainder at the back of the hand. The process is repeated to cause the reappearance of the other cards.

If the conjurer pleases he can show that the cards have completely disappeared even when they are held by his right hand ; that is to say, he shows both the back and the front of his hand. Suppose that the cards have been brought to the back in the way described. The conjurer bends his fingers, extends the second finger and with it pushes the cards from the top into the hand. The cards are not palmed in the usual way but are held by the edges between the first and second fingers and third and little fingers. They are then in readiness to be back palmed again.

One card is manipulated very easily in this way. Instead of using the second finger to push the card down into the hand, the magician drags the card down quickly by using his thumb. Simultaneously the hand is turned over, and the audience can see that there is no card at the back of the hand.

DIMINISHING CARDS.—The trick of making cards appear to diminish requires considerable skill. Here is the description and explanation :

The packs of cards you deal with are tied up with a thread. At the back of each pack there is a spring slip, into which the packet of the next size smaller is inserted. Having got the packs palmed in his left hand the conjurer volunteers to show the audience how it is all done.

He picks up a few cards, places his two hands together and exhibits the largest of the small packs and at the same time palms the big cards which he had picked up. With the excuse of showing how the cards have shrunk, the conjurer now picks up some more big cards with his right hand, and in returning them to the table returns the palmed cards with them. The audience now see the face of the top lot of cards reduced to the size of Patience cards. The conjurer now pretends to make these smaller, but he really pushes them down a little lower in his hands. Picking up a card from the table to show how small the cards are getting he continues the process, and puts the card down again. This card has a flap at the back. When the card is on the table it is flat, but when it is held with its face towards the audience the flap opens, leaving a little pocket, in which the first packet of small diminishing cards is dropped. The front card of the next size is a flap card, which can be opened to the size of a Patience card. The process is repeated ; each time the conjurer picks up a card to show how small the cards are getting. By means of the flap cards all palming of small packets is done away with.

THE SWINDLE TRICK.—The conjurer has a card selected and returned to the pack and the pack shuffled.

The cards are strewn about the table. The conjurer picks up the cards one at a time, turns each one over, looks at it, looks at the spectator who drew the card as though he would read his thoughts and then puts the card into his left hand.

He continues to do this until he has a number of cards in his hand, each one of which the spectator has seen. Among them is the card that the spectator originally drew and returned to the pack. Therefore, when the conjurer says: "The next card I turn over will be yours," the spectator, having seen that the card he chose has already been picked up and put in the conjurer's hand, will certainly say, "You're wrong." "Impossible," says the conjurer, "the next card I turn over will be yours." "But you've passed it," says the victim. "You're wrong," says the conjurer, and then takes a card from those in his hand —not one on the table, as the spectator thought—turns it over, and it is, of course, the selected card.

This is the way it is done. When the card is returned to the pack the conjurer holds his fingers under the pack and quietly bends a corner of the card. He is thus able to tell from feeling the card when he picks up the chosen one, and in putting it into his left hand he keeps his little finger on top of it. He takes care, of course, that the spectator gets a good view of this card, and then goes on picking up cards and looking at each one before he brings the trick to its conclusion.

THE MYSTERIOUS COUPLE.—Two cards are freely chosen and returned to the pack. The conjurer shuffles the pack, and, holding it in the left hand with the bottom card only visible, asks the first chooser if that was his card. The reply is negative. The conjurer deals this bottom card on the table, and, going to the second chooser, asks if the bottom card is his card. Again the reply is " No." From this point the patter is :

" My trick is fairly simple. I will first ask what were the chosen cards—the king of hearts and the three of diamonds. (They may, of course, be any other cards.) Very well. I think you all saw me place the two bottom cards of the pack—the five of diamonds and the ten of clubs (if those were the cards used)—on the table. What I propose to do is to ask the cards on the table to change places with those cards which were chosen. When you heard that little click (made by the riffle) the change took place, and if you now look at the cards you will see that the five of diamonds and the ten of clubs which I dealt on the table have returned to the pack and that the chosen cards —the king of hearts and three of diamonds—are on the table. There they are.''

This little piece of magic is brought about by means of half a card, or rather the halves of two cards, pasted together back to back. The conjurer hides this fake under the other cards when he has the two cards chosen. He brings the two chosen cards to the bottom of the pack, and keeps the faked card over one end. In holding up the pack for the first man to see, he keeps his hand in such a position that only the half-card is seen, and the junction between that and the real bottom card is hidden by the hand. When he turns the pack face downwards, and apparently draws out the card which has been shown to the member of the audience, the conjurer keeps hold of the faked card and draws out the bottom card, which is one of the two chosen cards.

The conjurer then turns the faked card over and repeats the process, and gets rid of the faked card in any way he pleases. The only part of the trick in which special care should be taken is in not allowing the two choosers of cards to take cards similar to those on the two sides of the faked card. It is, however, a comparatively simple matter to have these two cards and the faked half-card at the bottom of the pack before the commencement of the trick, and then there is no chance of a mishap.

BLINDFOLDING THE CARDS.—*Effect.*—The conjurer comes forward with three handkerchiefs, which he says he is going to use for the purpose of '' blindfolding the cards.'' He has the pack divided in halves. The person doing this is then invited to divide either half into three small heaps, and to wrap each heap in a handkerchief so chat the cards may be blindfolded. The person is then asked to choose one of the heaps. The conjurer takes this heap and holds it close to his forehead. He then calls out the names of several cards, and when the handkerchief is taken away the audience see that the cards named by the conjurer were those in the handkerchief.

Explanation.—A prearranged pack is used. When the person who has been helping the conjurer indicates which heap is to be used in the trick the conjurer says, " Very well, we shall not want these," and puts the other heaps on one side, but in doing this he secretly stretches the handkerchief, which should be a fine one, over the bottom card of the heap above the one chosen and sees the card through the handkerchief. He then takes up the chosen heap and holds it to his forehead. In doing this he stretches the handkerchief, sees the bottom card and, therefore, knowing the order of the cards, he can name those in the handkerchief, because knowing the bottom card of the next heap he is able to tell the top card of those he is holding.

CARDS AND A FAN.—*Effect.*—A spectator is asked to assist by freely choosing a card and writing upon it his initials. The card is placed in an envelope, which is closed and given to another member of the audience. The first assistant is now requested to shuffle the pack and fan it. The performer draws a card from fan, calls its name, and, initialling it, puts it in his pocket. These two cards change places and can be immediately shown and initials verified.

Method.—The only preparation necessary is to reverse the two bottom cards of the pack and initial the last one. The pack is false-shuffled, care being taken to keep reversed cards out of sight. The spectator freely chooses a card, and the performer, by fanning pack from top to centre, will prevent the bottom cards being observed. The chosen card is initialled, returned to top of pack, and is reversed before placing on the table. The performer lifts off top card, which is now really bottom card with his own initials, and lays it face down on table. He now lifts up pack and envelope and gives the latter for examination, meanwhile palming the original top card to trousers pocket. The card on the table is placed in an envelope. The remaining reversed card is now altered to agree with rest of pack, which is given to a spectator, who is asked to shuffle and fan. The performer picks a card, does not show it, but calls the name of the card he prepared beforehand. A pretence is made of initialling it. Finally it is placed on " top " of trousers pocket. Cards may now be commanded to change places, and pocket, by aid of " top " principle, may be shown empty after spectator's card is removed.

(This trick was devised by Margaret Mackey.)

CARDS RISING FROM THE POCKET.—*Effect.*—Three cards are selected and returned to the pack, which is then shuffled and placed in the outside breast pocket of the conjurer's coat. The conjurer asks the choosers of the three cards to name them and he calls upon them to come out of his pocket ; the cards obey him, and rise, one at a time, from the pocket.

Explanation.—The three cards are forced, therefore, after they are returned to the pack anyone is at liberty to shuffle the pack. Inside the pocket there is a little " buckram " partition with three duplicate cards threaded in the usual way. The end of the thread is passed out through the back of the coat and is attached to a spring ratchet winder sewn in the lining of the coat. To cause the cards to rise the conjurer stands, in a natural position, with his left hand on hip and presses on a little knob on the winder ; this releases the spring and winds up the thread, causing the first card to rise. The movement is repeated for the other two cards. This trick and the following one is the work of Elbert M. Morey.

THE SUSPENDED CARDS.—*Effect.*—Three cards are chosen, and returned to the pack. The conjurer, standing in front of a small black velvet screen, throws the pack up in the air. The three chosen cards remain suspended in the air, and the conjurer takes them and hands them out for inspection.

Explanation.—The screen is fitted with three short rods with a card concealed by means of black velvet at the end of each rod. The three cards, duplicates of the three which are forced on three members of the audience, are enclosed in little black velvet bags. These three rods work on three weak spring hinges, and when the cards are to be made to appear a pull at the back of the screen raises the three rods and thus brings the cards into view; as the rods are covered with black velvet the cards appear to be suspended in mid-air.

HERSCHELL'S ENVELOPES AND CARDS.—The following trick was invented by the late Dr. Herschell. Two cards, both of which may be examined before and after the trick, are placed respectively into two envelopes, each of which is provided with a round hole in the centre. By this provision, when cards are placed into envelopes, their centre pips (both cards being nines) are visible to the last moment. In spite of the apparent fairness of the preliminaries, the two cards manage to change places, the red taking the place of the black and vice versa.

Only two cards are used, and neither has any preparation in connection with it. Not so the envelopes. The front of each is made double to conceal a lever, the long arm of which carries a square piece of card on which is painted the pip of a card. One envelope has a club pip concealed, the other a heart.

The short arms projecting beyond corners of the envelope, a very slight pressure serves to bring the respective pips into view through the holes. Little more needs to be explained. The nine of hearts goes into the envelope containing the club lever; the nine of clubs goes into the one containing the heart lever. The envelopes are now placed on top of each other, and the levers moved to bring the faked pips into view. Whilst showing two tumblers, against which the envelopes are eventually lodged, the audience naturally fail to remember the positions of the respective cards. Each envelope is now shown and careful attention drawn to the respective positions of the cards. In turning the envelopes round so that the holes are away from the audience, the levers are pushed aside, so that the cards a few seconds later appear to have changed their positions.

THE HERSCHELL CARD-STABBING TRICK.—A selected card is revealed on the point of a dagger, although the spread pack is covered with a piece of newspaper.

The trick is simple, a faked sheet of newspaper being responsible for practically the whole mystery. A pocket made in a sheet of newspaper conceals a duplicate of the card, which is, of course, forced on a spectator. Let us imagine that the ace of spades is forced. A duplicate of this is " loaded " into the pocket of the paper, and if the paper is neatly faked there is no chance of its presence being detected. So soon as the card is returned to the pack, it is brought to top and palmed away. Ample opportunity for the necessary manipulation is afforded while a bandage for the eyes is examined.

The piercing of the duplicate with the dagger in these circumstances is not a difficult matter, as the performer knows the exact position of the pocket and stabs accordingly.

THE " MIRACLE."—A pack of cards in a case is handed to the audience by the conjurer, who asks someone to take out the cards, shuffle them, and select one card. The remainder of the pack is returned to the case, which is handed back to the conjurer, who slips it into his trousers pocket.

The person holding the card is asked to show it to several other members of the audience, and so that he shall not catch a glimpse of the card the conjurer turns his back on the audience for a moment. While he is in that position, the conjurer takes the case from his pocket and, holding it behind his back, asks the holder of the card to put it back in the pack, close the case, and put a rubber band round it. The performer turns round and immediately names the chosen card.

This is how it is done ! The performer is provided with two packs of cards and two cases just alike. One pack is prepared by having an index corner of each card cut out

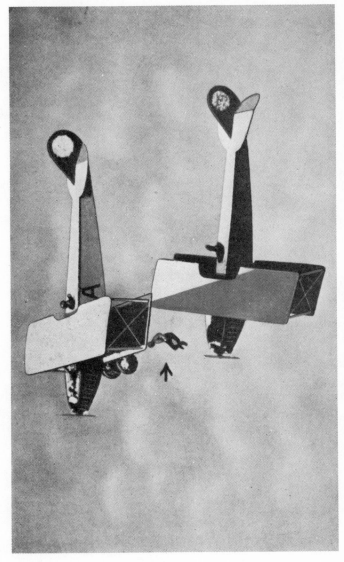

Houdini's daring jump from one aeroplane to another, from an actual photograph taken at the moment of jumping. The negative was touched up for the purpose of reproduction.

Houdini rehearsing his jump from one aeroplane to another.

of it. One case has a little piece cut out of the bottom right-hand corner. The space is equal in size to the index corner of a card. The prepared pack is placed in this case and just before he is going to do the trick the conjurer puts the case in his pocket.

The working of the trick, the invention of Hans Trunk, will now be clear. After the card has been chosen the conjurer puts the prepared case, with the case with the prepared cards in it, into his trousers pocket. He eventually takes out the prepared case and holding it behind him with the cut-out corner next to his body, invites the spectator to return his card to the case. Directly the performer brings the case in front of him he is able to see the index corner of the selected card.

THE THREE HEAPS.—*Effect.*—The spectator, having cut the pack into three heaps, is asked if he has cut them exactly where he pleased. The answer is, of course, " Yes." The conjurer says, " How curious that you should have cut them just where I wished—at the——" and names the top card of each heap.

Explanation.—The conjurer gets a glimpse of the bottom card and brings this to the top by a shuffle. To do this the conjurer picks up the cards in his right hand and turns them over so that the bottom card is facing him. In drawing off some cards with the left hand at the beginning of the shuffle the conjurer puts his thumb on this card and brings it singly into his left hand. The other cards may be fairly shuffled on the top, and then, when the pack is turned over, the card which was formerly at the bottom is now at the top. The spectator cuts the pack into three heaps. In naming the cards at the top of the three heaps the conjurer first names the card he knows is the top card of the pack, but he takes up the card of the middle heap and says " Right," as though he had actually drawn the card he named. He names this first card when he takes up the card of the lowest heap, and names this second card when he takes up the top card of the last heap. That card, being the original top card of the pack, is the card he named in the first place. Thus he has named all three cards.

THE FRIENDLY CARDS.—*Effect.*—The conjurer asks a member of the audience to choose a card and replace it in the pack. He then asks another spectator to think of any card in the pack. This being done the conjurer deals the cards from the bottom of the pack until he comes to the card of which the spectator is thinking. The next card he deals is the one which has been taken from and returned to the pack. In some way the two cards have shown themselves " friendly " and have appeared together.

Explanation.—There is no pretence about the spectator thinking of a card. The conjurer asks him what card he is going to think of. He has previously had the first card returned to the pack, and by bringing it to the bottom has it in readiness for the completion of his trick. He holds the pack in his left hand with the fingers on the bottom card. By using his third finger he draws this card back and deals out the other cards until he comes to the one which was thought of. The next card he takes out is the card chosen and replaced in the pack because he has had that card drawn back at the bottom of the pack all the time.

FLIGHT.—*Effect.*—The conjurer has a card selected and placed back in the pack. He asks the chooser to name any person in the room and announces that he will try and make the selected card fly invisibly across the room and into that person's pocket. Having pronounced a " magical password," the conjurer announces that the card has flown from the pack, but when the person chosen to receive it looks into his pocket the card is not there. The conjurer expresses surprise at this and asks the chooser of the card what card it was what he took from the pack. When he is told the name of the card the conjurer says that it is a special favourite of his, and that therefore the card never goes to a stranger, but always flies into his own pocket. He invites anyone to feel in his inside coat pocket, and when this is done the missing card is found there.

Explanation.—The conjurer has to force a card, the duplicate of which is already in his coat pocket. The chosen card is put back into the pack and, if the conjurer wishes to make the trick more effective, he brings it to the top by means of the pass and palms it off. He can either drop it behind a handkerchief on the table or slip it into his trousers pocket. The trick is then done. The surprise of the trick lies in the fact that the conjurer never goes to the pocket from which the card is subsequently taken.

A CARD TRAVELS INVISIBLY.—*Effect.*—The conjurer takes a card from the top of the pack and causes it to disappear for a second. He "finds" it again, and places it in the other hand. Then the card travels backwards and forwards from one hand to the other. It can be passed through the knees or through the body.

Explanation.—The conjurer has two cards alike on top of the pack. He takes these off and shows them as one card. Back palming these he reproduces one of the cards and leaves the other at the back of his hand. He takes the visible one with his left hand and back palms it, at the same time causing the one at the back of the right hand to appear in that hand. He continues the movements, back palming with one hand and causing the card in the other hand to appear. Then he holds the hands close to the body and makes the cards apparently travel right through the body. He can do the same thing by bending down and holding his hands close at the sides of the knees (the legs being close together) so that the card appears to travel through the legs. The cards are then put together as one card and replaced on the pack.

A CATALOGUE OF SELECTED DOVER BOOKS
IN ALL FIELDS OF INTEREST

A CATALOGUE OF SELECTED DOVER BOOKS
IN ALL FIELDS OF INTEREST

AMERICA'S OLD MASTERS, James T. Flexner. Four men emerged unexpectedly from provincial 18th century America to leadership in European art: Benjamin West, J. S. Copley, C. R. Peale, Gilbert Stuart. Brilliant coverage of lives and contributions. Revised, 1967 edition. 69 plates. 365pp. of text.

21806-6 Paperbound $3.00

FIRST FLOWERS OF OUR WILDERNESS: AMERICAN PAINTING, THE COLONIAL PERIOD, James T. Flexner. Painters, and regional painting traditions from earliest Colonial times up to the emergence of Copley, West and Peale Sr., Foster, Gustavus Hesselius, Feke, John Smibert and many anonymous painters in the primitive manner. Engaging presentation, with 162 illustrations. xxii + 368pp.

22180-6 Paperbound $3.50

THE LIGHT OF DISTANT SKIES: AMERICAN PAINTING, 1760-1835, James T. Flexner. The great generation of early American painters goes to Europe to learn and to teach: West, Copley, Gilbert Stuart and others. Allston, Trumbull, Morse; also contemporary American painters—primitives, derivatives, academics—who remained in America. 102 illustrations. xiii + 306pp. 22179-2 Paperbound $3.50

A HISTORY OF THE RISE AND PROGRESS OF THE ARTS OF DESIGN IN THE UNITED STATES, William Dunlap. Much the richest mine of information on early American painters, sculptors, architects, engravers, miniaturists, etc. The only source of information for scores of artists, the major primary source for many others. Unabridged reprint of rare original 1834 edition, with new introduction by James T. Flexner, and 394 new illustrations. Edited by Rita Weiss. 6⅝ x 9⅝.

21695-0, 21696-9, 21697-7 Three volumes, Paperbound $15.00

EPOCHS OF CHINESE AND JAPANESE ART, Ernest F. Fenollosa. From primitive Chinese art to the 20th century, thorough history, explanation of every important art period and form, including Japanese woodcuts; main stress on China and Japan, but Tibet, Korea also included. Still unexcelled for its detailed, rich coverage of cultural background, aesthetic elements, diffusion studies, particularly of the historical period. 2nd, 1913 edition. 242 illustrations. lii + 439pp. of text.

20364-6, 20365-4 Two volumes, Paperbound $6.00

THE GENTLE ART OF MAKING ENEMIES, James A. M. Whistler. Greatest wit of his day deflates Oscar Wilde, Ruskin, Swinburne; strikes back at inane critics, exhibitions, art journalism; aesthetics of impressionist revolution in most striking form. Highly readable classic by great painter. Reproduction of edition designed by Whistler. Introduction by Alfred Werner. xxxvi + 334pp.

21875-9 Paperbound $3.00

JOHANN SEBASTIAN BACH, Philipp Spitta. One of the great classics of musicology, this definitive analysis of Bach's music (and life) has never been surpassed. Lucid, nontechnical analyses of hundreds of pieces (30 pages devoted to St. Matthew Passion, 26 to B Minor Mass). Also includes major analysis of 18th-century music. 450 musical examples. 40-page musical supplement. Total of xx + 1799pp.

(EUK) 22278-0, 22279-9 Two volumes, Clothbound $17.50

MOZART AND HIS PIANO CONCERTOS, Cuthbert Girdlestone. The only full-length study of an important area of Mozart's creativity. Provides detailed analyses of all 23 concertos, traces inspirational sources. 417 musical examples. Second edition. 509pp. 21271-8 Paperbound $3.50

THE PERFECT WAGNERITE: A COMMENTARY ON THE NIBLUNG'S RING, George Bernard Shaw. Brilliant and still relevant criticism in remarkable essays on Wagner's Ring cycle, Shaw's ideas on political and social ideology behind the plots, role of Leitmotifs, vocal requisites, etc. Prefaces. xxi + 136pp.

(USO) 21707-8 Paperbound $1.75

DON GIOVANNI, W. A. Mozart. Complete libretto, modern English translation; biographies of composer and librettist; accounts of early performances and critical reaction. Lavishly illustrated. All the material you need to understand and appreciate this great work. Dover Opera Guide and Libretto Series; translated and introduced by Ellen Bleiler. 92 illustrations. 209pp.

21134-7 Paperbound $2.00

BASIC ELECTRICITY, U. S. Bureau of Naval Personel. Originally a training course, best non-technical coverage of basic theory of electricity and its applications. Fundamental concepts, batteries, circuits, conductors and wiring techniques, AC and DC, inductance and capacitance, generators, motors, transformers, magnetic amplifiers, synchros, servomechanisms, etc. Also covers blue-prints, electrical diagrams, etc. Many questions, with answers. 349 illustrations. x + 448pp. 6½ x 9¼.

20973-3 Paperbound $3.50

REPRODUCTION OF SOUND, Edgar Villchur. Thorough coverage for laymen of high fidelity systems, reproducing systems in general, needles, amplifiers, preamps, loudspeakers, feedback, explaining physical background. "A rare talent for making technicalities vividly comprehensible," R. Darrell, *High Fidelity*. 69 figures. iv + 92pp. 21515-6 Paperbound $1.35

HEAR ME TALKIN' TO YA: THE STORY OF JAZZ AS TOLD BY THE MEN WHO MADE IT, Nat Shapiro and Nat Hentoff. Louis Armstrong, Fats Waller, Jo Jones, Clarence Williams, Billy Holiday, Duke Ellington, Jelly Roll Morton and dozens of other jazz greats tell how it was in Chicago's South Side, New Orleans, depression Harlem and the modern West Coast as jazz was born and grew. xvi + 429pp.

21726-4 Paperbound $3.00

FABLES OF AESOP, translated by Sir Roger L'Estrange. A reproduction of the very rare 1931 Paris edition; a selection of the most interesting fables, together with 50 imaginative drawings by Alexander Calder. v + 128pp. 6½x9¼.

21780-9 Paperbound $1.50

THE ARCHITECTURE OF COUNTRY HOUSES, Andrew J. Downing. Together with Vaux's *Villas and Cottages* this is the basic book for Hudson River Gothic architecture of the middle Victorian period. Full, sound discussions of general aspects of housing, architecture, style, decoration, furnishing, together with scores of detailed house plans, illustrations of specific buildings, accompanied by full text. Perhaps the most influential single American architectural book. 1850 edition. Introduction by J. Stewart Johnson. 321 figures, 34 architectural designs. xvi + 560pp.
22003-6 Paperbound $4.00

LOST EXAMPLES OF COLONIAL ARCHITECTURE, John Mead Howells. Full-page photographs of buildings that have disappeared or been so altered as to be denatured, including many designed by major early American architects. 245 plates. xvii + 248pp. 7⅞ x 10¾. 21143-6 Paperbound $3.50

DOMESTIC ARCHITECTURE OF THE AMERICAN COLONIES AND OF THE EARLY REPUBLIC, Fiske Kimball. Foremost architect and restorer of Williamsburg and Monticello covers nearly 200 homes between 1620-1825. Architectural details, construction, style features, special fixtures, floor plans, etc. Generally considered finest work in its area. 219 illustrations of houses, doorways, windows, capital mantels. xx + 314pp. 7⅞ x 10¾. 21743-4 Paperbound $4.00

EARLY AMERICAN ROOMS: 1650-1858, edited by Russell Hawes Kettell. Tour of 12 rooms, each representative of a different era in American history and each furnished, decorated, designed and occupied in the style of the era. 72 plans and elevations, 8-page color section, etc., show fabrics, wall papers, arrangements, etc. Full descriptive text. xvii + 200pp. of text. 8⅜ x 11¼.
21633-0 Paperbound $5.00

THE FITZWILLIAM VIRGINAL BOOK, edited by J. Fuller Maitland and W. B. Squire. Full modern printing of famous early 17th-century ms. volume of 300 works by Morley, Byrd, Bull, Gibbons, etc. For piano or other modern keyboard instrument; easy to read format. xxxvi + 938pp. 8⅜ x 11.
21068-5, 21069-3 Two volumes, Paperbound $10.00

KEYBOARD MUSIC, Johann Sebastian Bach. Bach Gesellschaft edition. A rich selection of Bach's masterpieces for the harpsichord: the six English Suites, six French Suites, the six Partitas (Clavierübung part I), the Goldberg Variations (Clavierübung part IV), the fifteen Two-Part Inventions and the fifteen Three-Part Sinfonias. Clearly reproduced on large sheets with ample margins; eminently playable. vi + 312pp. 8⅛ x 11. 22360-4 Paperbound $5.00

THE MUSIC OF BACH: AN INTRODUCTION, Charles Sanford Terry. A fine, nontechnical introduction to Bach's music, both instrumental and vocal. Covers organ music, chamber music, passion music, other types. Analyzes themes, developments, innovations. x + 114pp. 21075-8 Paperbound $1.50

BEETHOVEN AND HIS NINE SYMPHONIES, Sir George Grove. Noted British musicologist provides best history, analysis, commentary on symphonies. Very thorough, rigorously accurate; necessary to both advanced student and amateur music lover. 436 musical passages. vii + 407 pp. 20334-4 Paperbound $2.75

A History of Costume, Carl Köhler. Definitive history, based on surviving pieces of clothing primarily, and paintings, statues, etc. secondarily. Highly readable text, supplemented by 594 illustrations of costumes of the ancient Mediterranean peoples, Greece and Rome, the Teutonic prehistoric period; costumes of the Middle Ages, Renaissance, Baroque, 18th and 19th centuries. Clear, measured patterns are provided for many clothing articles. Approach is practical throughout. Enlarged by Emma von Sichart. 464pp. 21030-8 Paperbound $3.50.

Oriental Rugs, Antique and Modern, Walter A. Hawley. A complete and authoritative treatise on the Oriental rug—where they are made, by whom and how, designs and symbols, characteristics in detail of the six major groups, how to distinguish them and how to buy them. Detailed technical data is provided on periods, weaves, warps, wefts, textures, sides, ends and knots, although no technical background is required for an understanding. 11 color plates, 80 halftones, 4 maps. vi + 320pp. 6⅛ x 9⅛. 22366-3 Paperbound $5.00

Ten Books on Architecture, Vitruvius. By any standards the most important book on architecture ever written. Early Roman discussion of aesthetics of building, construction methods, orders, sites, and every other aspect of architecture has inspired, instructed architecture for about 2,000 years. Stands behind Palladio, Michelangelo, Bramante, Wren, countless others. Definitive Morris H. Morgan translation. 68 illustrations. xii + 331pp. 20645-9 Paperbound $3.00

The Four Books of Architecture, Andrea Palladio. Translated into every major Western European language in the two centuries following its publication in 1570, this has been one of the most influential books in the history of architecture. Complete reprint of the 1738 Isaac Ware edition. New introduction by Adolf Placzek, Columbia Univ. 216 plates. xxii + 110pp. of text. 9½ x 12¾. 21308-0 Clothbound $12.50

Sticks and Stones: A Study of American Architecture and Civilization, Lewis Mumford.One of the great classics of American cultural history. American architecture from the medieval-inspired earliest forms to the early 20th century; evolution of structure and style, and reciprocal influences on environment. 21 photographic illustrations. 238pp. 20202-X Paperbound $2.00

The American Builder's Companion, Asher Benjamin. The most widely used early 19th century architectural style and source book, for colonial up into Greek Revival periods. Extensive development of geometry of carpentering, construction of sashes, frames, doors, stairs; plans and elevations of domestic and other buildings. Hundreds of thousands of houses were built according to this book, now invaluable to historians, architects, restorers, etc. 1827 edition. 59 plates. 114pp. 7⅞ x 10¾. 22236-5 Paperbound $3.50

Dutch Houses in the Hudson Valley Before 1776, Helen Wilkinson Reynolds. The standard survey of the Dutch colonial house and outbuildings, with constructional features, decoration, and local history associated with individual homesteads. Introduction by Franklin D. Roosevelt. Map. 150 illustrations. 469pp. 6⅝ x 9¼. 21469-9 Paperbound $5.00

ALPHABETS AND ORNAMENTS, Ernst Lehner. Well-known pictorial source for decorative alphabets, script examples, cartouches, frames, decorative title pages, calligraphic initials, borders, similar material. 14th to 19th century, mostly European. Useful in almost any graphic arts designing, varied styles. 750 illustrations. 256pp. 7 x 10.   21905-4 Paperbound $4.00

PAINTING: A CREATIVE APPROACH, Norman Colquhoun. For the beginner simple guide provides an instructive approach to painting: major stumbling blocks for beginner; overcoming them, technical points; paints and pigments; oil painting; watercolor and other media and color. New section on "plastic" paints. Glossary. Formerly *Paint Your Own Pictures*. 221pp.   22000-1 Paperbound $1.75

THE ENJOYMENT AND USE OF COLOR, Walter Sargent. Explanation of the relations between colors themselves and between colors in nature and art, including hundreds of little-known facts about color values, intensities, effects of high and low illumination, complementary colors. Many practical hints for painters, references to great masters. 7 color plates, 29 illustrations. x + 274pp.
22944-X Paperbound $2.75

THE NOTEBOOKS OF LEONARDO DA VINCI, compiled and edited by Jean Paul Richter. 1566 extracts from original manuscripts reveal the full range of Leonardo's versatile genius: all his writings on painting, sculpture, architecture, anatomy, astronomy, geography, topography, physiology, mining, music, etc., in both Italian and English, with 186 plates of manuscript pages and more than 500 additional drawings. Includes studies for the Last Supper, the lost Sforza monument, and other works. Total of xlvii + 866pp. 7⅞ x 10¾.
22572-0, 22573-9 Two volumes, Paperbound $11.00

MONTGOMERY WARD CATALOGUE OF 1895. Tea gowns, yards of flannel and pillow-case lace, stereoscopes, books of gospel hymns, the New Improved Singer Sewing Machine, side saddles, milk skimmers, straight-edged razors, high-button shoes, spittoons, and on and on . . . listing some 25,000 items, practically all illustrated. Essential to the shoppers of the 1890's, it is our truest record of the spirit of the period. Unaltered reprint of Issue No. 57, Spring and Summer 1895. Introduction by Boris Emmet. Innumerable illustrations. xiii + 624pp. 8½ x 11⅝.
22377-9 Paperbound $6.95

THE CRYSTAL PALACE EXHIBITION ILLUSTRATED CATALOGUE (LONDON, 1851). One of the wonders of the modern world—the Crystal Palace Exhibition in which all the nations of the civilized world exhibited their achievements in the arts and sciences—presented in an equally important illustrated catalogue. More than 1700 items pictured with accompanying text—ceramics, textiles, cast-iron work, carpets, pianos, sleds, razors, wall-papers, billiard tables, beehives, silverware and hundreds of other artifacts—represent the focal point of Victorian culture in the Western World. Probably the largest collection of Victorian decorative art ever assembled— indispensable for antiquarians and designers. Unabridged republication of the Art-Journal Catalogue of the Great Exhibition of 1851, with all terminal essays. New introduction by John Gloag, F.S.A. xxxiv + 426pp. 9 x 12.
22503-8 Paperbound $5.00

DESIGN BY ACCIDENT; A BOOK OF "ACCIDENTAL EFFECTS" FOR ARTISTS AND DESIGNERS, James F. O'Brien. Create your own unique, striking, imaginative effects by "controlled accident" interaction of materials: paints and lacquers, oil and water based paints, splatter, crackling materials, shatter, similar items. Everything you do will be different; first book on this limitless art, so useful to both fine artist and commercial artist. Full instructions. 192 plates showing "accidents," 8 in color. viii + 215pp. 8⅜ x 11¼. 21942-9 Paperbound $3.75

THE BOOK OF SIGNS, Rudolf Koch. Famed German type designer draws 493 beautiful symbols: religious, mystical, alchemical, imperial, property marks, runes, etc. Remarkable fusion of traditional and modern. Good for suggestions of timelessness, smartness, modernity. Text. vi + 104pp. 6⅛ x 9¼. 20162-7 Paperbound $1.25

HISTORY OF INDIAN AND INDONESIAN ART, Ananda K. Coomaraswamy. An unabridged republication of one of the finest books by a great scholar in Eastern art. Rich in descriptive material, history, social backgrounds; Sunga reliefs, Rajput paintings, Gupta temples, Burmese frescoes, textiles, jewelry, sculpture, etc. 400 photos. viii + 423pp. 6⅜ x 9¾. 21436-2 Paperbound $5.00

PRIMITIVE ART, Franz Boas. America's foremost anthropologist surveys textiles, ceramics, woodcarving, basketry, metalwork, etc.; patterns, technology, creation of symbols, style origins. All areas of world, but very full on Northwest Coast Indians. More than 350 illustrations of baskets, boxes, totem poles, weapons, etc. 378 pp. 20025-6 Paperbound $3.00

THE GENTLEMAN AND CABINET MAKER'S DIRECTOR, Thomas Chippendale. Full reprint (third edition, 1762) of most influential furniture book of all time, by master cabinetmaker. 200 plates, illustrating chairs, sofas, mirrors, tables, cabinets, plus 24 photographs of surviving pieces. Biographical introduction by N. Bienenstock. vi + 249pp. 9⅞ x 12¾. 21601-2 Paperbound $4.00

AMERICAN ANTIQUE FURNITURE, Edgar G. Miller, Jr. The basic coverage of all American furniture before 1840. Individual chapters cover type of furniture—clocks, tables, sideboards, etc.—chronologically, with inexhaustible wealth of data. More than 2100 photographs, all identified, commented on. Essential to all early American collectors. Introduction by H. E. Keyes. vi + 1106pp. 7⅞ x 10¾. 21599-7, 21600-4 Two volumes, Paperbound $11.00

PENNSYLVANIA DUTCH AMERICAN FOLK ART, Henry J. Kauffman. 279 photos, 28 drawings of tulipware, Fraktur script, painted tinware, toys, flowered furniture, quilts, samplers, hex signs, house interiors, etc. Full descriptive text. Excellent for tourist, rewarding for designer, collector. Map. 146pp. 7⅞ x 10¾. 21205-X Paperbound $2.50

EARLY NEW ENGLAND GRAVESTONE RUBBINGS, Edmund V. Gillon, Jr. 43 photographs, 226 carefully reproduced rubbings show heavily symbolic, sometimes macabre early gravestones, up to early 19th century. Remarkable early American primitive art, occasionally strikingly beautiful; always powerful. Text. xxvi + 207pp. 8⅜ x 11¼. 21380-3 Paperbound $3.50

VISUAL ILLUSIONS: THEIR CAUSES, CHARACTERISTICS, AND APPLICATIONS, Matthew Luckiesh. Thorough description and discussion of optical illusion, geometric and perspective, particularly; size and shape distortions, illusions of color, of motion; natural illusions; use of illusion in art and magic, industry, etc. Most useful today with op art, also for classical art. Scores of effects illustrated. Introduction by William H. Ittleson. 100 illustrations. xxi + 252pp.

21530-X Paperbound $2.00

A HANDBOOK OF ANATOMY FOR ART STUDENTS, Arthur Thomson. Thorough, virtually exhaustive coverage of skeletal structure, musculature, etc. Full text, supplemented by anatomical diagrams and drawings and by photographs of undraped figures. Unique in its comparison of male and female forms, pointing out differences of contour, texture, form. 211 figures, 40 drawings, 86 photographs. xx + 459pp. 5⅜ x 8⅜.

21163-0 Paperbound $3.50

150 MASTERPIECES OF DRAWING, Selected by Anthony Toney. Full page reproductions of drawings from the early 16th to the end of the 18th century, all beautifully reproduced: Rembrandt, Michelangelo, Dürer, Fragonard, Urs, Graf, Wouwerman, many others. First-rate browsing book, model book for artists. xviii + 150pp. 8⅜ x 11¼.

21032-4 Paperbound $2.50

THE LATER WORK OF AUBREY BEARDSLEY, Aubrey Beardsley. Exotic, erotic, ironic masterpieces in full maturity: Comedy Ballet, Venus and Tannhauser, Pierrot, Lysistrata, Rape of the Lock, Savoy material, Ali Baba, Volpone, etc. This material revolutionized the art world, and is still powerful, fresh, brilliant. With *The Early Work,* all Beardsley's finest work. 174 plates, 2 in color. xiv + 176pp. 8⅛ x 11.

21817-1 Paperbound $3.00

DRAWINGS OF REMBRANDT, Rembrandt van Rijn. Complete reproduction of fabulously rare edition by Lippmann and Hofstede de Groot, completely reedited, updated, improved by Prof. Seymour Slive, Fogg Museum. Portraits, Biblical sketches, landscapes, Oriental types, nudes, episodes from classical mythology—All Rembrandt's fertile genius. Also selection of drawings by his pupils and followers. "Stunning volumes," *Saturday Review.* 550 illustrations. lxxviii + 552pp. 9⅛ x 12¼.

21485-0, 21486-9 Two volumes, Paperbound $10.00

THE DISASTERS OF WAR, Francisco Goya. One of the masterpieces of Western civilization—83 etchings that record Goya's shattering, bitter reaction to the Napoleonic war that swept through Spain after the insurrection of 1808 and to war in general. Reprint of the first edition, with three additional plates from Boston's Museum of Fine Arts. All plates facsimile size. Introduction by Philip Hofer, Fogg Museum. v + 97pp. 9⅜ x 8¼.

21872-4 Paperbound $2.00

GRAPHIC WORKS OF ODILON REDON. Largest collection of Redon's graphic works ever assembled: 172 lithographs, 28 etchings and engravings, 9 drawings. These include some of his most famous works. All the plates from *Odilon Redon: oeuvre graphique complet,* plus additional plates. New introduction and caption translations by Alfred Werner. 209 illustrations. xxvii + 209pp. 9⅛ x 12¼.

21966-8 Paperbound $4.50

AGAINST THE GRAIN (A REBOURS), Joris K. Huysmans. Filled with weird images, evidences of a bizarre imagination, exotic experiments with hallucinatory drugs, rich tastes and smells and the diversions of its sybarite hero Duc Jean des Esseintes, this classic novel pushed 19th-century literary decadence to its limits. Full unabridged edition. Do not confuse this with abridged editions generally sold. Introduction by Havelock Ellis. xlix + 206pp. 22190-3 Paperbound $2.50

VARIORUM SHAKESPEARE: HAMLET. Edited by Horace H. Furness; a landmark of American scholarship. Exhaustive footnotes and appendices treat all doubtful words and phrases, as well as suggested critical emendations throughout the play's history. First volume contains editor's own text, collated with all Quartos and Folios. Second volume contains full first Quarto, translations of Shakespeare's sources (Belleforest, and Saxo Grammaticus), Der Bestrafte Brudermord, and many essays on critical and historical points of interest by major authorities of past and present. Includes details of staging and costuming over the years. By far the best edition available for serious students of Shakespeare. Total of xx + 905pp. 21004-9, 21005-7, 2 volumes, Paperbound $7.00

A LIFE OF WILLIAM SHAKESPEARE, Sir Sidney Lee. This is the standard life of Shakespeare, summarizing everything known about Shakespeare and his plays. Incredibly rich in material, broad in coverage, clear and judicious, it has served thousands as the best introduction to Shakespeare. 1931 edition. 9 plates. xxix + 792pp. 21967-4 Paperbound $3.75

MASTERS OF THE DRAMA, John Gassner. Most comprehensive history of the drama in print, covering every tradition from Greeks to modern Europe and America, including India, Far East, etc. Covers more than 800 dramatists, 2000 plays, with biographical material, plot summaries, theatre history, criticism, etc. "Best of its kind in English," New Republic. 77 illustrations. xxii + 890pp. 20100-7 Clothbound $10.00

THE EVOLUTION OF THE ENGLISH LANGUAGE, George McKnight. The growth of English, from the 14th century to the present. Unusual, non-technical account presents basic information in very interesting form: sound shifts, change in grammar and syntax, vocabulary growth, similar topics. Abundantly illustrated with quotations. Formerly Modern English in the Making. xii + 590pp. 21932-1 Paperbound $3.50

AN ETYMOLOGICAL DICTIONARY OF MODERN ENGLISH, Ernest Weekley. Fullest, richest work of its sort, by foremost British lexicographer. Detailed word histories, including many colloquial and archaic words; extensive quotations. Do not confuse this with the Concise Etymological Dictionary, which is much abridged. Total of xxvii + 830pp. 6½ x 9¼. 21873-2, 21874-0 Two volumes, Paperbound $7.90

FLATLAND: A ROMANCE OF MANY DIMENSIONS, E. A. Abbott. Classic of science-fiction explores ramifications of life in a two-dimensional world, and what happens when a three-dimensional being intrudes. Amusing reading, but also useful as introduction to thought about hyperspace. Introduction by Banesh Hoffmann. 16 illustrations. xx + 103pp. 20001-9 Paperbound $1.00

POEMS OF ANNE BRADSTREET, edited with an introduction by Robert Hutchinson. A new selection of poems by America's first poet and perhaps the first significant woman poet in the English language. 48 poems display her development in works of considerable variety—love poems, domestic poems, religious meditations, formal elegies, "quaternions," etc. Notes, bibliography. viii + 222pp.

22160-1 Paperbound $2.50

THREE GOTHIC NOVELS: THE CASTLE OF OTRANTO BY HORACE WALPOLE; VATHEK BY WILLIAM BECKFORD; THE VAMPYRE BY JOHN POLIDORI, WITH FRAGMENT OF A NOVEL BY LORD BYRON, edited by E. F. Bleiler. The first Gothic novel, by Walpole; the finest Oriental tale in English, by Beckford; powerful Romantic supernatural story in versions by Polidori and Byron. All extremely important in history of literature; all still exciting, packed with supernatural thrills, ghosts, haunted castles, magic, etc. xl + 291pp.

21232-7 Paperbound $2.50

THE BEST TALES OF HOFFMANN, E. T. A. Hoffmann. 10 of Hoffmann's most important stories, in modern re-editings of standard translations: Nutcracker and the King of Mice, Signor Formica, Automata, The Sandman, Rath Krespel, The Golden Flowerpot, Master Martin the Cooper, The Mines of Falun, The King's Betrothed, A New Year's Eve Adventure. 7 illustrations by Hoffmann. Edited by E. F. Bleiler. xxxix + 419pp.   21793-0 Paperbound $3.00

GHOST AND HORROR STORIES OF AMBROSE BIERCE, Ambrose Bierce. 23 strikingly modern stories of the horrors latent in the human mind: The Eyes of the Panther, The Damned Thing, An Occurrence at Owl Creek Bridge, An Inhabitant of Carcosa, etc., plus the dream-essay, Visions of the Night. Edited by E. F. Bleiler. xxii + 199pp.

20767-6 Paperbound $1.50

BEST GHOST STORIES OF J. S. LEFANU, J. Sheridan LeFanu. Finest stories by Victorian master often considered greatest supernatural writer of all. Carmilla, Green Tea, The Haunted Baronet, The Familiar, and 12 others. Most never before available in the U. S. A. Edited by E. F. Bleiler. 8 illustrations from Victorian publications. xvii + 467pp.   20415-4 Paperbound $3.00

MATHEMATICAL FOUNDATIONS OF INFORMATION THEORY, A. I. Khinchin. Comprehensive introduction to work of Shannon, McMillan, Feinstein and Khinchin, placing these investigations on a rigorous mathematical basis. Covers entropy concept in probability theory, uniqueness theorem, Shannon's inequality, ergodic sources, the E property, martingale concept, noise, Feinstein's fundamental lemma, Shanon's first and second theorems. Translated by R. A. Silverman and M. D. Friedman. iii + 120pp.   60434-9 Paperbound $2.00

SEVEN SCIENCE FICTION NOVELS, H. G. Wells. The standard collection of the great novels. Complete, unabridged. *First Men in the Moon, Island of Dr. Moreau, War of the Worlds, Food of the Gods, Invisible Man, Time Machine, In the Days of the Comet.* Not only science fiction fans, but every educated person owes it to himself to read these novels. 1015pp.   (USO) 20264-X Clothbound $6.00

LAST AND FIRST MEN AND STAR MAKER, TWO SCIENCE FICTION NOVELS, Olaf Stapledon. Greatest future histories in science fiction. In the first, human intelligence is the "hero," through strange paths of evolution, interplanetary invasions, incredible technologies, near extinctions and reemergences. Star Maker describes the quest of a band of star rovers for intelligence itself, through time and space: weird inhuman civilizations, crustacean minds, symbiotic worlds, etc. Complete, unabridged. v + 438pp. (USO) 21962-3 Paperbound $2.50

THREE PROPHETIC NOVELS, H. G. WELLS. Stages of a consistently planned future for mankind. *When the Sleeper Wakes,* and *A Story of the Days to Come,* anticipate *Brave New World* and *1984,* in the 21st Century; *The Time Machine,* only complete version in print, shows farther future and the end of mankind. All show Wells's greatest gifts as storyteller and novelist. Edited by E. F. Bleiler. x + 335pp. (USO) 20605-X Paperbound $2.50

THE DEVIL'S DICTIONARY, Ambrose Bierce. America's own Oscar Wilde—Ambrose Bierce—offers his barbed iconoclastic wisdom in over 1,000 definitions hailed by H. L. Mencken as "some of the most gorgeous witticisms in the English language." 145pp. 20487-1 Paperbound $1.25

MAX AND MORITZ, Wilhelm Busch. Great children's classic, father of comic strip, of two bad boys, Max and Moritz. Also Ker and Plunk (Plisch und Plumm), Cat and Mouse, Deceitful Henry, Ice-Peter, The Boy and the Pipe, and five other pieces. Original German, with English translation. Edited by H. Arthur Klein; translations by various hands and H. Arthur Klein. vi + 216pp. 20181-3 Paperbound $2.00

PIGS IS PIGS AND OTHER FAVORITES, Ellis Parker Butler. The title story is one of the best humor short stories, as Mike Flannery obfuscates biology and English. Also included, That Pup of Murchison's, The Great American Pie Company, and Perkins of Portland. 14 illustrations. v + 109pp. 21532-6 Paperbound $1.25

THE PETERKIN PAPERS, Lucretia P. Hale. It takes genius to be as stupidly mad as the Peterkins, as they decide to become wise, celebrate the "Fourth," keep a cow, and otherwise strain the resources of the Lady from Philadelphia. Basic book of American humor. 153 illustrations. 219pp. 20794-3 Paperbound $2.00

PERRAULT'S FAIRY TALES, translated by A. E. Johnson and S. R. Littlewood, with 34 full-page illustrations by Gustave Doré. All the original Perrault stories—Cinderella, Sleeping Beauty, Bluebeard, Little Red Riding Hood, Puss in Boots, Tom Thumb, etc.—with their witty verse morals and the magnificent illustrations of Doré. One of the five or six great books of European fairy tales. viii + 117pp. 8⅛ x 11. 22311-6 Paperbound $2.00

OLD HUNGARIAN FAIRY TALES, Baroness Orczy. Favorites translated and adapted by author of the *Scarlet Pimpernel.* Eight fairy tales include "The Suitors of Princess Fire-Fly," "The Twin Hunchbacks," "Mr. Cuttlefish's Love Story," and "The Enchanted Cat." This little volume of magic and adventure will captivate children as it has for generations. 90 drawings by Montagu Barstow. 96pp. (USO) 22293-4 Paperbound $1.95

THE RED FAIRY BOOK, Andrew Lang. Lang's color fairy books have long been children's favorites. This volume includes Rapunzel, Jack and the Bean-stalk and 35 other stories, familiar and unfamiliar. 4 plates, 93 illustrations x + 367pp.
21673-X Paperbound $2.50

THE BLUE FAIRY BOOK, Andrew Lang. Lang's tales come from all countries and all times. Here are 37 tales from Grimm, the Arabian Nights, Greek Mythology, and other fascinating sources. 8 plates, 130 illustrations. xi + 390pp.
21437-0 Paperbound $2.50

HOUSEHOLD STORIES BY THE BROTHERS GRIMM. Classic English-language edition of the well-known tales — Rumpelstiltskin, Snow White, Hansel and Gretel, The Twelve Brothers, Faithful John, Rapunzel, Tom Thumb (52 stories in all). Translated into simple, straightforward English by Lucy Crane. Ornamented with head-pieces, vignettes, elaborate decorative initials and a dozen full-page illustrations by Walter Crane. x + 269pp.
21080-4 Paperbound **$2.00**

THE MERRY ADVENTURES OF ROBIN HOOD, Howard Pyle. The finest modern versions of the traditional ballads and tales about the great English outlaw. Howard Pyle's complete prose version, with every word, every illustration of the first edition. Do not confuse this facsimile of the original (1883) with modern editions that change text or illustrations. 23 plates plus many page decorations. xxii + 296pp.
22043-5 Paperbound $2.50

THE STORY OF KING ARTHUR AND HIS KNIGHTS, Howard Pyle. The finest children's version of the life of King Arthur; brilliantly retold by Pyle, with 48 of his most imaginative illustrations. xviii + 313pp. 6⅛ x 9¼.
21445-1 Paperbound $2.50

THE WONDERFUL WIZARD OF OZ, L. Frank Baum. America's finest children's book in facsimile of first edition with all Denslow illustrations in full color. The edition a child should have. Introduction by Martin Gardner. 23 color plates, scores of drawings. iv + 267pp.
20691-2 Paperbound $2.50

THE MARVELOUS LAND OF OZ, L. Frank Baum. The second Oz book, every bit as imaginative as the Wizard. The hero is a boy named Tip, but the Scarecrow and the Tin Woodman are back, as is the Oz magic. 16 color plates, 120 drawings by John R. Neill. 287pp.
20692-0 Paperbound $2.50

THE MAGICAL MONARCH OF MO, L. Frank Baum. Remarkable adventures in a land even stranger than Oz. The best of Baum's books not in the Oz series. 15 color plates and dozens of drawings by Frank Verbeck. xviii + 237pp.
21892-9 Paperbound $2.25

THE BAD CHILD'S BOOK OF BEASTS, MORE BEASTS FOR WORSE CHILDREN, A MORAL ALPHABET, Hilaire Belloc. Three complete humor classics in one volume. Be kind to the frog, and do not call him names . . . and 28 other whimsical animals. Familiar favorites and some not so well known. Illustrated by Basil Blackwell. 156pp.
(USO) 20749-8 Paperbound $1.50

EAST O' THE SUN AND WEST O' THE MOON, George W. Dasent. Considered the best of all translations of these Norwegian folk tales, this collection has been enjoyed by generations of children (and folklorists too). Includes True and Untrue, Why the Sea is Salt, East O' the Sun and West O' the Moon, Why the Bear is Stumpy-Tailed, Boots and the Troll, The Cock and the Hen, Rich Peter the Pedlar, and 52 more. The only edition with all 59 tales. 77 illustrations by Erik Werenskiold and Theodor Kittelsen. xv + 418pp. 22521-6 Paperbound $3.50

GOOPS AND HOW TO BE THEM, Gelett Burgess. Classic of tongue-in-cheek humor, masquerading as etiquette book. 87 verses, twice as many cartoons, show mischievous Goops as they demonstrate to children virtues of table manners, neatness, courtesy, etc. Favorite for generations. viii + 88pp. 6½ x 9¼.
22233-0 Paperbound $1.25

ALICE'S ADVENTURES UNDER GROUND, Lewis Carroll. The first version, quite different from the final *Alice in Wonderland,* printed out by Carroll himself with his own illustrations. Complete facsimile of the "million dollar" manuscript Carroll gave to Alice Liddell in 1864. Introduction by Martin Gardner. viii + 96pp. Title and dedication pages in color. 21482-6 Paperbound $1.25

THE BROWNIES, THEIR BOOK, Palmer Cox. Small as mice, cunning as foxes, exuberant and full of mischief, the Brownies go to the zoo, toy shop, seashore, circus, etc., in 24 verse adventures and 266 illustrations. Long a favorite, since their first appearance in St. Nicholas Magazine. xi + 144pp. 6⅝ x 9¼.
21265-3 Paperbound $1.75

SONGS OF CHILDHOOD, Walter De La Mare. Published (under the pseudonym Walter Ramal) when De La Mare was only 29, this charming collection has long been a favorite children's book. A facsimile of the first edition in paper, the 47 poems capture the simplicity of the nursery rhyme and the ballad, including such lyrics as I Met Eve, Tartary, The Silver Penny. vii + 106pp. (USO) 21972-0 Paperbound $1.25

THE COMPLETE NONSENSE OF EDWARD LEAR, Edward Lear. The finest 19th-century humorist-cartoonist in full: all nonsense limericks, zany alphabets, Owl and Pussycat, songs, nonsense botany, and more than 500 illustrations by Lear himself. Edited by Holbrook Jackson. xxix + 287pp. (USO) 20167-8 Paperbound $2.00

BILLY WHISKERS: THE AUTOBIOGRAPHY OF A GOAT, Frances Trego Montgomery. A favorite of children since the early 20th century, here are the escapades of that rambunctious, irresistible and mischievous goat—Billy Whiskers. Much in the spirit of *Peck's Bad Boy,* this is a book that children never tire of reading or hearing. All the original familiar illustrations by W. H. Fry are included: 6 color plates, 18 black and white drawings. 159pp. 22345-0 Paperbound $2.00

MOTHER GOOSE MELODIES. Faithful republication of the fabulously rare Munroe and Francis "copyright 1833" Boston edition—the most important Mother Goose collection, usually referred to as the "original." Familiar rhymes plus many rare ones, with wonderful old woodcut illustrations. Edited by E. F. Bleiler. 128pp. 4½ x 6⅜. 22577-1 Paperbound $1.00

TWO LITTLE SAVAGES; BEING THE ADVENTURES OF TWO BOYS WHO LIVED AS INDIANS AND WHAT THEY LEARNED, Ernest Thompson Seton. Great classic of nature and boyhood provides a vast range of woodlore in most palatable form, a genuinely entertaining story. Two farm boys build a teepee in woods and live in it for a month, working out Indian solutions to living problems, star lore, birds and animals, plants, etc. 293 illustrations. vii + 286pp.

20985-7 Paperbound $2.50

PETER PIPER'S PRACTICAL PRINCIPLES OF PLAIN & PERFECT PRONUNCIATION. Alliterative jingles and tongue-twisters of surprising charm, that made their first appearance in America about 1830. Republished in full with the spirited woodcut illustrations from this earliest American edition. 32pp. 4½ x 6⅜.

22560-7 Paperbound $1.00

SCIENCE EXPERIMENTS AND AMUSEMENTS FOR CHILDREN, Charles Vivian. 73 easy experiments, requiring only materials found at home or easily available, such as candles, coins, steel wool, etc.; illustrate basic phenomena like vacuum, simple chemical reaction, etc. All safe. Modern, well-planned. Formerly *Science Games for Children*. 102 photos, numerous drawings. 96pp. 6⅛ x 9¼.

21856-2 Paperbound $1.25

AN INTRODUCTION TO CHESS MOVES AND TACTICS SIMPLY EXPLAINED, Leonard Barden. Informal intermediate introduction, quite strong in explaining reasons for moves. Covers basic material, tactics, important openings, traps, positional play in middle game, end game. Attempts to isolate patterns and recurrent configurations. Formerly *Chess*. 58 figures. 102pp. (USO) 21210-6 Paperbound $1.25

LASKER'S MANUAL OF CHESS, Dr. Emanuel Lasker. Lasker was not only one of the five great World Champions, he was also one of the ablest expositors, theorists, and analysts. In many ways, his Manual, permeated with his philosophy of battle, filled with keen insights, is one of the greatest works ever written on chess. Filled with analyzed games by the great players. A single-volume library that will profit almost any chess player, beginner or master. 308 diagrams. xli x 349pp.

20640-8 Paperbound $2.75

THE MASTER BOOK OF MATHEMATICAL RECREATIONS, Fred Schuh. In opinion of many the finest work ever prepared on mathematical puzzles, stunts, recreations; exhaustively thorough explanations of mathematics involved, analysis of effects, citation of puzzles and games. Mathematics involved is elementary. Translated by F. Göbel. 194 figures. xxiv + 430pp.

22134-2 Paperbound $3.50

MATHEMATICS, MAGIC AND MYSTERY, Martin Gardner. Puzzle editor for Scientific American explains mathematics behind various mystifying tricks: card tricks, stage "mind reading," coin and match tricks, counting out games, geometric dissections, etc. Probability sets, theory of numbers clearly explained. Also provides more than 400 tricks, guaranteed to work, that you can do. 135 illustrations. xii + 176pp.

20335-2 Paperbound $1.75

MATHEMATICAL PUZZLES FOR BEGINNERS AND ENTHUSIASTS, Geoffrey Mott-Smith. 189 puzzles from easy to difficult—involving arithmetic, logic, algebra, properties of digits, probability, etc.—for enjoyment and mental stimulus. Explanation of mathematical principles behind the puzzles. 135 illustrations. viii + 248pp.

20198-8 Paperbound $1.75

PAPER FOLDING FOR BEGINNERS, William D. Murray and Francis J. Rigney. Easiest book on the market, clearest instructions on making interesting, beautiful origami. Sail boats, cups, roosters, frogs that move legs, bonbon boxes, standing birds, etc. 40 projects; more than 275 diagrams and photographs. 94pp.

20713-7 Paperbound $1.00

TRICKS AND GAMES ON THE POOL TABLE, Fred Herrmann. 79 tricks and games— some solitaires, some for two or more players, some competitive games—to entertain you between formal games. Mystifying shots and throws, unusual caroms, tricks involving such props as cork, coins, a hat, etc. Formerly *Fun on the Pool Table*. 77 figures. 95pp.

21814-7 Paperbound $1.25

HAND SHADOWS TO BE THROWN UPON THE WALL: A SERIES OF NOVEL AND AMUSING FIGURES FORMED BY THE HAND, Henry Bursill. Delightful picturebook from great-grandfather's day shows how to make 18 different hand shadows: a bird that flies, duck that quacks, dog that wags his tail, camel, goose, deer, boy, turtle, etc. Only book of its sort. vi + 33pp. 6½ x 9¼.

21779-5 Paperbound $1.00

WHITTLING AND WOODCARVING, E. J. Tangerman. 18th printing of best book on market. "If you can cut a potato you can carve" toys and puzzles, chains, chessmen, caricatures, masks, frames, woodcut blocks, surface patterns, much more. Information on tools, woods, techniques. Also goes into serious wood sculpture from Middle Ages to present, East and West. 464 photos, figures. x + 293pp.

20965-2 Paperbound $2.00

HISTORY OF PHILOSOPHY, Julián Marías. Possibly the clearest, most easily followed, best planned, most useful one-volume history of philosophy on the market; neither skimpy nor overfull. Full details on system of every major philosopher and dozens of less important thinkers from pre-Socratics up to Existentialism and later. Strong on many European figures usually omitted. Has gone through dozens of editions in Europe. 1966 edition, translated by Stanley Appelbaum and Clarence Strowbridge. xviii + 505pp.

21739-6 Paperbound $3.50

YOGA: A SCIENTIFIC EVALUATION, Kovoor T. Behanan. Scientific but non-technical study of physiological results of yoga exercises; done under auspices of Yale U. Relations to Indian thought, to psychoanalysis, etc. 16 photos. xxiii + 270pp.

20505-3 Paperbound $2.50

Prices subject to change without notice.

Available at your book dealer or write for free catalogue to Dept. GI, Dover Publications, Inc., 180 Varick St., N. Y., N. Y. 10014. Dover publishes more than 150 books each year on science, elementary and advanced mathematics, biology, music, art, literary history, social sciences and other areas.